WHY WAR? WHY AN ARMY?

WHY WAR? WHY AN ARMY?

John M. House

An AUSA Book

PRAEGER SECURITY INTERNATIONAL
Westport, Connecticut • London

Library of Congress Cataloging-in-Publication Data

House, John M.
  Why war? Why an army? / John M. House.
    p. cm. – (AUSA book)
  Includes bibliographical references and index.
  ISBN: 978–0–313–36206–4 (alk. paper)
  1. War.   2. United States. Army.—Reorganization.   3. Military art and science.
I. Title.
  U21.2.H638   2008
  355.02—dc22   2008022563

British Library Cataloguing in Publication Data is available.

Library of Congress Catalog Card Number: 2008022563
ISBN: 978–0–313–36206–4

First published in 2008

Praeger Security International, 88 Post Road West, Westport, CT 06881
An imprint of Greenwood Publishing Group, Inc.
www.praeger.com

Printed in the United States of America

The paper used in this book complies with the
Permanent Paper Standard issued by the National
Information Standards Organization (Z39.48–1984).

10 9 8 7 6 5 4 3 2 1

Contents

Preface

Why study war? War is destructive. War causes great misery. Society praises men and women who promote peace. Society condemns people and nations who attack others without provocation. Regardless of these ills, war remains a component of our global environment. Studying definitions of war, the purpose of an army, war's natures, and how organizations implement change helps us understand why war remains a fixture in human interactions and how best to prepare for winning such a deadly contest.

A discussion of war must address many subjects. This discussion provides an overview, more as a primer for the study of war. This explanation of war's purpose, meaning, and characteristics is not intended as a repeat of American doctrine; however, much American doctrine fills these pages. New and old doctrinal terms mix within the text and attempt to prevent the discussion from bogging down into nothing more than a definition of doctrinal terms. The purpose of this book is to encourage thinking about why war is whatever it is. The text is army-centric because people live on land and armies conduct operations on land. In many cases "soldiers, sailors, airmen, and marines" could substitute for the term "soldiers" in the text. This focus is not intended to ignore the criticality of operations in the air or on the sea. Both are crucial to the success of a major power such as the United States. Future wars that involve large nations will always be multiservice. Nonetheless, nations exist on land because people reside there. Therefore, actions by armies and soldiers dominate this discussion.

War is a struggle for power, whether to impose one's will on another nation or group or to resist such imposition from outside. A nation or group's resources provide the means to conduct the military and nonmilitary actions associated with this struggle. These assets provide the capability for people to inflict pain and limit the ability of another nation or group to force it to act in accordance with their desires.

Military analysts, authorities, and doctrine use and have used a wide range of terms to define or describe military actions within the framework of warfare. While this terminology sometimes seems conflicting, anyone studying war needs a reasonable understanding of how to define war and types of wars in order to enter the discussion. The following text provides a summary of many of the terms and definitions used—but certainly not for every one of them. The range of terminology used in military doctrine and in military writings is too large to hope to cover all in one text such as this.

An army provides the land component of a nation's military forces. However, armies have utility beyond that of warfare. Armies provide a disciplined and organized body of people who are equipped to survive and function in an austere environment. Other military services provide similar capabilities on the sea and in the air. The focus here is on armies, this land element, because people inhabit the land, not the sea or air. Regardless of the outcome of operations on the sea and in the air, the effect on the land is the result that matters. That is where people are. These characteristics provide military forces unique capabilities beyond simply inflicting death and destruction. Using military forces for nonmilitary purposes brings risk because it diverts the military forces from their primary purpose. Nonetheless, such capabilities exist.

Levels of war provide a structure in which to allocate forces and capabilities and to describe the functions of leaders. Understanding this structure is important in characterizing and comprehending the effect of decisions and actions from the national level to the battlefield. The actions of national level leaders and platoon leaders are similar; however, they are not equal. The impact of the decisions and the resources available are different.

Another structure worth exploring is war's nature. This discussion divides war into physical, cognitive, and moral natures. By natures, the discussion seeks to explain the interaction of people and military forces within a framework that also describes how war affects them. The physical nature explains the environment in which war occurs. The cognitive nature examines the mental functions of leadership and resource use. The moral nature explores war's impact on people, particularly the soldiers who wage it.

This discussion of war then lays the foundation for an understanding of change as a process and as an essential component of military affairs. Militaries must change to cope with the changing environment in which they function. The U.S. Army has a robust process to guide this change in its combat developments community. Change is also present in the business world, as industry seeks a competitive advantage in order to survive and prosper. The present transformation initiatives in the U.S. Department of Defense seek to maintain the U.S. dominance in military capability in the world and to exploit the opportunities afforded by new technologies and concepts of organization and warfare that use those technologies. Several chapters address this process of change, transformation in the U.S. armed forces specifically, and the challenges associated with maintaining a program of change once begun.

The future of military requirements remains a challenge to define. The transformation process tries to define that future and the capabilities needed in order to maintain the security of the United States. Yet enemies of the United States and its allies also seek to predict and mold this future to their advantage. The rise of Islamic fundamentalists or radicalism has changed the global security environment. Western nations must prepare to defeat this threat that is not really new but has risen to new levels of ferocity and lethality.

Regardless of the changes in technology, organizational and operational concepts, and external or internal threats, people remain a constant as the crucial element in war. People make the decisions to use military and other elements of power to impose the will of a nation on another group or nations. People also comprise the military services and man the component systems within the services. Any study of war and warfare must address the impact that people make on the conduct of war and the effects of war on people. The political process always includes people. To paraphrase Carl von Clausewitz, war is a continuation of that political process. Leaders who make a decision to fight and those who lead those soldiers, sailors, airmen, and marines into battle must not forget that people implement those decisions and are the object of any offense or defense. Protecting the citizens of the United States is why this nation maintains military forces.

Acknowledgments

Why War? Why an Army? began as an attempt to capture my thoughts on warfare after graduating from the U.S. Army Command and General Staff College's School of Advanced Military Studies (SAMS) at Fort Leavenworth, Kansas, in 1989. My purpose has been to solidify my thoughts, understanding, and beliefs concerning war and the use of military forces in general. Many of the ideas discussed here have swirled inside my head for years. However, some only recently reached a level of clarity, where I decided to write them down. Regardless of how long these concepts have bounced around in my head, I owe this determination to put my ideas on paper to SAMS. Elements of my major papers from SAMS as well as ideas from papers while a student at the Naval War College and my Northcentral University doctoral program including my dissertation are in this book.

As a student in the Advanced Military Studies Program (AMSP) in SAMS, I studied war and the use of military forces more than I had done so in the past. As I neared graduation, I decided I had to write this book just to put my thoughts in order. SAMS was a tremendous experience, but it provided me so much information I was unsure I really understood what I had studied. Therefore, I put pencil to paper.

The ideas here are mine with regard to blame for their intent. However, I cannot take credit for all that is here. My fellow students and I read a tremendous amount of material in SAMS. I had also read quite a lot before starting the course. Hopefully, my notes and bibliography provide a sufficient link to those authors before me who wrote on such issues. My

SAMS seminar and the SAMS faculty must also receive credit. Eleven months of seminar discussions and exercises made it difficult to separate who first expressed an idea. I must specifically thank Dr. Jim Schneider from SAMS who encouraged me over the years to stretch my thinking and to write this book. Had he not provided encouragement at a couple of critical moments, I might have tossed these pages into a corner. The faculty at the Naval War College and Northcentral University also deserve my thanks, especially my dissertation committee chaired by Dr. Olin Oedekoven, now a brigadier general in the Wyoming Army National Guard. Without their tolerance and encouragement during my varied studies I would never have reached a point in my pondering where I felt confident to write down my ideas. Dr. Roger Cirillo from the Association of the United States Army was critical in my finding a publisher. I must also thank Mr. Adam Kane and the many other members of the Praeger Security International staff for working with me to publish the book. Without their help, I could not have completed this project.

I also must single out my wife and daughters for great thanks. Marilyn, the love of my life and best friend, has stood by me during good times and bad. She typed early versions of the manuscript, until I became comfortable with word processing. She also always served as a sounding board. Her ability to balance the needs of our family with my periodic bouts of writing madness kept all of us moving forward. My daughters, Shannon, Amanda, Mary, and Carole, continue to rank as my finest achievements. I often feel unworthy of them and all of their remarkable abilities. They deserve my thanks for allowing me to take the time to work on this book, as it stretched over many years in the making. Amanda especially deserves special credit for her initial editing recommendations, thanks to a degree in journalism and a willingness to critique dear old Dad for a change.

I hope my work helps others think about why nations require and use military power. My study has certainly helped me understand why I wore a uniform for so long. Understanding is essential in order to ensure success and the effective use of resources in any endeavor. When lives are in the balance, it is especially important for people who make tough decisions to understand why the decisions must be made. Those of us in public service owe the nation that much.

1

What's War All about?

WAR

War is man's most significant endeavor. Some people might argue against this assertion, but no other human endeavor affects the participants as war does. Once unleashed, the violence associated with war tends to dominate all aspects of life for the belligerents. States rise and fall through its workings. Societies prosper. Nations perish. Fortunes are won and lost. People win their freedom thanks to war. Losers may discover slavery or subjugation of their civilization and way of life. People die in war.

The effects of war generate fascination and repugnance. Books, stories, movies, and television shows try to explain, glorify, and demonize the actions and the participants in war. War is studied and explained. Regardless of whether someone endorses or opposes war, no one can deny the importance of understanding why peoples or nations fight. The impact of such violence affects many, so studying war is necessary in order to harness the violence and ensure that some good comes from it. People may argue that no good comes from war, but those who do so fail to understand the nature of man's interactions that have produced the world where we live. This is not to argue that violence is good, but sometimes it is necessary to right a wrong or provide a secure society in which to exist. War must remain the focus of study for professional soldiers and government leaders who ponder its use as a means to achieve a goal. For these, careful study is crucial.

Such leaders must not only determine if violence and bloodshed are appropriate means to achieve their ends, they must also determine the type of war or level of violence and degree of military force that will best achieve their goals. As Carl von Clausewitz said, "[T]he first, the supreme, the most far-reaching act of judgment that the statesman and commander have to make is to establish by that test the kind of war on which they are embarking."[1]

A discussion of war must touch upon many areas. This discourse will attempt to provide an overview, more as a primer for the study of war. This explanation of war's purpose, meaning, and characteristics is not intended as a repeat of American doctrine; however, much American doctrine will be included. New and old doctrinal terms fill out the discussion on the following pages. Such mixing is the result of trying not to get bogged down in a discussion of the ever-changing key words as doctrine matures. The purpose is rather to foster thinking about why war is whatever it is.

POWER

Power provides a nation or a people the ability to achieve goals or to act as they desire. The search for power over the environment or one's neighboring country, group, or individuals never ends because it provides the promise of a better or securer future. The desire for riches, the domination of others, or some other power brings people, and states, into conflict;[2] therefore, power provides the strength to achieve a future end state that is better than the present situation. Power is a means for achieving future goals. Conflict resolution pits opponents' powers against one another. The greatest power, or combination of types of power, will be victorious regardless of whether the struggle is peaceful or violent.

POLICY

Clausewitz said war is a continuation of policy.[3] What does that mean? Policy refers to governmental goals, actions, and decisions. Governments rule the affairs of a state. Governments establish goals that will enhance their power, solidify their control of their people and land, protect their rule, or enhance living conditions in their realms. Decisions lead to actions aimed at achieving these goals.

A government uses its power to execute these decisions—to take action. In other words, a government, or state, uses its power to enforce its will (i.e., decisions) on other states or people (whether they are citizens or not). War is one way a state may enforce its will on others. As Clausewitz stated, "War is thus an act of force to compel our enemy to do our will."[4] The failure to subordinate military objectives to political objectives leads to using military force only for the sake of doing so. That is immoral. War is too horrible and causes too much suffering to be a worthy endeavor for a state to conduct or endure if there is no purpose to justify it.

Policy then is a government's decisions and the actions that flow from those decisions. War is a means to achieve goals that government policy sets. But war is only one tool for a state to use. A state can use any power that it possesses in order to achieve its goals. To understand war's place in a state's possible courses of action, it is important to define power as it relates to states and conflicts among them. Power provides a state the ability to enforce its will or to resist the will of another.

Implementing policy requires a set of administrative structures and processes. In simple terms, public administration is "the activities of government that determine the supply of goods and services to the public."[5] Public administration describes the processes and organizations within the government that serve the public good. Some form of administrative process is necessary in order to control the activities of government agencies as they carry out public policy.

The purposes of government include protecting the lives, property, and rights of citizens, maintaining and securing a supply of necessary resources, supporting people unable to care for themselves, promoting economic growth, promoting an adequate quality of life, protecting the environment, and promoting scientific and technological advances. Governments must establish an organizational framework to provide such services.[6]

Governments use a variety of means to carry out the programs that provide support to their citizens. These "tools of implementation" include providing cash payments, constructing and maintaining public facilities, providing public services (such as health care, mail delivery, and public transportation), and regulating behavior. Maintaining the capability to govern, or to use these tools, supports these activities.[7]

An example of a government seeking a solution for a new threat against the lives and property of its citizens was the federal government's reaction to the terror attacks on September 11, 2001. These attacks destroyed the World Trade Center towers and damaged the Pentagon, which focused federal, state, and local governments on homeland security. President George W. Bush's decision to establish the Office of Homeland Security began a major restructuring of several federal government agencies. Funding and other resource allocations are the tools used by the government to carry out this purpose.[8]

An expansion of the previous definition of public administration in a democratic government system is "the process by which government organizations supply essential goods, services, and regulations, managing resources and resolving conflicts under a mandate of efficiency and fairness, while accounting to the public for both means and outcomes."[9] For a democracy, this adds the ideas of fairness and accountability to the basic premise of providing goods and services. In a democratic society, the public expects that services provided by the government will be administered in a fair manner and that those who provide those services will be held accountable for their actions. The political process will hold government administrations in the United States accountable for their actions to provide for homeland security subsequent to the September 11 terrorist attacks.

President Woodrow Wilson characterized administration as the "government in action."[10] Administration is the visible side of government. Citizens interact with the agencies of government in their daily lives, whether this involves driving down a road, sending children to school, or using electricity for heating and cooling. Even if these services are provided by a private organization, government regulation and oversight ensures that these services are provided in such a manner as to satisfy the desires of the collective citizenry. The oversight of the policies that govern the provision of such goods and services is public administration.

The term "bureaucracy" defines the formal, administrative structure of government. Richard Stillman credits Max Weber, a German social scientist, with providing a "classic" description of the characteristics of bureaucracy. Society's need to perform tasks such as building infrastructure, waging war, and collecting taxes made the growth of bureaucracy essential. Weber praised the rise of bureaucracy because of the improvements in "precision, speed, unambiguity, knowledge of the files, continuity, discretion, unity, strict subordination, reduction of friction and of material and personal costs." He goes on to state that bureaucracy removes emotions from government administration.[11]

John M. Gaus proposed that the ecology, or environment, of a bureaucracy is important in understanding how best to serve the public. He included several factors as important in the analysis of bureaucracy including "people, place, physical technology, social technology, wishes and ideas, catastrophe, and personality."[12] Such environmental factors affect the success of bureaucracy and how governmental agencies interact with people. Since any bureaucracy must act within an environment, it is important to understand that environment and the influence that these factors have on public expectations.

Within the American government, administrative organizations must interact with a variety of groups. This decentralized nature of our democratic system makes a clear consensus on a course of action difficult to achieve. Norton E. Long stated that power is the "lifeblood" of administration and warrants additional study.[13] The government's administrative organization must have the power to carry out its missions, but it is sometimes difficult to determine who is truly providing direction. Competition for resources and influence may cloud the tasks to be performed and identification of the element of the public to be served. This competition may also result in elements of the government administration working at cross-purposes. Assigning responsibility and accountability for actions can be difficult, but it remains very important.

Bureaucracy is the execution arm of a government. Bureaucrats issue regulations, apply laws and regulations, and manage staffs to execute these functions. Executives, legislatures, and courts may set policy, but bureaucrats execute those policies and fill in details when guidance from policymakers is too general in nature to meet the public need.[14]

Bureaucracy exists at all levels of government in order to perform the duties of the government in serving the public. The hierarchical nature of bureaucracies eventually leads to the election of an official, which provides a degree of accountability for public administration in a democratic society. Regardless of the strengths and weaknesses of bureaucracies, they are needed in order to carry out governmental actions. Policy execution in a complex world relies on a functioning bureaucracy.

ECONOMIC POWER

Power can take many forms. A nation's economy, geography, national will, military force, and political structure are different elements of power.[15] Economic power may provide one nation's government leverage over another. Trade is one example. Dependence on another state's exports is dangerous. If a state feels it must have an exported item, the exporting state may be able to influence the importing state's actions by withholding or threatening to withhold the desired item. The perception of need forms the basis for the power regardless of whether the perceived need is a real need. The concern of the industrialized world over the availability of Middle Eastern oil is an example of a resource that provides economic power, which could be used to influence another nation.

Internally to a state, economic power provides the basis for a citizenry's standard of living. This in turn affects the satisfaction that a state's citizens feel regarding the conditions in which they live as well as the ability of their leaders to provide a decent life. A satisfied population supports its government and the status quo. An unsatisfied population may oppose the same.

Physical survival is a basic human need. A state's economic system provides the food and shelter necessary to satisfy this requirement. A state's people must be able to eat and be comfortable in their environment for a government to realistically expect the population to be able to support it, let alone desire to support it.

A state's economic infrastructure also affects its ability to wield other forms of power including the use of military force. Industrial capacity provides the ability to produce weapons and equipment to outfit military forces. It affects the state's ability to provide equipment for soldiers and simultaneously maintain the citizenry's standard of living.

Aircraft, ships, and trucks have military as well as civil uses. Each can transport military or nonmilitary supplies. Roads provide the transportation network to support motor vehicle movement supplying products for consumers to purchase. They also serve as routes for ground military forces to use within a state's territory to change locations and move the supplies necessary to support military operations.

A state's financial system is another crucial element of its economic power. Money provides the means of exchanging merchandise within international and national market systems. Without a strong financial system, a state cannot trade within or outside its borders. The exchange of money for products allows the population to secure the items needed to satisfy its needs and desires.

The relationship of a state's corporations with those of other states will affect its interests in various parts of the world. These relations also will affect a state's desire (and possibly need) to control events outside its borders. If events in another country threaten the economic success or the survival of a nation's business community, that nation could decide to intervene militarily, economically, or diplomatically to support its industries. If such events threaten the lives of a state's citizens living abroad, the state might intervene to save those lives.

Business interests and the protection of American citizens prompted several interventions in the early twentieth century. For example, at the end of World War I, several states, including the United States, sent troops to northern Russia and Siberia. Though many factors influenced the decision to intervene, protecting American economic interests ranging from loans to U.S.-owned factories was an important consideration.[16]

GEOGRAPHY AND RESOURCES

Geography, another element of power, has several facets. A state's physical position grants it a certain degree of power. The ability to restrict movement grants one state power over another. For example, Iran influences other states because it sits on the northern side of the Strait of Hormuz, which provides entry into the Persian Gulf. Iran's actions can affect other states' actions by limiting or threatening to limit their ability to obtain oil.

Geography provides territory that can be easy or difficult to defend. It provides depth within which to fight an attacker. Landforms may compartmentalize the terrain to ease defense or inhibit lateral communications. Geography will affect the transportation network by facilitating or limiting vehicular movement. Military forces require physical space within which to operate. Geography will aid, inhibit, or be neutral to such a force's actions.

Switzerland's mountains provide protection from outside military attack because the terrain is difficult to move through. The losses an attacker would endure make an attack not worth the cost. This promotes Switzerland's neutral status and survival. Climate, vegetation, and soil conditions affect a state's agricultural system and thus its ability to feed itself or feed others.

Since food is necessary for basic survival, it is a critical national and natural resource. People must be able to satisfy their basic survival needs.

Population

A state's population is the manpower resource needed to work within its economic infrastructure. People work in factories, operate machinery, and provide the basis for a state's political system by consenting to be governed by those in political control. Without people, there is no economy, let alone state.

The population's education level affects the technological sophistication of the machinery industries can use and the weapons a state's military can employ. A better educated population can more easily adjust to the demands of new concepts and materiel. Technical specialization and sophistication in the civilian sector will affect the demands placed on weapon designers. American soldiers today have often had a great deal of exposure to computers while growing up. This facilitates their use of computers in the military services.

Natural Resources

Natural resources also provide a state power. They provide the raw materials necessary to support economic activity. A state must have the resources to be self-sufficient, or it must obtain the resources elsewhere. Self-sufficiency supports independence. If a state is not self-sufficient, it is subject to another state's will in order to obtain the natural resource it lacks. Need for raw materials supports international trade. The degree of impact of the lack of such resources will affect a state's perception of its need to use other elements of power to control the supplier's provision of the raw material. Withholding a raw material critical to another's survival can influence a state's action, but it could cause a violent counteraction.

Mineral and energy resources provide the raw materials to support a state's manufacturing capability. The vulnerability of these resources will affect the military power a state must devote to their protection. Resources that a state must import are a vulnerability that another state can exploit by threatening their importation. This again relates to a state's self-sufficiency. Protection of such resources includes physical protection from outside attack and safeguarding the necessary amount of the resources to satisfy its own needs and those of allied states whose survival is crucial.

NATIONAL WILL

National will is an element of power with two components—the will of the political leadership and the will of the state's citizenry. Both sustain and focus a state's goals and effort. The will of a government determines the allocation of resources. The will of a nation's citizens maintains the government's right to rule. This is true for both democratic and authoritarian governments. The timeliness of the effect may differ, but the necessity to maintain the will of the people through their consent, whether freely given or coerced, remains. As an example, the American people's lack of support for the war in Vietnam doomed the U.S. efforts there.

A diversion of the wills of the political leadership and citizenry will eventually cause the government to change. One need only look at the demise of Communism in eastern Europe to see that time is the enemy of an oppressive dictatorship. Repression can control a people only temporarily. Resentment will eventually overcome the fear of punishment.

A citizenry's attitudes, beliefs, and customs will affect a government's decisions. Of course, the degree of impact depends on the form of government—democratic or autocratic. Citizens in a democracy will have greater immediate impact than those in an autocracy. The state's social institutions, religious institutions, educational system, and family traditions will affect the society's cohesiveness and, hence, its collective will.

The will of the American people continues to be a major factor in U.S. foreign policy. Americans usually support the president if he decides he must commit military forces to protect American lives and property. The liberation of Grenada in 1983 and Panama in 1989 are examples. However, this support is transitory and less firm if the objectives of the intervention are unclear.

Vietnam was and remains a problem for the U.S. government. The complexity of a counterinsurgency war that also included conventional forces with significant limits imposed on their use resulted in the American people and eventually the government viewing the war as having no foreseeable end. Americans do not like open-ended wars and continue to resist any commitment of military force that resembles an open-ended one similar to their perception of the Vietnam War. The president and Congress struggle with each other as they confront this feeling and attempt to interpret the "will of the people," allocate resources, and ensure that neither branch of government becomes too powerful to be the sole arbiter of foreign policy.

Even as soldiers deployed to defend Saudi Arabia for Operation Desert Shield in August 1990, the specter of Vietnam hovered over the American government. However, President George H.W. Bush remained steadfast in his determination to support a distant ally. His moral courage in the face of a vocal opposition led the American people to support the deployment. Even though some may have felt that national will wavered, public opinion never forced the president to change his decision. The U.S. citizenry wholeheartedly supported the deployed soldiers, sailors, airmen, and marines. Their support had a positive impact on morale.

There is much discussion today over the wisdom of entering into a war in Iraq. There is little questioning of the reasons for attacking the Taliban forces in Afghanistan after they supported the terrorist attacks of September 11, 2001. There was little dissension in America when the United States invaded Iraq with weapons of mass destruction as the perceived justification. However, U.S. forces did not find evidence of a viable program to develop nuclear, chemical, or biological weapons at the time of the invasion. Saddam Hussein's previous abuse of his citizens and continuous attacks against American pilots enforcing the United Nations' "no fly zones" after Desert Storm seemed to mean little to the critics of U.S. policy. Regardless of one's views on the decision to depose Saddam Hussein, it is clear that American public opinion will affect the election of future leaders, which will then affect changes in U.S. policy toward Iraq and the time that U.S. troops remain there.

Not only a democratic government must consider its citizens' opinions, but an autocracy must also consider the will of its citizens in making foreign policy decisions. Anything that threatens the population's support or acquiescence in government decisions puts the survival of the government at risk. Certainly, an autocracy can disobey the people's will longer than a democracy because of its consolidation of power. However, ignoring the will of the people can eventually spark a revolt. As Nicolae Ceausescu discovered in Romania, a revolt can have deadly consequences for a deposed leader and his family.

MILITARY POWER

Military force is another element of power. It provides a nation the capability to impose its will on another nation through the threat or use of violence. Military force also provides a state the capability to resist another's coercive actions. The types of military forces required will depend on the state's physical characteristics and its enemies' capabilities. A landlocked state has little need for a navy. If a nation's opponent has a strong air force, then that nation should have strong air defenses.

The size and composition of military force available will dictate the types of operations a state may conduct. A landlocked power with no navy will never dominate the seas. A state without an air force or navy today will have great difficulty projecting and sustaining military forces over great distances. A strong army with no ability to move to another area has little impact on foreign policy, except on protecting its homeland.

The technological sophistication of its weaponry versus that of an opponent's will provide a state an advantage or disadvantage in projecting its will. All other things being equal, a state with weapons that can kill an opponent's soldiers faster and more efficiently than those of the opponent's has an advantage. Of course, rarely are all other things equal. Technological superiority can provide an advantage, but it cannot guarantee success.

Technology will also affect the state's ability to sustain its forces. Commonality of the civilian and military technological base will enhance logistical capabilities by making it easy for civilian industry to provide military forces the equipment needed. Technology can provide vehicles with greater haul capacity or speed, which could give one army a logistical advantage over another. If the needs of the civilian economy are such that vehicles or other equipment can support both military and civilian requirements, production costs will be less, since industry can capitalize on the economy of scale advantage. Lower production costs allow more vehicles or equipment to be purchased, so a greater capability is available for the same cost.

The location of military forces with respect to the theater of war and the enemy is another component of military power. If the military forces are near their wartime positioning, their deterrent and warfare capabilities are greater. For example, an American armored division stationed in Europe is more powerful than one in the continental United States (CONUS) when needed to prosecute a war in Europe. The division in Europe can much more quickly occupy a defensive position to oppose an attack. A unit that cannot deploy to a threatened area because of insufficient airlift or sealift has no value. It provides no addition to a state's military power.

The degree of civilian control and willingness to employ military force prescribes the manner in which a state may employ its military power. This point relates to the national will element of power. If the will to employ the military force available does not exist, the military force has no utility. No power results from the simple existence of the military force. Power results from the will to use military power, or at least an enemy's perception of the willingness to do so, and the capability of that military force to defeat an enemy.

Available reserves limit the duration of combat a state can endure. Once all the trained or trainable men and women are casualties, a state cannot continue. A state's manpower pool always serves as a limit on the size of the military force it can raise. Obviously, a state with a large population has an advantage over a state with a comparatively small population. Of course, the advantage is only decisive if all other national characteristics are equal.

Technology can overcome a manpower disadvantage by providing the capability to kill large numbers of enemy soldiers. Geography can also affect the value of a large manpower reserve because such a reserve is only useful if it can physically move to the theater of combat. China's manpower reserves exceed those of the United States; however, China's lack of a power projection navy results in that manpower advantage not being a major threat to the physical borders of the United States. This manpower may threaten other American interests or other nations' interests in Asia but not the physical border of the United States. Nation's without navies can provide a long range threat through the use of aircraft or missiles that have the range to reach and threaten hostile shores.

The composition of reserve forces also affects the options a state has in employing its military power. Mobilization time affects how quickly a state may employ its reserve military forces. If the reserve military forces are configured as light infantry, they will not be best suited to oppose an armor threat in open terrain. By the same token, mechanized reserves require heavy lift assets to deploy them. The mix of logistics versus combat units in the reserve and active forces will determine the importance of mobilizing reserve units based on the expected duration of the war.

The balance of combat, combat support, and combat service support units in the active and reserve forces is not a simple task. Providing an active force with a balanced mixture of all such units ensures that the government conducts operations without the need of calling up reserves. This provides the government the flexibility to respond to a citizen-soldier base. Mobilizing reserves implies a national commitment to resolve a conflict by force of arms. Relying on active duty forces, especially if they are volunteers, reduces the need for a national commitment.

The U.S. Army relies heavily on reserve component forces. Reserve component units provide critical supplies, transportation, military police, and medical support. They fight alongside their active brethren as seen daily in Operation Iraqi Freedom. They endure the hardships of war just as the active component soldiers do. Without the reserve component forces, regardless of the military service to which they are dedicated, the U.S. Department of Defense would experience great difficulty in executing the many operations that it must at all times.

Another aspect to this issue is the deterrent value of combat versus non-combat forces. Combat forces have immediate deterrent impact because they can destroy an opponent. In the short term, combat forces are more valuable because they can destroy the enemy. Combat forces bring the promise of the imposition of pain. However, if the conflict promises to last longer than the supplies organic to the combat force can last, an overreliance on combat units to the exclusion of support units can lead to disaster. A combat unit with no ammunition or fuel has little positive impact. Deterrence encourages a government to organize an unbalanced force with more combat force in the active component than can be supported for a long-term conflict. This relies on the threat that the combat power is so strong that it can crush the enemy before time causes supplies to be a problem.

If a government expects to fight a long conflict and places the majority of its support force in the reserves, it must mobilize those reserves before logistics cripple the active duty combat force. Mobilization time becomes critical. If it is not fast enough, the state will suffer defeat when the active component is forced to surrender, as the logistical deficiency forces the choice of surrender or annihilation. When a nation relies on reserve forces for much of its military power whether combat or support, it must also possess the will to mobilize those forces while acknowledging the impact on civilian society when the conflict is over. Using reserve forces diverts people, that most precious of resources, from their primary undertakings that provide the basis for economic well-being of society and often other security-oriented services in local governments. In the United States, there are plenty of reservists who are also police officers and firefighters, not to mention those who are entrepreneurs or teachers or are in other professions.

A state's military alliances provide opportunities and bring obligations. Alliances can provide additional military forces to employ. Alliances allow for the military forces of several states to combine to oppose a common enemy or enemies. Obviously, this makes possible the massing of more military power than that of any single state that is a member of the alliance. However, this combination comes with a price. All operations involving combined forces are inherently more complicated, and hence more difficult, than those involving a single state.

Language, customs, and technological levels are factors to consider and coordinate when considering coalition operations. Language will enhance or detract from the ability to interoperate. Different customs result in misunderstandings or unintended hostilities due to perceived but unintended insults. Differing technological levels can prevent interoperability because communication devices do not enable operational planning and control. Jealousy due to one nation's forces being more advanced than another can interfere with smooth operations. National pride can affect the willingness of one nation's forces to be subordinate to another.

Allies may have different types of weapons and equipment that will demand different logistical actions to supply a multitude of ammunition types, repair parts, and fuels. Training for the force as a whole is more complicated because each state's units may arrive with different levels of training behind them. If the different national forces attempt to use common equipment they have not used before, additional training will be necessary before combat operations begin. Differences in language will further complicate the training process because of the needs for translation and potential misunderstandings that can result from incorrect translations. Operations face the same language problems with potentially disastrous results if orders are misunderstood. Translation inherently increases the time to transmit orders between headquarters.

Alliances impose additional obligations on the use of military force. One potential danger associated with an alliance is that members are often obligated to protect one another from outside attack. This can result in one state gaining an enemy that was not an enemy before the alliance. Each alliance member must be prepared to accept the friends and enemies (past, present, and future) of the other members of the alliance.

Alliances also complicate decision-making because more governments are involved. Each government or its representative must have the opportunity to approve or disapprove decisions. Depending on the potential impact on the alliance, this delay to achieve consensus could make a decision pointless. Time is the enemy of decision-making.

The Allies' Siberian intervention after World War I provides an example of a solution to this decision-making problem. To supervise the critical railroad operations, the Allies formed a special committee and two special boards for technical and economic management and to coordinate military rail operations. These successful examples unfortunately were not repeated in all areas, so that competing national aims doomed the intervention from the start.[17] The purpose here is not to state that boards are the insurance against conflict among allies. Rather the purpose of this example is to demonstrate that conflict is a concern when more than one nation pools resources to take military action and that some means of coordinating that action is essential.

POLITICAL STRUCTURE

The national political system of a state is another element of power. The political system governs the selection of goals and the allocation of resources. Political goals focus the use of all other elements of power. Political ideas influence the actions that a state deems reasonable to take. Democratic states are more concerned with the rights of a country's citizens than autocratic ones. Actions that jeopardize the basic rights of people to live as they desire without excessive governmental interference are repugnant to democracies.

The values held by a national leader as well as influential groups within the state sway political decisions. Even a democracy will be subject to the desires of certain individuals over others. The people who hold high governmental positions will have more influence than those who do not. Additionally, people who provide opinions and advice to those in positions of authority also have more influence on political decisions than the average citizen.

The political system's ability to meld the various ethnic groups within the state into a cohesive group affects a government's ability to remain in power and use its resources to influence events beyond its physical boundaries rather than only maintaining internal control. A state that devotes all its time and energy to merely controlling its citizens has little ability to engage in international relations. Neglecting the international environment could lead to great surprise.

International political alliances provide additional partners in attempting to influence other states' decisions. However, as with military alliances, they also impose additional obligations and possibly constraints regarding permissible actions. Alliances force a state to consider the objectives and capabilities of its allies before deciding on a specific course of action.

WHY POWER?

People, nations, and groups seek power. But why? The answer is freedom—not that concept so cherished by people who yearn for the ability to live their lives as they desire. No, this freedom is more like control. It is the freedom to do as one wishes without interference from others, to control one's actions and the actions of others. Superiority in relative power provides a state or some other group the option to do as it wishes without fear of interference. Of course, the degree of superiority relative to opponents affects the degree of freedom.

This freedom comes from the power a state or group wields. More power brings more freedom to act. A lack of power reduces the options when choosing a course of action. A state or group may not be able to act in its own best interest because another state or group may limit its possible actions. One state may limit another's range of options by the threat of physical violence or the use of some other element of power.

This struggle for power is inherent in international relations. States seek an advantage over other states in order to ensure national survival and provide a better life for the controlling political power in the state. This controlling political power could be an individual in the case of a dictatorship or a state's citizens in the case of a democracy. This striving to secure an advantage may also be directed toward removing a threat to the status quo rather than toward improving it. If the political leadership is satisfied with the present situation, it will try to maintain it.

Another way to view this conflict between states is through the concepts of constraint and restraint. Constraining an opponent means compelling him to act as desired, to do one's will. This positive action is focused on forcing the opponent to do something. In other words, constraining an enemy requires a friendly plan. Otherwise no constraints can exist. Constraint is a positive tool because it enables one's freedom of action by compelling an opponent to act as desired.

Restraining an opponent limits an opponent's range of actions. This is a negative action in that it prevents an opponent from doing something. It focuses on the opponent's actions and will. The intent is to prevent an enemy doing as he desires.

Each opponent in this contest tries to constrain and restrain the other while removing any constraints or restraints placed upon itself. Constraining an opponent and reducing the constraints upon itself increases the degree of independence a state has. Restraining the enemy state prevents it from interfering with a state's actions. Independence, or the freedom to decide what actions to take, is at the root of all actions.

Constraining or restraining another may include the concept of punishment. One state may attempt to constrain or restrain another to punish it for previous or expected future actions. The damage caused by such actions serves as punishment for misdeeds. This may be done by using or threatening to use any of a state's elements of power as long as the state has a relative superiority of that power compared to the state that is the object of the constraining action.

Prevention is a related concept. Here the limiting action prevents one state from committing a misdeed. Such undesirable actions could include an attack on the country initiating the constraint or an attack on a third country. A state may try to protect itself or an ally by taking preventive action.

The power that states have is only important in relation to other states or groups with which the state must interact. These may be allies or enemies. Groups may be external or internal to the state. If a state does not interact with another state, its relative superiority or inferiority of power has no meaning because it cannot influence the actions of the other state.

States strive to maintain at least a balance of power. No government wants another government to have superior power out of the fear that it will lose its independence. A balance of power precludes one state or group of states from being able to force another to do its bidding. Certainly, any state or group of states would be pleased to have a superiority of power, whether it contemplated using that power to gain concessions from others or only protect itself from abuse by another. However, as long as there is a balance, one state cannot impose its will on another. If an imbalance occurs, states will consider joining together to consolidate their power to reestablish the balance of power, hence the rise of alliances. A balance of power is the minimum desired end state in order to maintain the freedom to select a course of action.

This explains why the events of the late fall of 1989 and winter of 1990 in eastern Europe were so troubling while also being exhilarating. Even though the Soviet Union and its Warsaw Pact allies posed a significant threat to the United States and its North Atlantic Treaty Organization (NATO) allies for years, the relative balance of power and threat of mutual destruction held the opposing sides in check. The loosening of control by the Soviets resulted in an unpredictable, revolutionary period in eastern Europe. The political changes threatened the balance of power between East and West, while the new governments sorted out internal reforms and future alliances.

The balance of power is important as it relates to a state or group of states and their aim to protect their security. Peace is only important if it preserves the security of the state(s).[18] A state will act to protect itself and reestablish the balance of power that assures its continued existence when its security is threatened. Failure to take such action is almost inconceivable. Such a course would be societal suicide. While it might be altruistically pleasing, such a course of action should not be expected from an opponent state or group.

A real or perceived imbalance may lead to overt conflict. The state with superior power may try to use that power to exact some payment, favor, or privilege from another. Resistance to such an attempt means conflict between the power holder and the target state. Surrender to an overt act may reduce the conflict, but it will also reduce the freedom of the state to decide its destiny. The conflict may not be violent, but it will exist at least to the degree implied by the loss of freedom by one state.

A balance of power prevents one state from rising to a position of strength that allows world domination. A world of many independent states limits the possibility of one state achieving such domination through the threat of the others banding together in opposition.[19] Of course, this only applies when those states recognize the need for such a balance and fear the consequences of conflict.

Fear of an attempt by a state with superior power to coerce some response from another could provoke a state or group of states to make a preemptive attack. Such an attack could include any or all types of power. Economic sanctions such as boycotts, diplomatic or political pressure such as resolutions through an international forum like the United Nations, and military action are methods of attack.

Generally, the international community objects less to nonviolent methods of coercion. Nonviolent options reduce the likelihood that other states will join to aid the state that is the object of the attack. However, violent options are usually faster means of achieving a goal. A state must carefully weigh the importance of speed versus the possible negative reaction resulting from the use of force before it selects the appropriate element of power to use.

NATIONAL SECURITY STRATEGY

This need to provide for security is basic for the survival of a government. A government must protect its citizens. Failure to do so would mean suicide for the government and its people. A secure environment allows not only survival but also economic growth. There is no other basic duty inherent in the role of governing. However, the actions that may be taken to provide that security are many. Gazing into the future to select the right path demands a clear focus on the desired end, the wisdom to chart the course, and the will to carry out the decisions required. A nation's interests serve to focus a nation's actions.

Several theories compete to serve as the framework for the national security strategy path that a nation might take to protect its interests. These include isolationism, primacy, selective engagement, and collective security with cooperative security as a similar concept to the last. All have strengths and weaknesses. The selection of one as the guiding theory for national security will affect decisions regarding conflicts a state enters and the resources needed to support those decisions.

NATIONAL INTERESTS

A critical factor in all national security discussions is the characterization of national interests to describe events or actions of sufficient importance to warrant interventions or not. One way to describe interests is to divide them into two categories—vital and secondary. Vital interests concern the survival of the state and are worthy of military action to protect them. All others are secondary and subject to compromise.[20]

Interests can also be defined as vital, important, or marginal. In this paradigm, vital interests affect the security of the nation. Protecting them is worth risking war. Important interests are worthy of extensive diplomatic and economic effort with limited military action as the last resort. Marginal interests warrant attention, but they are not worthy of major resource expenditures to address.[21]

Regardless of how interests are characterized, military operations are an option when protecting the interests of a nation. However, the inherent risk of casualties associated with military action requires careful consideration before committing military forces, especially if national survival is not an issue. Each of the national security theories mentioned earlier propose to protect the United States—but in different ways.

ISOLATIONISM, PRIMACY, AND SELECTIVE ENGAGEMENT

Isolationism demands that a nation retreat behind the protection of its geography. For the United States, this means retreating behind the two oceans. Massing military power to reach across either ocean is no simple task. However, an asymmetric attack as carried out by al Qaeda on September 11, 2001, can reach across these protective bands of water. For an isolationist, the only vital national interest is protecting that national territory. If no other state can threaten a nation's borders, foreign intervention is unlikely. Promoting national economic health then is a matter for the private, not the public, sector. Intervention overseas breeds resentment and does not serve such a nation's interests. Obviously a force structure oriented on defending the territory of an isolationist nation rather than deploying overseas would flow from this strategy.[22]

Primacy demands "a preponderance of power" to ensure peace. National security and a stable world demand that a nation retain its dominant position in the world. The intent of such a strategy would be to preclude any challenger from threatening a nation's supremacy politically, economically, or militarily. Superior military power capable of deploying worldwide would be essential. For the United States, maintaining its present single su-perpower status would be an example of following primacy as a strategy.[23] Primacy demands a large force structure of all types. A nation relying on this strategy would have to be ready to deploy unilaterally to fight to protect its interests worldwide.

Selective engagement recognizes that scarce resources limit a nation's actions. Only the actions of countries that have the industrial and military potential to pose a threat would warrant a nation's concern when relying on this strategy. A nation's interests would determine its actions abroad. Military forces would have to be of sufficient size and type to combat those nations that could threaten another's interests.[24]

COLLECTIVE SECURITY AND COOPERATIVE SECURITY

Collective security focuses on peace as opposed to power. International organizations coordinate the military actions of several countries to end conflicts. The goal is that the threat of collective military intervention by several states will dissuade an aggressor from attacking another.[25]

Though the actual definition may vary depending on the theorist be-ing quoted, one way to look at collective security is as a "rejection of al-liances." Security comes from the guarantee of "united reaction against all who transgress." President Woodrow Wilson championed this concept in his Fourteen Points and the League of Nations.[26] An international approach should ease the financial and other resource burdens faced by a nation adopt-ing this course because it would not bear the cost of intervention alone.[27] Collective security attempts to focus national interests, so that they enhance international security.[28]

There are several potential problems with a strategy of collective secu-rity. Punitive action against an aggressor is designed to return the situation to the status quo whether it is a desired one or not. Deciding who the ag-gressor is requires the consensus of several states whose interests and frames of reference may not coincide. Collective security also precludes alliances organized with particular state names as the security concern. Members of the collective security organization sacrifice a degree of independence to the centralized decision-making of the group.[29] Parties to the agreement must be willing to abide by the security obligations of the group, or the agreement has no meaning.

Cooperative security is related to collective security through its focus on peace and the coordinated actions of several countries. However, coopera-tive security demands action to counter threats before they arise. Collective security uses the threat of force to dissuade aggression and military force to defeat them after they occur.[30] Cooperative security's requirement to inter-vene in a threatening situation earlier is supposed to reduce the chance the situation will get out of hand.[31]

Cooperative security is similar to collective security because both strategies demand a united, multinational, shared security posture. However, cooperative security demands a preventive capability—the option to use military force to prevent an aggressor from attacking. Cooperative security tries to prevent physical conflict by "eliminating the material basis for organized aggression."[32] The multinational or coalition requirements of these strategies requires either harmony in national objectives, domination by one party or small group regarding the philosophical use of force, or a perfect willingness to place one nation's interests subordinate to the group as a whole. While this certainly seems reasonable because this is a requirement to a degree in any alliance, the degree of subjugation may make such a strategy unworkable in times of great stress or great threat. People still compose governing bodies, and people remain human in their desires to maintain the freedom to act as they desire.

WAR AND VIOLENCE

War is one means of achieving political goals associated with these ideas of constraint and restraint as well as with a balance of power. Though defining war may be difficult, most people can at least agree that war is the use of coercive military power. Violence is inescapable if military power is involved. Michael Howard wrote that men fight because they perceive a threat and choose to act upon that perception. The "diversity of interests, perceptions, and cultures" produce international conflict that results in war. Howard posits that war can be prevented through "patience, empathy, prudence, and the hard, tedious, detailed work of inconspicuous statesmanship."[33]

As Clausewitz said, war means bloodshed.[34] Military forces train in the art and science of destruction. Even though an army may have the capability to support actions not associated with war and violence, armies and other military forces organize and train to kill people and destroy things. There is no way to escape this conclusion. War means violence in order to achieve some goal.

Though war means violence, using military power does not necessarily require killing. The threat of bloodshed may be sufficient to achieve a state's goals. Military power may also be useful in public support such as disaster relief, exploration, and law enforcement after the violent phase of the conflict ends. Restoring governmental control and public services is an essential activity once the violence concludes. Failure to do so will only prolong the discomfort of the populace and foster discontent. This can lead to future violence.

Conflict among states and groups of people occurs due to this struggle for power in order to achieve the independence of freedom to act. In the past, nations have sought the power that more natural resources might bring, an advantage over a neighbor in order to enhance their citizens' standard of living or ability to survive. Nations have fought over ideology or religious views rather than exhibit tolerance of another's beliefs. Today we see the potential for conflict arising from fundamental cultural beliefs with a foundation in religious intolerance.

Samuel Huntington has warned of conflict between Western civilization's values and the values of other civilizations in contact with the West. The rise of religious intolerance particularly as espoused by radical Islamic beliefs has led to opposition of Western culture and influence around the world. Huntington writes that the reasons for conflict include the traditional ones that have long generated hostilities including "the control of people, territory, wealth, and resources, and relative power, that is the ability to impose one's own values, culture, and institutions on another group." These conflicts combined with conflicts based on "personal, tribal, racial, [and] civilizational" conflict fueled by the human tendency to hate have spawned conflict around the world.[35] When reviewing the actions of terrorists such as Osama bin Laden with the attacks on the United States and other Western or relatively pro-Western countries, it is fairly easy to see justification for Huntington's writings, which occurred well before the infamous September 11, 2001, attacks.

Nations and groups of people fight in order to enhance their power or gain some sort of freedom to act or think. Islamists fight Western culture today because they see it as a threat to their way of life. Civil wars occur because one group in a nation strives to dominate another or to gain freedom from oppression. Insurgents have fought colonial powers in order to gain freedom for their people or support another cause in a neighboring country. The competitive nature of people underscores the violence that people are willing to inflict on one another in order to achieve some level of advantage over an opposing person or group.

Consequently, war means the violent use of military power to constrain another state, group of states, or hostile group of people from some action. This constraint depends on the relative power of the states and groups involved. The outcome of the struggle will determine which states or groups have the independence, or freedom, of action to do as they wish and not be forced to act as another wishes. However, many would argue that the issue is much more complex than this definition implies. They are correct. The spectrum of conflict addresses that complexity.

2

Types of Wars

WAR, PEACE, AND MILITARY POWER

The spectrum of conflict is a term sometimes used to describe the range of types of activities in which military forces may find themselves. Such phrasing is an attempt to categorize military actions into more descriptive terms than simply war and peace. However, this terminology can be misleading because the term categorizes military actions in ways that can be difficult to comprehend. War and peace alone are insufficient because war implies extreme violence as discussed earlier. However, military forces may attempt to limit rather than increase the level of violence. On the other hand, peace implies a lack of violence, but military force always includes the potential for violence. Some authors use the spectrum of conflict as a way to differentiate among the various ways a government uses military power. Depending on the definitions presented, these ways may include violent or nonviolent uses of military forces.

Regardless of the use of military force, it remains a tool or instrument available to resolve a conflict. The conflict may be internal or external to a nation. Resolving conflict may include the violent or nonviolent use of this tool. The availability of military force provides power to the government or organization that directs the use of this instrument. This power provides the ability to act without interference except from the holder of a greater degree of power.

Warfare is a complex endeavor. While the characteristics of war may change over time, Clausewitz's linkage of war and policy remains valid. Clausewitz's conceptual description of war as a continuation of government policy remains correct, even though the methods of warfare may have changed. Whether a nation's government or the leader of a revolutionary band decides to make war, the head of a body of people is continuing its policy (or actions inherent to ruling) when it selects war as a course to follow. The fact that groups of people other than nations make war does not mean Clausewitz's idea is dead.

CONFLICT INTENSITY

One way to view this spectrum is as consisting of low-, mid-, and high-intensity conflicts. These categories generally relate to the perceived intensity of combat due to the lethality of the weapons used on the battlefield and the importance of battlefield actions over nonmilitary operations such as providing medical care to civilians. The idea being that the overall level of violence would translate into different levels of perceived intensity of violence. In the theoretical sense, this might work. However, the soldier being fired at might have practical difficulty attempting to differentiate among the levels in each category.

The 1981 version of the Army's *Field Manual (FM) 100-20: Low-Intensity Conflict* used the type of weapons as a way to differentiate between high- and mid-intensity conflicts. High-intensity conflict included the use of nuclear and chemical weapons. Mid-intensity conflict excluded nuclear but included chemical weapons.[1] Low-intensity conflict included two types of operations or conflicts: Type A was "internal defense and development operations involving actions by U.S. combat forces" to establish internal control within a country. Type B included the same types of operations but not by U.S. combat forces. Instead, U.S. advice, combat support, and combat service support would assist host nation forces in establishing internal control. These definitions also indicated high- and mid-intensity conflicts were between nations. Low-intensity conflict involved internal rather than external threats.

Barry Crane, Joel Lesan, Robert Plebanek, Paul Shemella, Ronald Smith, and Richard Williams differentiated between low-intensity conflict and conventional war by categorizing military operations by seven characteristics. Here, conventional war encompassed mid-intensity and high-intensity conflicts. The characteristics included objectives, parties to the conflict, conflict termination, limitations on military actions, source of direction of effort, sizes of units involved, collateral damage, and cost.[2]

These authors considered the primacy of political objectives in low-intensity conflict and the primacy of military objectives in conventional war to be the basic difference between low-intensity conflict and conventional war. Low-intensity conflict was often a conflict between a state and a non-state group. Conventional war was a conflict between states. Belligerents terminate a low-intensity conflict by controlling the populace and ultimately the government. A conventional war terminates through the defeat of military forces and is generally on a shorter timeline than a low-intensity conflict.[3]

Another highlighted difference was in the primacy of the government agencies involved. A wide range of government agencies participate in low-intensity conflict in order to win support from a nation's people. Since military actions are the key in conventional war, the military provides the central direction of such a war effort. Low-intensity conflict also differs from conventional war in the character of tactical engagements. In low-intensity conflict, small units conduct most combat operations. In conventional war, large units conduct combat operations.[4]

Collateral damage was another difference between low-intensity conflict and conventional war. Low-intensity conflict requires the careful use of firepower to avoid injury to the nation's citizenry. Population support is essential for success. An insurgent will hide among the populace for support and protection. Conventional war requires the destruction of military forces and the industrial base that supports large armies. Civilian deaths are not a primary objective but will undoubtedly occur.[5]

The last difference in the types of war addressed by these authors was the resources available. Low-intensity conflict often involves unsophisticated weaponry and equipment. Conventional war requires the most sophisticated weaponry and equipment available to best counter another nation's military forces.[6]

Another way to view this conflict spectrum is through the ideas of limited and unlimited war. Clausewitz discussed how war tends toward the absolute.[7] A nation will use its power to reach its objectives. If one level of violence or power will not suffice, the nation will increase the level of violence or increase the amount of its power used until it achieves its objectives. Consequently, war tends toward an extreme. That does not mean all war is unlimited. It only means nations should use their power to ensure success. Therefore, a nation will escalate the use of its power until it has no more to use, or it achieves its goals. If all power available is used, the war is unlimited. If any power is held back, the war is limited. But war is not that simple.

Nations are not always willing to use all of their available power. Limited objectives may restrict the need to use maximum force. Fear of international condemnation may limit the force used. Fear of reprisal may also restrict the force options available.

Limited objectives may mean the use of limited power because a nation may not need unlimited power expenditures to achieve the objectives. If one nation does not need to destroy another nation, it does not need to use an amount of power that will result in destruction. Using more power than required ensures that some amount of power or resources is wasted. War is certainly not the most efficient of human endeavors. Effectiveness is more important than efficiency. It is better to maximize efficiency and effectiveness if that is possible as long as effectiveness is dominant.

International condemnation may limit the use of certain types of power. The international condemnation of nuclear, biological, and chemical weapons makes their use a special consideration. International society views such weapons of mass destruction as morally wrong. Even though using such weapons could achieve a nation's war objectives, international reaction could make subsequent victory a hollow one. The limiting factor is the pain the user of the weapons will face. If the user will face damaging economic boycotts or the loss of key allies, the use of condemned weapons could ultimately be more painful than the consequences of not using them. Of course, if the condemnation is verbal with no damaging substance to it, using condemned weapons may be worth the price paid.

Fear of reprisal can restrict the use of certain weapons. The world fears the use of nuclear weapons because of the belief that a strategic exchange could radically alter worldwide environmental conditions and cause unspeakable levels of death and destruction. The entire planet might suffer due to the acts of a small group. This concern acted as a restraint on the use of tactical nuclear weapons for years out of concern that their use would have automatically escalated to a strategic exchange between nations such as the United States and the Soviet Union. There is no reason to use a weapon that will result in your own destruction by provoking a similar response from an opponent.

For the threat of reprisal to be a restraint, the object of the promised reprisal must view the threat as a real one. The nation or group must possess the power to inflict the promised pain. It must have the instrument, whether a weapon or some other element of power, that will cause the desired pain. The nation or group must have the will to use the threatened form of attack or at least be able to convince the nation being threatened that the will to use the weapon exists.

Nuclear weapons by their nature then limit a nation's ability to use them. The lethality of a nuclear war exercises a restraint on the use of this weapon. While on one hand the use of nuclear weapons would follow from Clausewitz's discussion of war tending toward an absolute, their very destructiveness then precludes their use. This dilemma then in a sense poses as a limitation on the applicability of Clausewitz's concept of war and its absolute tendency when dealing with rational actors because such responsible nations always impose a limit on the weaponry that they are willing to use. Extreme circumstances such as national survival would be one such justification for the use of a weapon as destructive as a nuclear device as keeping in line with the concept of war's tendency toward an absolute.

An irrational actor, as seen from a Western democratic liberal society point of view, might very well follow Clausewitz more closely. A terrorist organization motivated by the promise of heavenly reward for inflicting pain and suffering on unbelievers might very well see great utility in using a weapon as destructive as nuclear systems in line with war tending toward an absolute. If a heavenly reward awaits the instigator of such destruction, why accept a limitation?

Another problem with the limited–unlimited characterization of war is that of the opponent's point of view. A war may be limited to one nation but unlimited to another with regard to the objective or outcome. For example, a nation may feel it can achieve its goals without using all its power or that world opinion prevents it from using all its resources to defeat another. However, the second nation may not be as rich in power as the first and may have to use all available assets to survive. How does one categorize such a conflict? The United States fought a limited conflict in Vietnam. It did not come close to fully mobilizing the nation to defeat the insurgency or North Vietnam. However, the conflict was not limited from the South Vietnamese government's viewpoint. It lost and ceased to exist after the North Vietnamese invasion. The United States fought a limited war. National survival was not at stake. This was not the situation faced by North Vietnam or South Vietnam.

North Vietnam was in a struggle for national survival with uniting all of Vietnam into one nation as a goal. That eventually happened. North Vietnam was fighting an unlimited war. It had to use all available resources or risk failure. Had it failed, Vietnam would not be one nation today. Failure risked extermination of the idea of a united Vietnam under the control of the North Vietnamese government. If the North Vietnamese government had failed to view the war as unlimited, that view would have resulted in national suicide.

South Vietnam faced the same dilemma. We now have proof of the consequences of defeat. South Vietnam's loss of the war resulted in the extinction of the South Vietnamese nation-state. For South Vietnam to have viewed the war in any terms other than unlimited (tending toward the absolute in Clausewitz's words) would have been foolish.

CONVENTIONAL VS. UNCONVENTIONAL WAR

Another way to view this spectrum of conflict is to consider war to be conventional or unconventional. Conventional war involves standard military formations like brigades and divisions fighting other standard military formations. Unconventional war does not include large formation combat but instead includes guerillas and special formations like rangers or some type of commando force. Tactics, support requirements, and political implications will differ. Conventional tactics are those automatically associated with military forces. Armies, navies, and air forces battle each other using infantry, tanks, artillery, battleships, aircraft carriers, bombers, fighters, and all those expensive items of hardware that seem to be the focus of constant government debate. This is the vision associated with George Patton's Third Army racing across France in World War II.

Supporting such forces requires massive amounts of trucks, fuel depots, ports, airfields, and trained technicians. Conventional war implies a political decision to achieve a battlefield victory over another nation's military power. This military victory will lead to the enemy government's surrender and agreement to subjugate its will to the victor's. Everyone will know who won. Victory is obvious. The war cannot last forever because each nation has a finite amount of military power. One nation will eventually overcome the other, unless both are so evenly matched that they stop fighting due to mutual exhaustion. Unconventional war includes the use of nonstandard military forces. Guerilla warfare and commando raids require different tactics from those required to maneuver a division through the European countryside. Guerillas must blend with the population to survive. They generally operate in small groups and use hit-and-run attacks and ambushes. Guerillas do not normally stand their ground and slug it out with an enemy force. Raids by their nature are operations of a short duration designed to achieve a specific objective requiring quick action.

Support to unconventional war must occur covertly. Guerillas depend on the population for materiel and moral support. Logistical requirements are much less than those for a modern, mechanized conventional warfare force. It takes less tonnage to support a soldier with a rifle who must carry everything he or she owns than it does to keep a tank or armored personnel carrier operational. Special operations forces do not need long-term support during operations because their operations must not last a long time by nature. Unconventional warfare requires a different political viewpoint as well. Victory will probably not come from a single, decisive battle. More time will be necessary to ensure the cumulative effect of the unconventional operations breaks the will of the opponent. The population may be an integral component of the battlefield as in guerilla operations, which adds pressure on the government to resolve the conflict in order to protect its citizens.

The 2005 U.S. National Defense Strategy refers to traditional, irregular, disruptive, and catastrophic challenges. Traditional challenges correspond to conventional war as discussed here. Irregular challenges include terrorists and insurgencies, where such opponents take a long-term view and seek to "erode influence, patience, and political will." Extremist ideologies and failing governments have given rise to these threats. Catastrophic challenges rely on the use of weapons of mass destruction to cause massive casualties or to threaten such action. Disruptive challenges seek to exploit a vulnerability or offset a present technological capability.[8]

Terrorism would fall in the unconventional category and is an exception to the idea that a decisive battle will normally not decide victory. Terrorism is also a category that is difficult to define. Most would agree that the slaughter of civilians, generally assumed to be innocent persons, at an airport as an act of protest against some government's decision or action is terrorism. The terrorists might disagree, especially if they view no civilian as "innocent." After all, any adult civilian can choose which government to support. Injuring or threatening to injure children is a way to punish parents and society. Killing children threatens the future of a nation or culture. Allowing them to live produces future enemies.

Still, most people can accept the idea that terrorism is an act of violence perpetuated against a person who cannot resolve a grievance but whose injury can influence the actions of a third party (such as a government) not directly involved in the violent act. The definition is a little cloudy, however, when the object of the attack is armed to defend itself and/or is a direct representative of a government. The bombing of the U.S. Marine barracks in Beirut in 1983 is an example of where there may be room to argue whether the act was terrorism or an act of someone who was desperate and determined to fight for a cause.

The bombing of the Marine barracks certainly had some of the characteristics of terrorist attacks. An individual drove an explosive-laden truck into the building and killed himself as he blew up the truck and destroyed the barracks. The intent was apparently to protest the American presence and to influence the American government's future decisions affecting that region. However, one could also argue that this act was that of a patriot fighting for his version of freedom in his land. Our own pages of history are filled with soldiers sacrificing themselves for the cause of freedom. What is the difference between soldiers, sailors, airmen, or marines dying for their compatriots and the suicide of a Moslem trying to drive the United States out of his or her country? After all, the marines were armed and capable of defending themselves had their defenses been designed to do so. The difference is perspective. Some Arabs resent the U.S. actions in the Middle East. Some Arabs or Moslems would undoubtedly refer to the dead Moslem as a hero, a freedom fighter. On the other hand, Americans would probably continue to define this as an act of terrorism by a Moslem fanatic whose sneak attack prevented the Marines from defending themselves.

Another point worth consideration is that of a decisive battle in these operations outside the normal definition of war. Since the United States withdrew its military forces from Lebanon after the bombing, this may very well be an example of a decisive battle. A difficulty in defining any event as "decisive" is that it being decisive depends on the viewpoint of the decision-maker. An event is decisive if the event results in a decision that alters national policy or forces a new course of action. Therefore, a terrorist act can be decisive if it causes such a change.

Of course, conventional and unconventional operations can occur simultaneously to complement one another. Guerillas or commandos can operate behind an enemy's front lines while conventional forces fight as expected. During World War II, Russian and French partisans harassed German supply lines, while conventional operations continued unabated.

TYPES OF WEAPONS

Types of weapons can characterize the spectrum of conflict. Categories could include nuclear war and nonnuclear war or war with nuclear, biological, and chemical weapons and war with conventional weapons. Certain weapons cause a dramatic change in the inherent characteristics of war. Their use changes the rules that govern decisions by political and military leaders. Nuclear weapons provide an example.

The use of nuclear weapons has inspired countless hours and pages of debate. Their destructive power is acknowledged by all. However, some people feel their power is so great and the psychological impact of their use so severe that the weapons are inherently evil. War is different when nuclear weapons are involved.

Nuclear weapons provide the capability to destroy an enemy with unprecedented speed and efficiency. Compared to the physical cost of maintaining the same capability using nonnuclear forces, nuclear weapons are cheap. In this manner nuclear weapons bring a dramatic change to warfare. They consolidate incredible destructive power in the hands of a few people.

If one assumes the use of one nuclear weapon will automatically lead to the use of more, so that escalation will continue into a massive exchange of national nuclear arsenals, then nuclear weapons change war because the use of one weapon will lead to the destruction of the enemy and possibly the nation itself. This automatic escalation leading to mutual destruction (or even worldwide destruction) is why some people view nuclear weapons as inherently evil. Of course, to follow this line you have to believe several things.

First, you must believe that a massive exchange of nuclear weapons will render the target nations unlivable. The human ability to adapt must be considered inapplicable or too feeble to make a difference. Targeting efficiency must be assumed so high that sufficient weapons will strike the targeted country and detonate so that the destruction is complete. You also must assume that the political leaders involved will condemn millions to their deaths by following through with such a plan or that such an exchange will just "happen."

These assumptions are questionable. Targeting efficiency of any weapon is rarely as good as first thought. Regardless of how horrible the destruction, a few people will probably survive even if the political leaders are sufficiently mad to follow such a course of action. Circumstances could certainly prove these objections wrong. Nations spend a great deal of money ensuring that they hit a target. If sufficient numbers of weapons launch, enough may get through to kill everyone. Finally, madmen do sometimes rise to national leadership. Adolf Hitler proved that.

Nuclear weapons provide the opportunity for war to tend toward the extreme (with an acknowledgment of Clausewitz) that includes total destruction of the enemy. This threat is particularly useful if the opponent lacks such weapons or only has a few of them. However, the threat is only useful if the object of the threat perceives that the nation with the nuclear weapons has the will to use them.

This threat of massive and possibly mutual destruction is why nuclear weapons have served as a deterrent to war between major powers since World War II. No nuclear power has used nuclear weapons as tools to settle a dispute. Nuclear weapons have exerted a restraint on major powers settling disputes by strength of arms.

GEOGRAPHY

War can also divide along geographical lines. A war could be global because it includes operations around the world. World War II was obviously global. War could be regional because operations are confined to a particular group of countries located near one another. The Napoleonic Wars were regional because they were generally confined to Europe. War can be international because the fighting is between two nations or internal because it occurs between belligerents within one country. The Vietnam War was international and internal. The United States and South Vietnam fought North Vietnam—the international component. The South Vietnamese fought an internal conflict because it battled South Vietnamese guerillas, the Viet Cong.

WAR AND OPERATIONS SHORT OF WAR

Another way to look at the types of wars is to divide military operations into war and operations short of war. War then includes military conflict between nations where a variety of weapons may be used, including nuclear, chemical, and conventional. Weapon selection would depend on objectives, resources, and outside or self-imposed restraints regarding the carnage allowed. Operations short of war would include actions normally associated with low-intensity conflict, unconventional operations, and special operations not supporting war. As always, though, defining war and differentiating between the two categories is difficult.

This differentiation remains challenging because there are a variety of types of military operations or functions that can occur simultaneously. War is reasonably easy to characterize because the use of violence while not desired at least is obvious and easy to explain. Everything else tends to fall into the operations other than war or military operations other than war.

The simultaneity of a variety of such operations while violence is ongoing makes the explanation or characterization difficult.

REVOLUTION AND COUNTERREVOLUTION

Revolution and counterrevolution relate to the survival of the government of a nation. For this reason categorizing them as components of low-intensity conflict or limited war is not a good fit. A small or weak nation could be fighting a counterrevolutionary war against a revolutionary group. If the weak nation has a superpower such as the United States as an ally, the superpower may conduct a limited war to support its ally. Operations could be conventional or unconventional. Types of weapons and actions could simultaneously fit into mid-intensity or low-intensity conflict as well. Theoretically, one nation could even use nuclear weapons in a counterrevolutionary war if it were willing to significantly damage a portion of itself and face the public outcry that would most certainly result.

A revolution seeks a major change in society. Any types of operations conceivable could be used. However, revolutions are typically conducted by some segment of society that is not in control. Revolutionaries want to overthrow the existing government and possibly society in general. Therefore, revolutions tend to include unconventional operations by the revolutionaries. Selected violence to effect change is used. Seemingly random violence can be useful if the intent is to show government inability to maintain public safety and control. Major combat actions between large formations do not occur because the revolutionaries normally have no large formations able to carry out such operations.

Of course, if the revolution includes some element of a nation's military force or the revolution lasts long enough for the revolutionaries to form large units, major combat operations may occur. When the American colonies first revolted against Great Britain, they had militias and volunteers. Once time and resources were available, the Continental Army came into being and was able to conduct large unit operations against the conventional British Army units in conjunction with French army and naval assistance.

FULL SPECTRUM OPERATIONS

Operations in the early part of this new century have included modifications to the terminology used to describe military operations in situations that include all of the complexities imaginable. The difficult and dangerous work to rebuild Iraq after the defeat of Saddam Hussein's military forces and the efforts to establish and support democracy in Afghanistan after the defeat of the Taliban fit this mold. The U.S. Army defined full spectrum operations as operations that "combine offensive, defensive, stability and reconstruction, and civil support operations."[9] The new terms in this definition are stability and reconstruction operations.

The 2005 version of *Field Manual 1: The Army* defines stability and reconstruction operations in the following manner:

> *Stability and reconstruction* [italics in original] operations sustain and exploit security and control over areas, populations, and resources. They employ military capabilities to reconstruct or establish services and support civilian agencies. Stability and reconstruction operations involve both coercive and cooperative actions. They may occur before, during, and after offensive and defensive operations; however, they also occur separately, usually at the lower end of the range of military operations. Stability and reconstruction operations lead to an environment in which, in cooperation with a legitimate government, the other instruments of national power can predominate.[10]

The same doctrinal manual also points out that these operations may occur at the same time by noting "[s]imultaneity is at the heart of how the Army operates: Army forces conduct offensive, defensive, and stability and reconstruction operations at the same time throughout a campaign."[11]

This discussion makes it clear that one cannot divide war into specific types that fit in some sort of linear projection. Operations designed to kill an enemy combatant and those required to help the civilian populace may occur at the same time within a given geographic area. Physical separation may exist in a matter of feet or city blocks. Death and injury may threaten any or all of the missions and people, whether combatants or not, regardless of the actual intent of the combatants. The idea of simultaneity is truly crucial. These types of military operations do not necessarily grow from one to another in a simple line.

CONSTRAINT, RESTRAINT, AND FREEDOM

The concepts of constraint, restraint, and freedom to act are the key factors in any competitive struggle between nations. Nations seek to constrain and restrain the actions of other nations, groups, and people in order to enhance or maintain power. Nations also strive to reduce the constraints and restraints placed on them by other nations, groups, or people. Freedom of action results from a lack of such limitations. Focusing on the environmental conditions, including weaponry, as a way to explain a theory of war diverts attention from the central issues of constraint and restraint, as they provide freedom of action.

Limiting an opponent's actions, the objective of conflict between nations, should drive the decisions concerning tactics and weapons used. The

goal of the commander or leader is to select the proper methods and resources to achieve the objectives. Combinations of various methods and
resources may be best.

Weaponry, such as nuclear and chemical weapons, should not be used
to categorize war. They are tools that a general or a terrorist could use.
Availability, objectives, and accepted restraints govern their use. Weaponry
should not be part of the definition of the spectrum of conflict or an attempt
to categorize types of war. The weaponry used is a function of resource
availability, not some identifiable characteristic of one war that makes it
different from another.

Defining the spectrum of conflict by using tactics also results in a grave
error because it attempts to divorce various techniques from one another.
Conventional and unconventional operations can complement each other.
Large military formations can operate in conjunction with guerillas or special
operations raiding forces. Partisans and regular units have cooperated in
conflicts as different as the American Revolutionary War, World War II, and
Vietnam. The tactics used do not adequately serve to differentiate among
different types of conflicts.

Using weaponry or tactics to differentiate among different types of conflict also ignores the connection among political decisions and military force.
Political decisions should determine the tools used by a government. The
tools should not drive the decision. Military force is one tool. Diplomatic
persuasion and economic policies are others.

POWER AS A TOOL

Any type, or element, of power is a tool for a government to use. A
nation should not automatically accept or reject any available means of
enforcing its will. A nation must carefully weigh the resources and methods
available that can accomplish the task and make a choice. A nation must
also carefully consider the consequences of using the methods and resources
that are viable choices. The cost of using certain ones may exceed the benefit.

A linear spectrum of conflict is wrong because it ignores the complexity
of warfare. Theory must include the many types of military operations.
However, theory must not put types of wars in boxes that hide the overlap
between such categories and the combinations of military activities available
to a commander to help him achieve success. If theory portrays simplicity
rather than the complexity of reality, theory only serves to confuse, not bring
clarity. Simplicity can aid understanding, but it must not blind the student
to the complexity.

This is not to say that all things in war are complex. The basic idea
of competition or constraint and restraint through the use of military and
other types of power is simple. Violence in itself can be very simple. Killing
people is simple and final. However, the combinations of types of power,

methods of using the types of power, the variety of resources available, and the personalities of the leaders make execution of decisions a very complex affair. Using military power alone is very complex because of the different types of forces, weapons, and tactics from which to choose. Combining effects of various elements of power increases the complexity of military operations. Leaders must synchronize such combinations, so that all actions work together to achieve the ultimate goal. If such actions are only combined rather than synchronized, certain actions may actually negate the outcome of other actions.

The spectrum of conflict is really a collection of many options concerning how to use power to achieve goals. Violence is only one way to gain a desired effect. Before deciding on the type of conflict in which to engage, the political leadership must determine the desired end state. Failure to do this will result in an uncoordinated (therefore, unsynchronized) application of power. Only luck will bring success. Excessive damage to enemy resources and neighboring nations may result. Resource application will at least be inefficient if not ineffective.

Assuming the leaders decide upon a satisfactory end state, they must then select the type(s) of power that can achieve the end state desired. This selection must consider the ability of the type of power to achieve the end state without violating any applicable restraints. These restraints may come from internal or external sources and include such concerns as acceptable noncombatant suffering, actions other allies and enemies may take, and the allowable degradation of the type of power used considering other potential uses of that power.

If decision-makers select military power as part of the solution, they enter the arena often called the spectrum of conflict. Of course, even the use of nonmilitary power could be considered part of the spectrum of conflict. When one nation's goals or decisions threaten another's goals or decisions, they are in conflict. Any power used to resolve this disagreement becomes part of the general spectrum of conflict. However, my study of conflict has focused on uses of military power. Therefore, this discussion will do the same.

The terms limited and unlimited have value only as they describe a particular belligerent's commitment to the struggle at hand. Most wars are limited because nations rarely use absolutely every shred of power available to annihilate an enemy. However, it can occur, and each belligerent may view the war differently. A powerful nation may fight limited war against a less powerful nation that may have to fight an unlimited war or immediately surrender.

The intensity of conflict as a descriptor is misleading. The person being shot at will view the war as high-intensity regardless of the category someone else tries to apply to the conflict as a whole. Weapons certainly should not be used as the way to differentiate among these levels of intensity because weapons are tools. Their use depends on their availability and the desired effects. Nuclear, biological, and chemical weapons are prime examples.

Military forces or groups may use nuclear, biological, or chemical weapons if they must rapidly inflict massive numbers of casualties on the opposing force. A terrorist could use them—too. Such weapons may bring special considerations to warfare with regard to noncombatant casualties and international condemnation. These considerations may bring additional complexity to decision-making. However, the basic problem of matching resources to the desired end state remains. As with any course of action, the decision-maker must carefully weigh the benefits of using a resource versus the consequences of its use. This is an obvious concern when considering weapons of mass destruction.

The spectrum of conflict then is really the collection of different missions that a military force may have. A military force could have a mission requiring it to attack, defend, delay, conduct a raid, perform reconnaissance, conduct peacekeeping or peacemaking operations, rescue hostages, protect a prospective target, enforce law and order, build roads, and many other tasks. Each type of mission has different training, force structure, and support requirements. Tactics may vary from mission to mission. Weapons and other equipment are the tools used to accomplish the mission.

For this reason the apparent automatic linkage today between special operations and the many operations that indicate military operations in other than major combat operations (including terms such as insurgency, counterinsurgency, combating terrorism, stability operations, and others) is unfortunate. Special operations forces possess a wide range of skills that are valuable in many types of operations or types of wars. Equating low-intensity conflict operations or operations other than major combat operations with special operations makes it too easy for the majority of a nation's military forces to ignore such operations. This could bring disastrous consequences, if units other than special operations forces are needed. It is clear in operations in Iraq, while this manuscript is under production, that all types of units may engage in combat, and operations other than combat that support national political goals.

3

The Purpose of an Army

MILITARY POWER

What does an army do? Why do nations have an army or any military force? The answer involves much more than parades and inspections. Military force exists in order to provide military power—the use or threat of violence in order for a nation or group to force its will on another nation or group. However, a nation may use military power to do things not normally associated with military forces. These nonmilitary tasks may actually be the primary use of military forces during peacetime.

First of all, military forces are necessary to fight. If the existing power relationships are such that a nation must have the capability to cause bloodshed, the nation needs military power to do so. Death is very serious and is without a doubt final. There is no recovery, short of that associated with religious beliefs.

This is the violent aspect of military power. Threats or the actual imposition of violence in order to inflict death or injury on another nation or group is the primary purpose for having military power. If violence is not necessary, there is no need for military power. People being people, there will always be a need for coercive violence as a threat or for actual implementation of one nation's will over another. Mankind is clearly not yet ready to live together in peace and harmony. Anyone who believes that competition for domination of one's neighbors is not a factor in international relations is not paying attention to present events.

However, military forces can do much more than fight. Military forces provide a source of disciplined personnel trained to function as a unit. This can be useful in many ways. Anytime a nation needs a disciplined body of people to perform a specific task, military forces are potential tools. These missions could include fighting forest fires, assisting in disaster relief, and patrolling a border otherwise open to smugglers or other illegal entrants to the country.

DEFENSE AGAINST ALL ENEMIES

The U.S. military enlistment oath provides a key to understanding what an army can do. In that oath, soldiers pledge to protect the constitution against all enemies, foreign and domestic.[1] The phrase "all enemies" provides a tremendous degree of latitude in determining the U.S. Army's missions. Anything that threatens the ability of the constitution to continue to serve as the foundation upon which our government rests is an enemy that soldiers pledge to fight. American soldiers do not swear allegiance to any elected official or military officer. They pledge to protect the foundation of this nation's system of government—the U.S. Constitution. In this way, they obligate themselves to protect the very essence of our nation and our way of life.

This pledge certainly includes defending the United States from aggression by another nation. Few, if any, people would question the use of armed force to protect the United States during a war such as World War II. Nations have the right to defend themselves just as an individual does. International law and custom do not require a nation to commit suicide by refusing to defend itself. Soldiers provide the violence-producing capability to defend the nation against aggression.

One of Alexander Hamilton's arguments for the foundation of strong central government was the concern over an attack by an outside power. Standing armies were necessary to prevent an invader from conquering a nation before it could mobilize its citizens to repel the assault.[2] War is so dangerous and events can move so quickly that there is no questioning the need today of a standing military force. The size and composition of that force is worthy of much debate. However, a standing force capable of defending a nation is essential, if that nation plans to exist very long.

Should an internal or revolutionary threat exist, military forces again provide the capability for a nation to use violence to defeat the threat. Since this again involves protecting the nation, or at least the present government, from extermination, a nation has the right to use military forces in that way. Hamilton also warned of the need to consider using military force to quell insurrection to prevent the dissolution of a government.[3] National or governmental suicide is not required. Violence or the threat of violence is one means of enforcing domestic policy.

Of course, there are limits on the degree of violence the international community condones, even when national or governmental survival is at stake. The Geneva Convention is one attempt to civilize war to protect those no longer a military threat, such as prisoners. Various agreements limit the use of weapons that cause undue suffering, such as biological and chemical weapons. Generally, a nation that willfully attacks civilians not directly part of the war effort (for example, children), mistreats prisoners, attacks enemy medical facilities, or uses nuclear, biological, or chemical weapons risks international condemnation. However, since this condemnation generally does not include a violent reaction by the international community, the threat may not be persuasive.

Another limiting factor is the response of the opponent.

If one nation engages in excessive violence against another, the target nation may reciprocate. Therefore, the use of any element of military power may result in a similar reaction by an opponent. This could lead to an intolerable situation in the nation originally contemplating excessive violence.

This covers the obvious purpose of military force, but what else does an army do? The list is only bounded by the imagination and includes tasks such as nation-building, exploration, enforcing law and order, and governing. Various nations have had different experiences with their military forces performing these missions. Some have been bad. Some have been good. The danger always exists that military forces trained to cause violence may have a difficult time showing restraint in situations where violence is inappropriate.

NATION-BUILDING

Nation-building or reconstruction as is often used today is one use of military force. An example is civil works. Armies have engineers who have the ability to construct bridges, roads, airfields, ports, and buildings. Such construction is a way for an army to help its political leaders by improving the citizenry's standard of living. This subsequently increases the population's satisfaction with the political system and their leaders. The end result is domestic political stability. A satisfied population will not demand radical change. The government can focus on external concerns rather than internal ones, if the domestic situation is favorable. Medical facilities, schools, roads, and housing help a nation's citizens. Since winning the hearts and minds of the people is essential to ensure political stability, support of a nation's economic and social well-being is important.

This recognition of the importance of nation-building is not new. During the pacification of the Philippines after the 1898 Spanish–American War, the American Army built schools, reorganized governmental activities, and improved the local public health facilities. This improved the standard of living in the Philippines and reduced the resistance faced by the Army.[4]

Tremendous governmental and health problems also faced the U.S. forces in Veracruz, Mexico, in 1914. U.S. Army personnel established courts, collected and distributed taxes, collected import and export duties, ran the post office, and maintained schools. Public health was a special problem with such diseases as malaria, smallpox, meningitis, gonorrhea, syphilis, tuberculosis, and dysentery rampant. Efforts to clean up the city were so successful that the death rate for the Mexican population in the city dropped 25%.[5]

Even in the United States, this nation-building support, or support to civilian authorities, is evident. Recent years have seen American active duty soldiers fighting forest fires in Western states and providing disaster relief in Southern states after hurricanes. This is a far cry from defending the nation against a foreign invasion. However, it certainly is in line with the concept of protecting the nation against domestic enemies as long as one is willing to accept a threat to public safety as an enemy worthy of committing all available resources to fight.

Another nation-building type activity conducted within the United States includes the multitude of U.S. Army Corps of Engineers projects. The Army has performed a tremendous service to the nation by supporting the country's inland waterway and power systems. A nation cannot afford to neglect any resource when providing a better life for its citizens.

EXPLORATION

Exploration is another way an army can help a nation. The U.S. Army played a key role in developing the nation by supporting the exploration and expansion westward. By the nature of their training and experience, soldiers are well prepared to endure the hardships and accept the risks associated with exploration. Whether considering land, sky, sea, or space, military forces are always interested in the environment where they may have to operate. This need to understand their operating environments makes exploration an obvious goal of military forces. Therefore, a nation tasking its military forces to explore is actually providing its military forces a reason to do something it wants to do anyway.

LAW ENFORCEMENT

Enforcing law and order is another potential use of military force. The U.S. Army was one source of government control and law enforcement as the nation expanded westward. Until citizens established sufficient local government structures through towns and states, federal troops had to fill the void.

As part of its nation-building operations in other countries, the Army has established law and order. This work has included maintaining law and order using its organic capability. It also included training host nation police forces to do the same. One of the Army's postoperation requirements in Operation Just Cause in Panama was to establish a civilian government–controlled police force to replace the Panama Defense Force. Maintaining law and order was a critical problem.

The military's role in domestic law enforcement continues to be a topic of debate today. In the United States, posse comitatus restrictions limit the use of the military services. For example, should the U.S. government use military forces to combat the drug trade? Armed forces have sophisticated communication hardware, intelligence systems, and transportation capabilities that can help police forces detect drug producers and traffickers and mass the necessary personnel to interdict the drug flow. The use of military forces to combat national level problems such as this will vary by nation, depending on its laws and experiences in using the military as a force resembling a national police force or an army typically focused on combating other armies.

Craig Trebilock has stated that the Posse Comitatus Act was originally passed in 1878 to preclude the use of the U.S. Army as a national police force. Congress became concerned that the Army's actions in Reconstruction-era South and the stationing of Army troops at polling sites risked politicizing the Army.[6] However, John Brinkerhoff disagrees with Trebilock and has written that Congress passed the act to prevent the local law enforcement officials from requiring local Army units to assist in law enforcement activities.[7] The act does not specifically prohibit the use of the Navy, Marines, or National Guard in law enforcement, even though the Department of Defense has considered all military forces to fall under the same restrictions.[8]

The U.S. president is also required to maintain law and order. If local or state agencies are unable to maintain law and order, the president can order the secretary of defense to employ federal military forces to restore order, such as after the riots in Los Angeles in 1992.[9] Exceptions passed to the restrictions on use of the military specifically allow the use of military forces when nuclear or other weapons of mass destruction are involved. The secretary of defense may also allow military personnel to support counterdrug operations by training law enforcement personnel in the use and maintenance of military equipment. The Posse Comitatus Act does not preclude the use of the military for law enforcement operations, but it does impose limits on the use of military forces.[10] Such limitations then are planning considerations that leaders must include in their decision process when selecting an appropriate reaction to an internal problem.

The use of military forces in this manner in order to enforce laws embroils military units in a mission not traditionally associated with military force. This does not mean that military units cannot conduct law enforcement operations. However, it does mean that government leaders must carefully consider the costs associated with such a use of military power.

Certain military forces have utility in a law enforcement role, and such operations are very close to their traditional missions. For example, transportation assets such as helicopters and trucks can transport police forces or military personnel performing law enforcement duties generally like they move standard military units. Radars can also provide electronic surveillance to report activity in a particular area. However, problems may arise once contact with a suspected criminal activity occurs.

A danger is that soldiers trained to use deadly force as a general rule rather than as an exception could unintentionally harm innocent people. Historical concerns over due process and the accused being innocent until proven guilty could become virtually meaningless. Negative reaction to the actions of British soldiers in colonial America certainly influenced many people in their decision to support the founding of the United States.

Military forces traditionally train to find and destroy hostile military forces. Police forces capture suspected criminals, so that the judicial system can try them. As long as the judicial system considers a suspected criminal to be innocent until proven guilty, no alternative exists. Disregarding this principle could result in the incarceration, injury, or death of innocent people who are suspected criminals.

Obviously, such a legal system demands that restraint in using force to apprehend individuals be essential. Failure to show restraint could result in violation of this basic tenet of American law, where people are innocent until proven guilty. However, military forces traditionally do not train to show restraint. They train to use violence to destroy. Therefore, the type of action traditionally required of military forces is very different from that associated with police forces. If military forces charged with a law enforcement mission cannot make this change, a catastrophe will result. The relatively free application of violence will result in the injury or death of innocent people—bystanders due to collateral damage or suspected criminals who may be innocent or at least not legally guilty. Either outcome is unsatisfactory.

Another related problem is the negative impact on the military force's ability to perform its traditional wartime mission. If the military force succeeds in altering its mindset so that it shows restraint, it will again have to change if it must fight another military force. Soldiers are not robots with an on/off switch to facilitate the enforcement of certain behavior. Training would be essential in order to help soldiers and units transition between these functions.

Corruption is also a danger when using military force as a tool of law enforcement. Soldiers receive very little pay compared to the vast sums of money involved in drug trafficking. They could become targets of bribes to influence operations in order to prevent apprehension of certain criminals. Corruption or even allegations of corruption could weaken the faith the citizenry has in its military forces.

The danger of corruption also exists with regular police forces; however, there is an added danger when a nation's military forces are involved. The danger is that the nation will lose faith in the government's ability to protect it from external aggression. This would result in a loss of will, an element of power. It could also encourage an external enemy to take advantage of this loss in power to take action injurious to the nation such as an attack on the nation or an ally.

This discussion is not intended to indicate that military forces cannot or should not perform law enforcement operations. One could easily argue that the American Army and Marine Corps are performing these functions daily in Iraq in the aftermath of the 2003 Operation Iraqi Freedom defeat of the Iraqi military and government. Soldiers and marines have provided law enforcement functions and support before and will probably do so in the future. However, law enforcement operations include certain considerations. Leaders empowered to make such resource allocation decisions must carefully weigh the benefits and risks or costs of such a decision.

GOVERNING

Military forces can also perform a governmental role. If no government authority exists, a military force can establish population control and societal structure to govern an area or country. The coercive nature of military power's dependence on violence provides the means to ensure obedience to laws or rules established. The authoritative hierarchy inherent in a military force provides the necessary structure to replicate political activities.

The U.S. military has acted as a government when no civilian authority existed. Such actions should be temporary but are nonetheless critical until civilian control is possible. A rapid return to local civilian control is essential to provide legitimacy to the civilian government that eventually comes to power. People do not want to be ruled by an outsider. The longer another nation's military remains in control, the greater the risk that civilians who run the government will face accusations that they are dupes of the occupying power. Stability comes from the population's satisfaction with its government. The population will not be satisfied if it views its leaders as puppets of another nation. This ability to threaten violence as a means of establishing control forms the basis for military forces to control or overthrow civilian governments. Recent events in the underdeveloped regions of the world show that the threat of a military coup is very real in some countries. The American tradition of civilian control over the military is a very important means of preventing such problems in the United States.

Fortunately, all coups do not result in a permanent loss of democracy or civilian control. Turkey provides a ready example, since the Turkish military has overthrown its government and returned it to civilian control several times. This is a remarkable achievement and an indication of the dedication to civilian governmental control and the concern for its nation that the Turkish military leadership has held.

SOCIALIZATION

A by-product of drawing together people from different social backgrounds to serve in a military force is socialization. Forcing people with different backgrounds to live and work together helps people discover similarities in beliefs. Such close contact may eventually reduce prejudices held by various groups toward others. This breaking down of social barriers is necessary for a military force to develop sufficient unit cohesion to withstand the rigors of combat.

People who serve in a nation's military will take these lessons learned back to society. If their group is large, their experiences will begin to change society. Of course, this process is not instantaneous. As more people serve, the socialization process spreads.

SUMMARY

An army or military force can have many functions. The overriding purpose is to protect the nation through the use or threatened use of violence. The ability to inflict pain is essential. However, as a source of disciplined manpower with many varied skills, military forces can do much more. They can perform disaster relief, conduct nation-building operations, explore uncharted territory, enforce law and order, and govern. The list may very well only depend on the imagination of the leaders deciding how to resolve a nation's problems. However, the leaders must carefully consider the impact of diverting military forces from their primary mission.

Use of military forces to conduct operations other than their traditional one of fighting other military forces risks a loss in the ability to fight an external aggressor. Leaders must carefully assess this risk before diverting military resources. The benefit may be worth the risk. The decision-maker must understand the risk and make a rational decision.

Military forces can do many things. All deserve recognition as well as inclusion in the range of options for using military power to accomplish national goals. The uses of military forces vary by the needs of the situation. All types of operations occur in violent and nonviolent environments. The critical point is for the leader responsible for taking action to make a careful appraisal of the desired objective and select the forces that can best succeed.

Regardless of the mission assigned, military forces must not lose the ability to fight. Defeating external and internal threats remains the principal purpose of military forces. Disregarding that key point could eventually result in an impotent military, a tool without the ability to perform its primary mission. When a nation's military forces lose the ability to use violence to inflict pain on an enemy, they are no longer an element of power.

4

Levels of War

LEVELS

Military theory and American military doctrine today accept three levels of war—strategic, operational, and tactical. No specific levels of command or types of forces are exclusively associated with any single level. Technological change has ensured that distinct boundaries do not exist among them. The effect of an action regarding its impact on objectives determines whether an action is strategic, operational, or tactical.[1] The meanings of the strategic, operational, and tactical levels of war have changed over time. The history of each provides a basis for understanding.

STRATEGIC LEVEL OF WAR

Strategy has had various meanings over the years. Clausewitz defined strategy as "the use of engagements for the object of the war."[2] Jomini defined strategy as "the art of making war upon the map." He defined grand tactics as "the art of posting troops upon the battlefield according to the accidents of the ground, of bringing them into action, and the art of fighting upon the ground, in contradistinction to planning upon a map." Jomini related strategy and grand tactics by stating strategy determined "where to act," while grand tactics determined "the manner of execution and the employment of the troops."[3] These definitions grew from the authors' analyses of Napoleon's conduct of war. These definitions also guided military thought for years.

Baron von der Goltz explained strategy as the "science of directing armies."[4] When John Burr described warfare during the early years of World War II, he associated strategy with the conduct of campaigns and planning where, how, and with what force to strike an enemy. Burr included an army's movements before contacting an enemy as part of strategy. Strategy was important to position forces to ensure a successful battle.[5]

Other definitions of strategy included managing operations, gaining an advantage during a campaign,[6] or determining whether to use nuclear or nonnuclear forces.[7] Trevor Dupuy described strategy as planning and managing all types of resources to wage war. He wrote that national strategy includes combining political, economic, psychological, social, and military resources in war and peace to support national policies. Military strategy focuses on using military resources in war to support national policy.[8] Liddell Hart defined strategy as "the art of distributing and applying military means to fulfill the ends of policy." Edward Luttwak concluded that strategy includes "the conduct and consequences of human relations in the context of actual or possible armed conflict."[9]

Soviet military theory considered military strategy as "the highest level of military art." Military strategy included studying and preparing for war.[10] Strategy was a combat activity focused at national and theater levels.[11] Soviet General Aleksandr A. Svechin defined strategy as "the art of combining preparations for war and the grouping of operations for achieving the goal set by the war for the armed forces."[12]

The U.S. Army has used a variety of definitions of strategy. Before World War II, strategy referred to maneuvering or concentrating forces in a theater of operations to facilitate battle.[13] After World War II, strategy expanded in scope to include a direct linkage between military and national strategy. For example, the 1962 *FM 100-5: Field Service Regulations—Operations* defined military strategy as the use of military means to further national strategy.[14] The 1982 *FM 100-5: Operations* discussed military strategy as the use of armed forces or the threat of their use to attain national policy objectives.[15]

The U.S. Army's 1986 *FM 100-5* defined military strategy as "the art and science of employing the armed forces of a nation or alliance to secure policy objectives by the application or threat of force."[16] Companion doctrinal manuals stated that the combination of military objectives, concepts, and force were necessary to meet national security policy objectives. National strategy included using political influence, economic resources, psychological actions, military power, and national will to achieve national objectives during peace, crisis, or war.[17]

The 1987 Joint Chiefs of Staff *Publication 1 (JCS Pub 1)* defined strategy as "the art and science of developing and using political, economic, psychological, and military forces as necessary during peace and war" in support of policies to increase the chance of victory and lessen that of defeat. National strategy focuses on using these elements of power "to secure national objectives." Military strategy concerns using military power to do the same.[18]

The U.S. Army's 2001 *FM 3-0: Operations* defined strategy as "art and science of developing and employing armed forces and other instruments of national power in a synchronized fashion to secure national or multinational objectives." The updated 2008 version of *FM 3-0* changed the definition to "a prudent idea or set of ideas for employing the instruments of national power in a synchronized and integrated fashion to achieve theater, national, and/or multinational objectives" and references the 2006 *Joint Publication (JP) 3-0: Joint Operations*.[19] The 2001 *Joint Publication 3-0: Doctrine for Joint Operations* used a very similar definition of strategy—"[t]he art and science of developing and employing instruments of national power in a synchronized and integrated fashion to achieve theater, national, and/or multinational objectives."[20] The 2006 *JP 3-0* with Change 1 dated 2008 defined the strategic level of war as

> [t]he level of war at which a nation, often as a member of a group of nations, determines national or multinational (alliance or coalition) strategic security objectives and guidance, and develops and uses national resources to achieve these objectives. Activities at this level establish national and multinational military objectives; sequence initiatives; define limits and assess risks for the use of military and other instruments of national power; develop global plans or theater war plans to achieve those objectives; and provide military forces and other capabilities in accordance with strategic plans.[21]

The ninth edition of *Merriam-Webster's Collegiate Dictionary* lists several definitions of strategy. One definition is "the science and art of employing the political, economic, psychological, and military forces of a nation or group of nations to afford the maximum support to adopted policies in peace or war." Another definition is "the science and art of military command exercised to meet the enemy in combat under advantageous conditions." More general definitions include "a careful plan or method" and "the art of devising or employing plans or stratagems toward a goal."[22]

Strategy means a variety of things based on the context of the term's use. It varies from a general planning process to an activity related to achieving national objectives. When used in a military context, strategy refers to actions regarding the use of national level resources and national policies. The strategic level of war includes the decisions and policies of a nation's seniormost leadership. In order to set bounds on this discussion of the levels of war, tactics addresses the lower end of the hierarchy. Lower in this instance refers to actions near the physical point of impact in battle as opposed to the senior levels of command and leadership.

TACTICS

The meaning of tactics is relatively constant throughout a number of sources, unlike that of strategy. Clausewitz defined tactics as "the use of armed forces in the engagement."[23] Jomini viewed tactics as the art of using military forces where they have concentrated.[24] John Burr defined tactics as handling troops in combat.[25]

Other definitions of tactics include managing "military operations in direct contact with the enemy"[26] and the "technique of deploying and directing military forces... in coordinated combat activities against the enemy in order to attain the objectives designated by strategy or operations."[27] Liddell Hart explained tactics as applying strategy "on a lower plane."[28] The Soviet Army viewed tactics as the level of combat activity conducted at division and below.[29]

Before World War II, the Army considered tactics to be "the art of executing the strategic movement prior to battle and of employing combat power on the field of battle." Tactics included movement to the battlefield, protecting the army, deploying for the battle, conducting the battle, and reacting to the success or failure of the battle.[30] This definition differs little from the 1982 *FM 100-5: Operations*. The manual described tactics as techniques used by smaller units to win battles and engagements. Tactics included moving, positioning, and sustaining forces on the battlefield before, during, and after engagements.[31] The 1986 *FM 100-5* defined tactics as "the art by which corps and smaller unit commanders translate potential combat power into victorious battles and engagements. Engagements were small conflicts between opposed maneuver forces... Battles consist of a series of related engagements."[32]

The 1987 *JCS Pub 1* provided two definitions for tactics: "1. The employment of units in combat. 2. The ordered arrangement and maneuver of units in relation to each other and/or to the enemy in order to utilize their full potentialities."[33] A Webster's dictionary defined tactics as "the science and art of disposing and maneuvering forces in combat."[34]

More recent American doctrinal manuals provide similar definitions. The 2001 *FM 3-0* defined tactics as the employment of units in combat. Tactics included the ordered arrangement and maneuver of units in relation to each other, the terrain, and the enemy to translate potential combat power into victorious battles and engagements. A battle consists of a set of related engagements that last longer and involve larger forces than an engagement. Battles can affect the course of a campaign or major operation. An engagement is a small tactical conflict between opposing maneuvering forces, usually conducted at brigade level and below. The 2008 *FM 3-0* updated the definition of tactics to mean "the employment and ordered arrangement of forces in relation to each other."[35]

Joint doctrine also has addressed the meaning of tactics. The 2001 joint dictionary defined the tactical level of war as

> [t]he level of war at which battles and engagements are planned and executed to accomplish military objectives assigned to tactical units or task forces. Activities at this level focus on the ordered arrangement and maneuver of combat elements in relation to each other and to the enemy to achieve combat objectives.[36]

These definitions of tactics are similar. All focus on the battlefield and military forces smaller than a nation's entire military structure. Tactics is qualitatively different from strategy. Tactics is the up close and personal fight where soldier faces soldier, weapon faces weapon. The tactical level of war is the personal level of war, where killing takes place. The contest of wills shows its ugly and brutal nature here. Life and death are tactics' most precious commodities. Warriors dwell here. Yet something must link the higher level plans and decisions of strategy to the direct actions of tactics. The operational level of war forges that bond.

OPERATIONAL LEVEL OF WAR

Warfare changed in the nineteenth century due to the political, social, and economic turmoil of the times.[37] The rise in population supported mass armies. Political alliances led to multinational armies. The rifled musket, conoidal bullet, breech loading mechanism for weapons, rifle magazine, and smokeless powder increased the tactical depth of the battlefield. The telegraph and railroad increased the depth of armies.[38] These changes led to battles of long duration and great spatial scope.[39] German and Russian theorists began to hypothesize that another level of war existed between strategy and tactics in order to explain the need to conduct successive battles to defeat an enemy.[40] This recognition of a change in warfare led to the Army's use of the term operational art.[41]

Before World War II, the Army called these actions strategy.[42] However, the 1986 *FM 100-5* defined operational art as "the employment of military forces to attain strategic goals in a theater of war or theater of operations through the design, organization, and conduct of campaigns and major operations."[43] Several terms were clearly important: theater of war, theater of operations, campaign, and major operation.

The 1987 *JCS Pub 1* defined a theater as a "geographical area outside the continental United States for which a commander of a unified or specified command has been assigned military responsibility." Unified and specified commands were major commands in the U.S. Department of Defense that employed military forces in specific geographic regions or for specific activities. The U.S. Central Command, a unified command, employed military forces from all services (hence a unified command) as required to accomplish U.S. objectives in southwest Asia. The U.S. Strategic Air Command was a specified command that planned and conducted operations using long range U.S. Air Force assets. However, the 1987 *JCS Pub 1* referred the reader to an area of war for a definition of a theater of war. An area of war was the "area of land, sea, and air which is, or may become, directly involved in the operations of war."[44]

The 1982 *FM 100-5* linked operational art to a theater of war, but historically the theater of war has always been associated with strategy and not operational art. The 1986 *FM 100-5* added the theater of operations to the operational level but did not clearly define either.[45] However, the 1986 *FM 100-5* stated that a theater of war may contain more than one theater of operations.[46] The 1987 *JCS Pub 1* failed to define theater of operations. Instead it referred the reader to "area of operations," which was "that portion of an area of war necessary for military operations and for the administration of such operations."[47] The 1987 *FM 100-6* stated a theater of war commanders may divide their theater of war into multiple theaters of operations if they need to employ forces on multiple, independent lines of operations. Logistics, political concerns, personal relations with other commanders, or other reasons may make a theater of war commander want to establish subordinate theaters of operations.[48]

Since a theater of operations involves the operational level of war, John Meechan postulated that it "may have its own strategy to support both the strategy of the theater of war and the national military strategy."[49] The 1986 *FM 100-5* defined a campaign as "a series of joint actions designed to attain a strategic objective in a theater of war." Simultaneous campaigns may occur when a theater of war contains multiple theaters of operations.[50]

Additional sources stated that these operations focus on the same enemy force[51] or involve "simultaneous and sequential battles."[52] Webster's dictionary defines a campaign as "a connected series of military operations forming a distinct phase of a war."[53] Colonel William H. Janes, a former director at the Army's School of Advanced Military Studies (SAMS), said that planning a campaign and fighting offensively were the "essence" of operational art.[54]

The 1987 *JCS Pub 1* did not define a campaign, but it did define a campaign plan as "a plan for a series of related military operations aimed to accomplish a common objective, normally within a given time and space."[55] The Army's *FM 100-6* explained that the campaign plan provided guidance to subordinates on the use of available resources to accomplish strategic objectives.[56]

The campaign plan lays out a commander's vision of the sequential and simultaneous operations required to achieve the desired objective.[57] The

1986 *FM 100-5* explained major operations as "the coordinated actions of large forces in a single phase of a campaign or in a critical battle. Major operations decide the course of campaigns."[58]

Other definitions expand the meaning of operations to include a group of actions in a theater of war that consists of concentrations, marches, occupying positions, and battles that follow each other in a logical sequence. Multiple operations make a campaign.[59] Baron von der Goltz explains operations as a "group of actions . . . composed of marches, the assumption of positions, and combats."[60] Trevor Dupuy defined operations as "the control and direction of large forces (usually armies or army groups) in combat activities within a single, discrete theater of combat."[61]

Wayne Hall posited that the operational level of war focused on the mind of the enemy commander, while tactics tried to destroy enemy forces. Operational commanders focused on the future, while tactical commanders focused on the present.[62] The operational level of war includes time and space considerations that are qualitatively different from those in tactics and strategy. As used today, tactics focuses on near-term events and forces in contact. Strategy focuses on far-term events and national resources. The time and space necessary to marshal and employ resources are obviously different between these levels of war. The operational level fills the void between these extremes. The actions of large forces within the framework of a campaign or major operation require more time and greater space, or depth, than tactical actions require. Such time and space requirements also increase between the operational and strategic levels of war.

Dwight Adams and Clayton Newell linked specific levels of command to levels of war such as a theater of war commander in chief being at the strategic level and a theater of operations commander in chief being at the operational level.[63] The U.S. Army reported that the Soviet Army described "levels of combat activity" as: strategy, national and theater level; operational, fronts and armies; and tactical, division and below.[64] Chris Donnelly stated that the Soviets divided operational art into three levels: operational, strategic (front); operational (army); and operational, tactical (corps).[65]

Soviet military theory viewed operational art as "a framework for studying, understanding, preparing for, and conducting war." The tasks of operational art included investigating combat action rules, developing the means to prepare and conduct combat operations, determining "the function of large units and formations," and specifying "organizational and equipment requirements."[66]

Viewing the operational level of war as a process or activity highlights the point that it seeks to integrate military force actions to achieve a higher goal. It includes selecting the methods necessary to reach "a desired end."[67] Planning, coordinating, and integrating the results of tactical actions (whether victories or defeats) to attain an objective greater than that possible as a sum of the results of the individual engagements is also a description of the operational level of war.[68]

Richard Simpkin wrote of three meanings of the operational level of war. He reported that the Germans and Russians viewed the operational level as having a direct relationship to combat operations as opposed to administration or logistics. A second meaning was that it related to an organization level from division to theater. However, this use was obsolete, since small units had operational capability due to technology. Simpkin's third meaning included actions that had five criteria: having a mission one step removed from a political-economic aim; having a "dynamic, closed-loop system, characterized by speed and appropriateness of response"; having three components with at least one being the enemy's will; being synergistic so that the value of the whole is greater than the sum of the individual parts; and being "self-contained within the scope of its mission."[69]

U.S. Army and multiservice, or joint, doctrines also define the operational level of war. The 2001 *FM 3-0: Operations* explained the operational level of war as the level at which campaigns and major operations are conducted and sustained to accomplish strategic objectives within theaters or areas of operations (AOs). The 2001 and 2008 versions of *FM 3-0* linked the tactical employment of forces to the purpose of achieving strategic objectives. The focus at this level is on operational art—the use of military forces to achieve strategic goals through the design, organization, integration, and conduct of theater strategies, campaigns, major operations, and battles. A campaign is a related series of military operations aimed at accomplishing a strategic or operational objective within a given time and space. A major operation is a series of tactical actions (battles, engagements, strikes) conducted by various combat forces of a single service or several services, coordinated in time and place, to accomplish operational, and sometimes strategic, objectives in an operational area. These actions are conducted simultaneously or sequentially under a common plan and are controlled by a single commander. Operational art determines when, where, and for what purpose major forces are employed to influence the enemy disposition before combat.[70]

The 2001 joint dictionary *JP 1-02* described the operational level of war as the level of war at which campaigns and major operations are planned, conducted, and sustained to accomplish strategic objectives within theaters or other operational areas. Activities at this level link tactics and strategy by establishing operational objectives needed to accomplish the strategic objectives, sequencing events to achieve the operational objectives, initiating actions, and applying resources to bring about and sustain these events. These activities imply a broader dimension of time or space than do tactics. They ensure the logistic and administrative support of tactical forces, and provide the means by which tactical successes are exploited to achieve strategic objectives.[71] The 2001 *Joint Publication 3-0* defined operational art as "[t]he employment of military forces to attain strategic and/or operational objectives through the design, organization, integration, and conduct of strategies, campaigns, major operations, and battles." The 2006 version of *Joint Publication 3-0* with the 2008 update included the importance of the "creative imagination by commanders and staffs" in this process. This recent version also pointed out that operational art "integrates ends, ways, and means across the levels of war."[72]

This discussion does not propose to address every document that has addressed some aspect of the levels of war or the meaning of such concepts as operational art. Nonetheless, the documents described provide a representative sample of the intellectual effort devoted to defining these concepts. Clearly the operational level of war is essential in order to link tactical actions to strategic decisions due to changes in warfare requiring the sequencing and combinations of battles into operations and campaigns. This cognitive act is necessary in order to ensure that tactical actions fulfill a purpose when viewed from national levels.

STRATEGY VS. TACTICS VS. OPERATIONAL ART

If military strategy is using an armed force to accomplish national objectives, and tactics means using military power to win battles and engagements, do we have operational art if one battle determines whether the national objective is met? If campaigns and operations alone are the foundation of operational art, then the answer is no. The inability to force a decisive battle to meet a strategic objective due to technological and societal changes is the reason operational art was born. However, decisive battles are still possible, even though they have changed in form from those of Napoleon's day. The truck bombing of the Marine barracks in Beirut in 1983 was a decisive battle that the United States lost in a conflict that probably seemed like war to the marines, sailors, and soldiers on the ground even if today we might refer to the operation as peacekeeping or stability operations. A few years ago, American doctrine would have referred to such military actions as low-intensity conflict.

The battle or engagement to defend the barracks was a decisive one that the United States lost. The result of the destruction of the barracks was that the U.S military personnel left Beirut. On a larger scale, nuclear weapons could result in such devastation on the battlefield or homeland that the political will of a government could break. Certainly many factors affect such decisions, but the decisions rest in people's minds. People are not necessarily rational. They may think they have lost when they have not. They may not quit when others think they should. A battle is decisive because of the effect it has on the opponent's will, not because of the destruction involved.

Thomas Schelling stated that strategy includes the "exploitation of potential force," not the application of force. He related conflict to bargaining because for both parties involved the ability to satisfy one's aims depends on the choice of the other participant in the process. Deterrence flowed from this potential force because the threat influences an opponent's behavior.[73]

Dr. James J. Schneider wrote that General Ulysses S. Grant was the first true practitioner of operational art. The American Civil War was the first time the conduct of war involved a series of operations distributed in time and space in order to achieve a specific goal. Grant's simultaneous use of William T. Sherman's march through Georgia, Nathanial P. Banks' attack from Mobile toward Atlanta, and his operations in Virginia destroyed the Confederate war-making ability.[74]

Operational art required distributed operations where classical warfare demanded concentration at a single point. Armies moved and fought as a concentrated mass. The collision of opposing armies (or masses) resulted in battle. Changes on the battlefield resulted in the birth of a new type of warfare.[75]

Increased weapon lethality forced armies to dispense to survive. Battlefield expansion doomed concentration at a single point. This distribution of forces resulted in distributed operations. Hence maneuver in order to attack an enemy distributed in depth became the norm. Campaigns could no longer consist of a single action. Campaigns contained operations consisting of several battles and maneuvers. This is the trademark of operational art that distinguishes it from classical military strategy.[76]

This description of operational art describes a dramatic change in the way military leaders conduct war. Operational art in this sense is a creative activity aimed at the destruction of an enemy through the combined effect of military actions distributed in time and space.

Constraint and restraint as activity limitations are another way to explain war. Each opponent in a conflict attempts to constrain the other within friendly desires and to restrain the enemy from achieving his ends. Each also tries to reduce these limitations placed upon him by his opponent so as to attain assigned goals as efficiently as possible. The concepts of constraint and restraint apply whether talking about levels of war or anything else. At the operational level the means of constraint are maneuvers and engagements. All conflict participants seek freedom of action toward goal attainment while trying to deny freedom of action to an opponent. Constraint and restraint are unifying factors in war. The objective is to devise the appropriate sequence of actions to maximize the limitations on an enemy and minimize them on one's own actions. This concept applies to all military operations as well as other actions that focus on resolving a conflict.

Operational art involves the combination of the effects of several events to achieve this limitation upon enemy actions. The results of the battle may not be as important as the use of the results in denying the enemy his campaign objectives.[77] However, combinations of events are also important in the activities called tactics and strategy.

When battalion commanders maneuver their companies on different axes, pass units through or around others, employ fire support assets before an attack, and perform their many other duties, they are combining sequential actions that in turn restrict the actions of an opponent. They should also have contingency plans to address all enemy capabilities and plans for actions after they reaches their objective. This is not meant to show that a battalion commander is an operational commander. The point is that tactical commanders also combine and plan for actions as operational commanders do. A tactical commander who fails to consider simultaneous and sequential actions is one who will not succeed often.

Strategy also involves combinations of such limiting events. In World War II, the Allies agreed to defeat Germany and then Japan. The sequential combination of actions inherent in defeating Germany and then Japan was necessary to win the war. Nations must also plan for actions to defeat all enemy capabilities or risk defeat by being unprepared. Strategic leaders must perform the same types of tasks as operational level commanders.

The point is that conducting warfare requires the integration of simultaneous and sequential actions by the forces concerned. The complexity of this activity increases as the force size and the types of resources increase. However, the dual objectives of constraining and restraining an opponent as well as the need to reduce these limitations on oneself through the integration of simultaneous and sequential actions remain the conceptual foundation of modern operational warfare. These concepts apply to all types of warfare and military operations regardless of the doctrinal term applied to them.

LEVELS OF WAR SUMMARY

National strategy then is a nation's plan to meet national objectives at the strategic level of war. The tactical level is the battlefield use of resources. The linkage between strategy and tactics is the operational level of war.

Strategy then is the cognitive activity that includes establishing the goals to attain as well as allocating the resources to enable the achievement of national level objectives. Strategy requires an understanding and synchronization with governmental policy. Political leaders must establish objectives and select the tools to achieve those ends. Each tool (such as military force) must then be used to support the attainment of the strategic objective. The strategic level of war then is the command level where a national leader performs this cognitive function.

Operational art is the cognitive activity where a military leader defines a series of actions (or operations) that achieve the strategic objective. The types of operations (land, sea, air, economic, etc.) depend on the resources under the control of the leader assigned this function. Sequencing actions to accomplish a mission is nothing new or extraordinary; however, it certainly is complex and more difficult as the size of force and types of resources increase. When taking a theater view, this function clearly includes campaigns. The operational level of war is the command level where someone performs this cognitive function.

Tactics governs the use of these resources on the battlefield and is composed of techniques and procedures, the manner in which these tools are physically used to have the effect they are designed to produce. The tactical level is the command level, where a military leader performs this cognitive function.

Shimon Naveh discussed at length the ground-breaking theoretical work by the Soviets that later heavily influenced American doctrine after the war in Vietnam diverted American theoretical exploration for years. This cognitive function "is not confined to a specific echelon."[78] From an American perspective, operational art is a style of warfare birthed in the American Civil War and the changes that occurred in warfare in the nineteenth century. The battlefield and forces available expanded, so that a single battle could no longer determine the victor. Operational art is the creative process to combine the effects of multiple actions, or operations, distributed in time and space in order to win. Victory flows from the combined effect of the operations rather than a single action focused on a single point.

War, however, cannot be explained simply as the purpose for gaining power or a series of levels of type action or command. An understanding of how war affects the people who engage in it and attempt to harness it is necessary. This discussion necessitates a review of war's three natures.

5

The Physical Nature of War

There are many ways to segment a study of war and war's elements. One way is to explain war as having three natures—physical, cognitive, and moral. The physical nature encompasses the physical aspects of the area of operations. The cognitive nature refers to the mental contest in war. The moral nature addresses the human element in war.

James Schneider considered the physical nature to include "the role of technology, terrain, logistics, etc."[1] This includes elements of power previously discussed such as natural resources and geography. Natural resources provide the materials upon which to build economic strength and a system of trade. Demographics form a subset of natural resources because armed forces are composed of people. The number of military-age people and their physical and mental capabilities will affect the technological requirements of weaponry and the training necessary to field an armed force.

This explanation of the physical nature includes the three components of geography, maneuver and logistics, and technology. Geography includes all environmental and physical characteristics that affect operations. Maneuver and logistics are the military activities affected by geography. Technology provides armies the ability to overcome or enhance the impact of geography.

GEOGRAPHY

The physical nature is the theoretical construct that relates geography to military operations. All military operations occur within some physical area whether land, sea, air, or space. Additionally, one element of a nation's power is its geography, which includes the nation's location in relation to other nations and its natural resources.

Therefore, all military operations must consider the physical characteristics that support or restrain action in the area where operations take place. These characteristics will influence the size and type of forces required, tactics, and time needed to accomplish the assigned mission.

The first geographical division relating to military operations is the theater, defined in U.S. doctrine as "[t]he geographical area for which a commander of a combatant command has been assigned responsibility."[2] A theater of war is

[d]efined by the President, Secretary of Defense, or the geographic combatant commander, the area of air, land, and water that is, or may become, directly involved in the conduct of major operations and campaigns involving combat. A theater of war does not normally encompass the geographic combatant commander's entire area of responsibility and may contain more than one theater of operations.[3]

The theater of operations is the next geographical division. U.S. doctrine defines the theater of operations as

[a]n operational area defined by the geographic combatant commander for the conduct or support of specific military operations. Multiple theaters of operations normally will be geographically separate and focused on different missions. Theaters of operations are usually of significant size, allowing for operations in depth and over extended periods of time.[4]

Military forces occupy a position within the theater of operations. From that position, they execute campaign plans. This position includes the complete operations and support structure of the force employed by a given commander. Commanders plans to conduct battles within the general confines of their position if in a defense. However, they should seek to fight an opponent within the opponent's position if in the offense.

The battlefield is where military forces engage one another. The battlefield may include all or part of a position depending on the ability of the force concerned to project violence through the extent of the position. A force executes battle plans here. Conceptually, this is where bloodshed should occur if the forces actually use their weapons to kill people and destroy equipment. If the threat of violence on the battlefield is sufficient to force a decision, this area is still the battlefield.

On the battlefield, each unit occupies a point in time and geographic space. Time constantly changes and is important as it affects the relationship of one unit to another. If two units occupy the same geographic space at different times, no conflict occurs. Occupying the same geographic space at the same time provides the potential for conflict.

This geographic space has changed over the years. Other than the height advantage offered by hills and mountains, warfare was generally two-dimensional, until armies began to use balloons for observation. This three-dimensional consideration became significant with the airplane. All military operations today must consider surface and air forces. The air provides a medium for observation and attack.

Land warfare generally neglects subsurface operations. However, mines dug beneath defensive positions are not impossible as shown by the battle of Petersburg, Virginia, in the American Civil War, where a mine packed with explosives dug from the Union to the Confederate lines blew a large gap in the Confederate position, leaving a huge crater. Naval forces must never neglect subsurface operations because of the use of submarines to attack surface craft and launch missiles.

Today's third dimension has expanded to include outer space. Modern communication and navigation systems rely heavily on satellites. During 1991's Persian Gulf War, handheld and vehicle-mounted global positioning systems were essential for the rapid victory of the U.S.-led coalition forces. They provided precise locations for navigation and for indirect fire systems (weapon and target location). Without them, maneuver would have been slower and less precise, and the danger of fratricide due to disoriented units would have dramatically increased. Obviously, satellites can also provide a means to observe the ground and sea. Surface operations must consider the support of space systems and the danger of discovery by an enemy space observation platform. Warfare today must also include decisions on whether to destroy hostile satellites. The possibility of destroying satellites or spacecraft immediately raises the issue of how to protect them as well.

Given space operations, how do military forces destroy and defend space systems? How do military forces hide a satellite? How does a nation harden a satellite or manned platform such as a space shuttle or space station, so that it can survive an attack and still be sufficiently lightweight to allow its launch? If a nation establishes a base on the moon, an asteroid, or a planet, what are the means required for protecting it? Such a presence would constitute a surface or an air and surface entity to be protected. As nations launch more systems into space, the answers to these questions will grow in importance. Any military force that uses space-based systems must plan for the contingency that an enemy will destroy the systems. Any commander who has operational control or command over a space-based system must include its defense in his, or her, plans.

Another way to look at the physical nature is through the construct of the U.S. Army's doctrine that debuted a few years ago and divided battle into three components—close, deep, and rear. This division of the battle-field addressed operations in time and geographical space in AirLand Battle doctrine.[5] Close, deep, and rear operations were components of one battle. Each related to the other. Commanders and their respective staff would have to synchronize all of them or risk defeat.

Close operations concerned those actions where the main forces of the opposing armies are engaged in combat. Close operations ultimately determined victory or defeat. However, AirLand Battle doctrine as outlined in the 1986 *FM 100-5: Operations* stated that if an activity supported current operations, it was part of the close operation.[6] This mixture of time and geography in one term is unfortunate. The usage of the term "close" to describe a geographic position relative to the main force engaged is better than including time as part of the definition.

Deep operations were directed against reinforcing/follow-on/second echelon forces not engaged in combat at the forward line of troops (FLOT). Since the outcome of the battle would depend on the close operation, deep operations had to support the close fight. Deep operations would do this by preventing reinforcements from reaching the close fight and by destroying an opponent's long range fire support assets that could attack the main force but were located in the enemy's rear.

Rear operations were behind the FLOT that supported the close operations by ensuring the commander had the freedom to act in the close fight. This included sustaining the close operation forces and protecting those logistical assets responsible to provide support. It also included protecting reinforcements for their future use.

U.S. Army doctrine changed its representation of the close, deep, and rear paradigm in 2001. The 2001 *FM 3-0* referred to "decisive, shaping, and sustaining operations" conducted in the spatial areas categorized as close, deep and rear. The doctrine emphasized that these areas were characteristics of linear operations, which were being replaced by nonlinear operations on the battlefield. However, the 2008 *FM 3-0* rescinded the concepts of and the terms close, deep, and rear areas. This latest doctrinal publication used the term close combat to refer to actions that occurred in the close area.[7]

The 2001 *FM 3-0* stated, "[T]he close area is where forces are in immediate contact with the enemy and the fighting between the committed forces and readily available tactical reserves of both combatants is occurring, or where commanders envision close combat taking place. Typically, the close area assigned to a maneuver force extends from its subordinates' rear boundaries to its own forward boundary." Commanders planned and conducted "decisive maneuvers" within the close area. Most maneuver forces were positioned within the close area. Forces providing direct support fires and logistics support were also positioned within the close area.[8]

Commanders used the deep area, which was forward of the close area, to shape enemy forces before they reach the close area. Army doctrine stated, "[T]he deep area extends from the forward boundary of subordinate units to the forward boundary of the controlling echelon. Thus, the deep area relates to the close area not only in terms of geography but also in terms of purpose and time." Maneuver forces might have operated in the deep area; however, most maneuver forces remained in the close area.[9]

Most sustainment, or logistical, operations occured in rear areas. U.S. Army doctrine stated, "Operations in rear areas assure freedom of action and continuity of operations, sustainment, and C2." Commanders would have to provide for the protection of sustainment forces in rear areas, since they usually lacked the combat power to defend against an attack.[10]

Operations in close, deep, and rear areas occurred in present time within those geographic regions. Future operations whether in close, deep, or rear areas were the focus of staff planning. Staffs planned the actions within close, deep, and rear areas that would some day be conducted in the present time. The physical distances on a linear battlefield often caused deep operations and rear operations to be viewed as having a "future" time function, in that they influence future actions in close areas.

Military planners and operators must not confuse geography with time. Close, deep, and rear refer to physical locations on the battlefield. They provide a conceptual framework for orienting actions on the linear battlefield. The words current and future address time and separate current operations from planners. Time must link close, deep, and rear operations because one may become or at least affect another operation as time progresses. However, close must not mean current. Deep and rear operations also have a current phase. Deep does not equate to future, even though shaping operations in deep areas affect the success of operations in close areas.

U.S. Army doctrine continues to evolve based on the environments in which the Army finds its forces fighting and as technology and other factors influence requirements. The physical division of the battlefield into close, deep, and rear areas has faded. The complexity of operations in the early twenty-first century has focused thought on a nonlinear battlefield, where combat and stability operations occur simultaneously. Divisions into deep, close, and rear are not as useful as when the U.S. military faced a hostile Soviet Union in Europe during the latter half of the twentieth century. U.S. Army Training and Doctrine Command (TRADOC) pamphlets on the Army's conduct of joint operations and tactical maneuver discuss close combat, close engagement, deep objectives, deep engagement, and rear area security.[11] The construct of deep, close, and rear areas is absent. Nonetheless, the physical nature of operations will force commanders to contend with action in close proximity to their main forces. Commanders must also consider forces not in contact and at a distance, where they can reinforce actions at the point of engagement. Commanders must also remember operations to their rear, whether combat or providing logistical support. Combat and other military operations will occur within the physical aspect of terrain. Success demands consideration of the influences of friendly and enemy actions in all directions, at all distances, and within the time associated with the mission at hand.

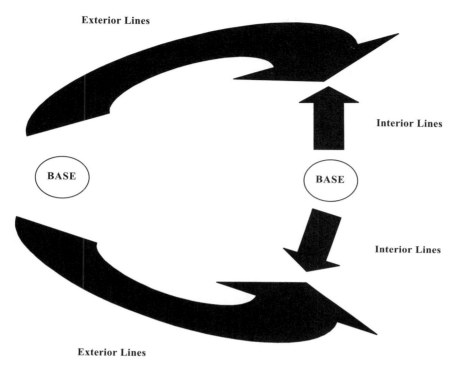

Figure 5.1: Interior and Exterior Lines.

GEOMETRY

Jomini's writings provide a foundation for reviewing the geometry of the battlefield, another component of the physical nature. Numerous lines and points compose operations. These lines and points provide a geometrical framework within which to study the physical nature.

Lines of operations are the axes that link a military force with its base and indicate the direction in which forces are moving or toward which they are oriented. They are generally referred to as lines of communications, rather than operations, when discussing logistics support to a unit.

A unit operates on interior lines when its lines of operations project outward from a central point toward various objectives. Enemy action along such lines generally pushes the force toward its base. Exterior lines refer to the situation where a focus converges on an enemy from directions that do not point toward its base in a straight line. An enemy reaction does not push the force directly toward its base. Figure 5.1 also illustrates operating on interior and exterior lines.

Either interior or exterior lines may offer an advantage depending on the situation. Interior lines provide the opportunity to concentrate against individual threats one at a time. One force may defeat another in detail by using interior lines. Reverses experienced during combat allow a unit to decrease its logistical problems by falling back toward its base for recovery. Exterior lines provide the opportunity to crush an opponent, to annihilate it. An army can force an enemy to collapse and cut off its line of retreat by exploiting exterior lines.

Another important element of Jomini's discourse was the decisive point. A decisive point grants the holder an advantage over his opponent who does not hold it. Jomini stated that every battlefield held a decisive point that was the key to victory if the appropriate forces massed at that spot.[12]

American joint doctrine defined a decisive point as "[a] geographic place, specific key event, critical factor, or function that, when acted upon, allows commanders to gain a marked advantage over an adversary or contribute materially to achieving success."[13] The 2001 *Joint Publication 3-0* defined a center of gravity as "[t]hose characteristics, capabilities, or sources of power from which a military force derives its freedom of action, physical strength, or will to fight." The 2006 version of *Joint Publication 3-0* with Change 1 dated 2008 modified the definition to "[t]he source of power that provides moral or physical strength, freedom of action, or will to act."[14]

Clausewitz called battle the center of gravity of the war because it is the "fight of the main force." He described a "great battle" as the "provisional center of gravity of the entire campaign." In a later portion of *On War*, Clausewitz said the center of gravity "is always found where the mass is concentrated most densely." The cohesion of an armed force helps produce a center of gravity.[15]

Clausewitz expanded the concept in Book Eight of *On War* to include the idea of the center of gravity being the "hub of all power and movement." He stated that "everything depends" on this point and all effort should be focused on it. Then Clausewitz wrote that the center of gravity could be a capital, an ally's army, the interests solidifying an alliance, personalities of leaders, or public opinion.[16]

These explanations of the term center of gravity have caused some confusion. Clausewitz appears to state in one place that the center of gravity is the mass of the enemy army, where in another place he seems to have said it can be something as intangible as public opinion. Clausewitz's definition is unclear as translated.

An explanation of some of the confusion may be in the translation of the word "*schwerpunkt*." Some authors translate *schwerpunkt* as the main effort,[17] point of effort,[18] or thrust-point.[19] These concepts allude to the forces or locations on which commanders focus their efforts to defeat an enemy. This is more like Clausewitz's idea of a concentrated mass of forces. However, modern firepower allows a greater dispersion of forces to achieve the same power relative to an enemy than in Clausewitz's time. At the same time these renderings of the German term often lead one to equate center of gravity with Jomini's decisive point, a term that is fundamentally different.

Identifying the center of gravity is an important activity but not an end in itself. A commander must plan a way to attack it and be prepared to change objectives if the center of gravity changes or it is discovered that the original perception was incorrect.[20] Regardless of whether a planner selects a center of gravity that is a military force or political will or any other concept, the purpose of the analysis remains to select an objective that will lead to mission accomplishment.[21]

If the center of gravity is a source of strength, it should not be considered to be a vulnerability to be protected; however, attacking it is important because defeating it will remove an enemy's strength. Since it is physically strong, a direct attack upon it may not be the wisest course. Command and control centers, logistics bases, and lines of communication are not inherently strong physically. The concentrated mass of an army is. These two categories of military elements should not be mixed. The term decisive point is a bit simpler to understand.

In Jominian terms, decisive points can be geographical or accidental. Geographic decisive points are decisive due to their physical characteristics or location that includes the Army doctrinal concept of key terrain. Accidental decisive points depend on the maneuver of the opposing forces.[22]

Time is also a component of a decisive point. Any point is decisive or not as it relates to actions on the battlefield. Since battles do not last forever, a point cannot be decisive forever. A point is only decisive as long as the area concerned is potentially a battlefield. An area may possess a geographic feature that is decisive such as a piece of terrain that dominates the area due to its height. However, if the area is not a battlefield because it is not to be the scene of combat, the point cannot be decisive.

There may also be a decisive point in time to conduct a particular action. For example, a unit may have to temporarily assume a hasty defensive posture in order to recover from the effects of fighting. That time could be a decisive point for an opponent if the balance of power is in its favor. Of course, this time is only really decisive if the opponent attacks the force that is pausing before continuing operations.

CULMINATING POINT

This idea of time relates to Clausewitz's culminating point. If a force attacks beyond its culminating point, it risks defeat due to a counterattack. This moment of varying length becomes a decisive point of time if the other belligerent realizes the overextension has occurred.

The idea of a culminating point is also an important concept in U.S. doctrine, which has defined it as

> the point at which a force no longer has the capability to continue its form of operations, offense or defense. a. In the offense, the point at which continuing the attack is no longer possible and the force must consider

reverting to a defensive posture or attempting an operational pause. b. In the defense, the point at which counteroffensive action is no longer possible.[23]

Clausewitz also presented several factors that might cause an attacker to reach a culminating point: losses in battle, lengthening supply lines as the army advances, a change in alliances, or increased enemy resistance.[24] Anything that causes an attacker's strength relative to the defender's to decrease so that the defender is superior may cause an attack to culminate.

Another way to look at the concept is in terms of friction, fog, and the superiority of the defense. Friction reduces the strength of a force and may cause culmination. The fog of war can hide the approach of a culminating point, which may result in the attacker reaching the point but not realizing he has. A defender normally has the advantages of time to prepare and knowing the terrain to help him select positions. The relative reduction of the attacker's strength over time brings about culmination.[25] Clausewitz called the concept of culmination the "keystone for most plans of campaigns." Victory depends on one side having superior strength through a combination of physical and psychological means.[26]

Clausewitz noted that a successful attack depends on superior strength. Therefore, an attacker must stop once his strength is reduced to the point where he is only strong enough to establish a defense and sue for peace. Continuing an attack beyond that point invites a counterattack by a superior force. Determining the culminating point before reaching it is crucial.[27]

An attacker risks defeat if he continues beyond his culminating point. The attacker's strength is important only in relation to the defender's strength. Therefore, one argument about the culmination point states that an attacker does not reach a culminating point if he is successful or the defender fails to act when the attacker is overextended.[28] A unit's culminating point is an absolute, but passing it is immaterial if the defender does not take advantage of the event.

Clausewitz also discussed a defender's opportunity to defeat an attacker by judging when the attacker would reach his culminating point. He explained that once an attacker sets his mind on a certain course of action, he may not realize he has reached his culminating point. Even if the attacker knows this has occurred, he may find that continuing the attack is easier than stopping. Clausewitz related this to the difficulty of stopping a horse that is pulling a load up a hill. Stopping is too difficult. This problem provides the defender the opportunity to defeat the attacker.[29]

Though Clausewitz did not explicitly state so, the point on which a defender goes on the offense—"the flashing sword of vengeance"—should be when an attacker reaches his culminating point. Clausewitz does state that a defender must be aware of reaching his culminating point because he "must make up his mind and act." There is no reason to continue waiting because there will be no additional advantage in doing so.[30]

The offensive nature of the culminating point concept should also apply to a defender's counterattack. During his counterattack, the defender becomes the attacker. Failure to judge his strength correctly may result in his passing his culminating point and the counterattack failing.

TERRAIN

Of course, any description of the physical nature must include terrain. Land forces move on the ground. Movement rates depend on the trafficability of the ground whether cross-country or via roads. Air forces fly over it. The height of landforms will affect the altitude at which aircraft must fly. Sea forces move on water. The depth of the water will limit the size of the ship that can use the waterway.

The U.S. Army has used an acronym to summarize the effects of terrain that a commander must consider—OCOKA. The letters stand for Observation and fields of fire, Cover and concealment, Obstacles and movement, Key terrain, and Avenues of approach.[31] Commanders and staffs must analyze the terrain on which they sit and also which extends to the front, flanks, and rear to ensure they understand its effect on enemy actions before contact and impact on future operations.

Observation provides the ability to determine an enemy's actions as well as to interdict that action. A military force must be able to observe its enemy in order to fire at it. Fields of fire are the areas where one force or weapon system may engage another. Terrain and weapon characteristics will determine the size, shape, and location of the field of fire.

Today observation means more than that visible to the naked eye. We must also consider electronic observation. Terrain will limit those areas open to visual and electronic sight. Planners and operators must consider landforms and foliage. The air provides an opportunity to escape the confines of the ground with regard to observation and fields of fire. Of course, using the air to gain better observation of the ground also opens oneself to observation and subsequent attack from the ground. Military air planners must also consider the impact of weather, curvature of the earth, and high landforms, as they can obscure potential targets.

The sea is of course relatively flat. Observation is more a factor of distances than the impact of terrain on the sea except for the hindrance of the earth's curvature, intervening landmasses such as islands, and the effects of weather on the ocean surface.

In space, we are only in our infancy determining the factors to consider. As on the sea, little hinders observation when comparing the impact of terrain as on the ground. However, objects in space would naturally limit observation. Stars may make observation difficult in certain directions due to their brightness and proximity to the observer and the object. If trying to observe the surface of a planet from space, the observer must consider the effect of weather conditions (such as clouds) and the limitations on observation due to the characteristics of the planet's surface. Trees will limit observation from space just as they will from the air and on the ground.

Cover protects a unit from observation and fire. Concealment hides a unit from observation. A force can build structures such as bunkers for cover or use the natural characteristics of the terrain. The uneven surface of the ground provides natural cover.

Anything that prevents observation provides concealment. Obviously, vegetation can hide forces, people, and equipment. Camouflage helps people and equipment blend with their surroundings to enhance concealment.

Obstacles hinder movement. They may prevent or only slow movement in a certain direction. They may channel a force into a certain position or in a certain direction. Mountains, swamps, forests, ditches, and embankments are examples of obstacles. Man-made obstacles such as minefields can enhance the effect of natural obstacles. Mountains can interfere with air assets striking a target by making the approach particularly steep or forcing the aircraft to fly very high, which may allow air defense weapons to engage it. Reefs and the ocean bottom can be obstacles to shipping by limiting the movement of watercraft.

Key terrain affords the holder an advantage over his opponent. High ground offers an obvious advantage because it affords better observation and reduces the interference of lower ground with fields of fire. Whether looking at land, air, or sea operations, high landmasses may be key terrain because of the impact they can have. But other terrain may also be key terrain. Land forces must consider narrow passes that constrict and slow movement. Road intersections that are critical to the transportation network may be key terrain. Air forces need flat ground for airstrips. Naval forces need sheltered ports to rearm, refit, and escape dangerous weather. Terrain is key terrain because it can provide an advantage, not because it is a particular type of landform. The commander and staff officer must look at the terrain from the perspective of the friendly and enemy commanders to determine the impact of the terrain and whether it meets the definition of key.

Avenues of approach provide a route for a unit to move within the constraints of the terrain. The avenue's value will depend on its characteristics and those of the armed force. A swamp is not an avenue of approach for a mechanized force; however, it could be for a dismounted infantry force planning to surprise an opponent. A swamp also could be an avenue for a force possessing small watercraft that can negotiate the narrow channels within it. If aircraft are going to use the terrain, valleys may provide air avenues of approach as long as they lead to the desired point. Channels between islands may be sea avenues of approach if they shorten a route and do not increase the danger to the force to an intolerable level.

Weather is another key element of the physical nature. It affects the human and technological aspects of battle. Obviously, soldiers experience physical comfort or discomfort depending on the temperature, humidity, precipitation, wind speed, and other weather conditions. Weather may obscure an enemy or oneself. It may favor one force over another, if one force is better prepared to overcome the weather conditions through tougher physical conditioning or superior technology providing weapons not limited by weather effects. Examples of weather effects include reducing observation and weapon employment ranges, enhancing or degrading the use of smoke or chemical weapons, limiting the use of aircraft, and impeding ship cargo discharge operations.

MANEUVER AND LOGISTICS

Two additional points of discussion are maneuver and logistics. Maneuver is the movement of a unit in relation to another in order to give battle. Logistics is the support provided to a maneuvering force. The two concepts cannot be separated. A force cannot maneuver for very long without logistical support. Logistics has no purpose if it does not support the maneuver necessary to achieve a commander's objectives.

Maneuver includes direct and indirect fire. Maneuver is important because it positions one unit so it can engage another. This engagement may include any weapons used by the opposing force.

One way to look at maneuver is the relationship between the direction in which the attacker is moving and the direction the defender is facing. Jomini stated that there were three directions possible when attacking an enemy. An attacker could go to the left, right, or center.[32] Of course, Jomini was describing a Napoleonic battlefield, where armies faced one another in linear formations, and a commander could generally see his entire army. Yet even given this context, Jomini's description is generally correct for ground combat forces.

Today we talk about frontal attack as one where a force moves directly at another. This generally pits brute strength against brute strength. Casualties are often high. The most powerful belligerent wins, or at least survives.

A flank attack attempts to avoid an opponent's strength by skirting to one side or the other of the enemy position. By avoiding the front of a position, the attacker's casualties should be lower and the chances of success greater. This maneuver is also known as an envelopment.

A turning movement is a deep envelopment that forces the defender out of his current position to reorient the direction of his defense. A deep operation may result in a turning movement that can unhinge a defense.

Air operations today add a vertical dimension to the concept of envelopment by going over rather than around a defensive position. Air defense is a critical element of a defensive operation to prevent a vertical envelopment.

Though not often addressed, tunneling is another means of adding a third dimension, as the North Koreans have shown for years along the Korean Demilitarized Zone (DMZ).

Logistics includes the sustainment necessary to provide the force the freedom to maneuver. Jomini considered logistics to be the art of moving armies.[33] Logistics must consider such actions and needs as movement routes, required supplies, maintenance, health support, and personnel replacement. The type and degree of support needed will vary based on the type of force involved. Obviously, the needs of a mechanized force are much different than those of a light infantry, air, or naval unit.

Logistics enables maneuver. It may also prevent successful maneuver by the limitations imposed on the force size that can continue to operate. Without supplies, no military force can continue to fight indefinitely. Germany did not have the raw materials, reserve stocks, or transportation assets to sustain its invasion of the Soviet Union in World War II. Neither did it have the port capacity or the transportation system within north Africa to support Erwin Rommel's Libyan operations.[34] In both examples, logistical support limited the force size that could operate in the theater and was a factor that encouraged the eventual German defeat. Logisticians must strive to support operators. Operators must never forget logisticians.

The speed associated with the movement of large military forces has dramatically increased. Motorized vehicles, whether on land or sea or in air, have the ability to move much faster than ever before. However, the complexity of the logistical system has also increased, as the distance involved in operations and support requirements of modern mechanized forces have risen. Whether the actual overall speed of operations will rise is open to debate.[35] However, the criticality of logistical support remains.

Maneuver and logistics have aspects of art and science in them, but maneuver is more art than science. Logistics is more science than art. Maneuver demands artistic creativity to devise an action or series of actions that will achieve the desired effect. Logistical actions are based on quantifiable requirements and capabilities.

TECHNOLOGY

Technology has a profound impact on war. Technology provides the machines used to fight. These machines include weapons and the devices that support the weapons. As time has progressed, technology has continuously changed the battlefield. Technology will continue to change warfare into the future.

The Army expends a large amount of resources trying to best utilize technology. There is a constant tension between whether new concepts should lead technological research and development and whether we should develop concepts to exploit the technology that exists. The issue is not a simple one.

In a time of limited resources, the Army must carefully spend its time and money. Insufficient resources exist to do everything. If by deciding on a concept the Army can focus technological development to maximize the use of the limited resources, the Army will waste less resources than it would by allowing research to continue in multiple directions. The danger, of course, is that a concept may ultimately not be technologically supportable. Should that occur, a great deal of time and money would be wasted.

Focusing on best utilizing existing technology to develop concepts does not focus research toward a specific goal. It also may preclude the Army's developing a revolutionary concept. Here technology constrains conceptual thought.

Technology forms a key link in the combat development process. It can drive materiel and force design and force structure developments. It provides the physical means required to execute command decisions and conceptual requirements.

One of the principle ways technology has affected warfare is in lethality. A machine gun will kill more people at a greater range and more rapidly than a sword. Obviously, changes in technology have provided weapons with a greater destructive capability. However, the lethality may be perceived rather than actual when looking at the battlefield as a whole.

This increased lethality required military forces to disperse. Soldiers had to separate to avoid presenting a large target and to seek cover. Dispersion leads to decreased casualties because it results in a reduced target array within a given area. Nuclear and chemical weapons are examples of weapons that force military forces to disperse to avoid mass destruction. Both types of weapons affect large amounts of territory. However, if the opponents fail to use such weapons after dispersing, they risk defeat by failing to mass sufficient power at the decisive point. This tension always exists when operations principally include the use of conventional weapons but have the threat of nuclear and chemical weapons hanging over them.

Dispersion increases the feeling of loneliness on the battlefield because soldiers are in close contact with fewer people than if they are not dispersed. Dispersion increases the need for small unit cohesion to provide the moral support necessary to sustain the soldiers' will to fight. As explained in my discussion of the moral nature, this loneliness is a critical concern.

Dispersion makes leadership more difficult and more important. It is physically more difficult to communicate instructions and supervise their execution as the distance between leaders and subordinates increases. Therefore, leaders must ensure their subordinates understand the essential components in the plan and their respective leader's intent for the battlefield outcome, so that subordinates continue to act in consonance with the leader's will even if the leader cannot directly communicate with the subordinate.

Weapon lethality also has separated the leaders from the led. Leaders cannot always lead from the front if they are to survive. Certain situations may require a leader's presence at the front to inspire his troops. However, the complexity of modern operations and the danger in being at the front will often force the commander rearward.

Once the commander cannot rely on his physical presence to exert control, he must rely on technology to support his command and control from a distant location. Thus, sophisticated communication and information processing systems become critical. The commander must use technology to provide him the information needed to make a decision. He must also rely on technology to help him enforce the action required by the decision.

The expanded battlefield puts added demands on junior leaders who must cope with greater time and distance factors than before. If a senior leader cannot directly control events on the battlefield, he must rely on junior leaders to exercise the required control.

Modern communications provide the means for commanders to talk over great distances. Such systems allow commanders to continue to control their units when separated from them. Radio has freed the commander from having to be physically present on the battlefield to issue instructions and receive reports. He does not have to physically see the entire battlefield in order to control events on it. Today's commander does not have to rely on his own eyesight alone. He can use every subordinate's vision of the battlefield as long as he and the subordinate can talk on a radio.

Today's intelligence collection assets allow commanders to see the battlefield at a greater depth than before. Direction finding and communication intercept provide the opportunity to identify enemy capabilities by analyzing the electronic order of battle.

Technology has also brought us automation. Computers provide the capability to process quickly huge amounts of information. The Army uses computers to perform such diverse functions as tracking supply actions and artillery fire control. They are marvelous tools, as long as their information processing is harnessed to serve, not dictate, decisions. Computers are only as good as the information and programs they contain. If either the information or programs are bad, the computers' answer will be bad. If the computers are deemed infallible, the users are in trouble. Computers cannot think. They can only provide a programmed response.

Technology has worked to expand the battlefield in addition to the effect of weapon lethality. This has manifested itself in a number of ways. Unit dispersion has expanded the amount of ground a unit occupies. This has expanded the distances over which a military force must maneuver, communicate, and sustain itself.

As mentioned before, the separation of the commander from his unit to escape the lethality of modern weapons has also expanded the battlefield.

In order to survive, commanders must avoid enemy fires. To do this, commanders must protect themselves while maintaining communications with their soldiers in order to exert control. If they fail to protect themselves and become casualties, they are no longer of any use to their soldiers. However, commanders could separate themselves so far from their soldiers that they may not be able to control their forces. Consequently, the need to avoid weapon lethality can cripple command and control.

This battlefield expansion caused by weapon technology forces a corresponding reaction by technology that supports command and control. If command and control technology can keep pace with the need to avoid weapon lethality, no degradation in command and control will occur.

Technology has also expanded the battlefield by increasing the depth of the position a force can occupy and remain within logistical support. For example, human porters and horse-drawn wagons cannot support as large a force over a given distance as motor transport and railroads. Air transport can now move critical supplies over thousands of miles if needed. This long distance logistical tail increases the distance or depth of position that a commander must consider when developing a plan or executing decisions.

Modern vehicles can carry significantly greater tonnage than horses and wagons. Bigger and faster ships, aircraft, and trucks have provided a greater haul capacity over time than was there in the days of sail and horse and buggy.

Technology has also placed different types of requirements on the logistical structure. The complexity of modern machinery has increased the need for specially skilled repairmen. Special skills require special education. Complex skills require intelligent soldiers.

Today's armored forces require tremendous amounts of fuel and ammunition tonnage to sustain their operations. Without the necessary support structure, these war machines are useless hunks of metal. Technology has added a large supply requirement that other technology must then provide the means to transport.

As units have become heavier, the criticality of strategic transportation has increased. The weight and cube size of armored forces make deployment a costly affair. Airlift and sealift are essential to support any force, but the needs of supporting an armored force over great distances of air and water is a factor no commander can afford to overlook. An army of tanks and armored personnel carriers in the continental United States is of no value if it cannot deploy to the desired battlefield. If U.S. Army transformation is successful, the United States will gain an army that is as lethal as the armored force could today be but much more strategically mobile.

From the U.S. Army's perspective, joint operations are essential. The Army cannot sustain itself outside the nation's borders without support from the Navy and Air Force. If they fail to provide sufficient ships and aircraft to lift and sustain the Army's force, the Army cannot perform its assigned mission. The Department of Defense must develop its plans within this frame of reference. Combat elements alone have no value. They only have value if the sustainment package required is also available. Plans must include combat and sustainment forces.

Indirect fire systems also have forced headquarters and logistical facilities to occupy positions farther rearward from the front line. This need to escape the effects of fires coupled with the ability to transport supplies over greater distances than before has increased the depth of the battlefield as discussed earlier. Recent improvements in terminal guidance systems for artillery munitions have made indirect fire systems a threat to armored point targets as well as the traditional area fire capability against soft targets.

Today we have a three-dimensional battlefield whether over land or sea. Aircraft work with land and naval forces. The Army relies on the Air Force to provide close and deep aerial fires. The Army also has helicopters to provide deep aerial maneuver and transport forces. The Navy always links submarine, surface, and air assets to provide a balanced capability to attack an enemy.

CONCLUSION

The physical nature of war remains a combination of the impact of the characteristics of the environment (or geography) on military units that maneuver and support forces within that environment. Technology provides the capability to overcome or enhance the effects of the environment. The tension between these elements is a critical element in war because it limits a commander's options in war.

Geography provides the situational framework within which military forces operate. "[T]erritory is the clearest expression of a state's political sovereignty," and military forces maintain the security of that territory with ground forces serving as the principal means to dominate land.[36] The characteristics of the physical environment affect the types of units and equipment most suitable for employment. The command and control structure relating to areas of responsibility and action determine the commander who controls operations within a certain physical space.

Maneuver and logistics define how forces use the space allotted. Units must position and move in consonance with the mission as restricted or aided by the characteristics of the physical space they occupy. Logistic capability must support the maneuver, or the maneuver will fail.

Finally, technology provides the capability to overcome the physical characteristics of the area where a force operates. Technology has expanded the battlefield and increased the capabilities of weapons and supporting equipment. This expansion of the battlefield, in part due to enhanced weapon lethality, has changed how leaders command and control units.

The physical nature includes the resources a belligerent must use or overcome to fight an opponent. It establishes the basic battlefield structure as a frame of reference for developing plans and executing them. A leader must use the physical nature to his advantage. The cognitive nature addresses how.

6

The Cognitive Nature of War

The cognitive nature addresses the mental contest inherent in war, which includes the command and control of military forces. Communications and intelligence support this process. Leadership of people and management of resources are essential in military operations. The cognitive process establishes the direction the force will take and provides a mechanism for the commander to control the actions of the forces. Several national level elements of power also affect this aspect of war.

Leadership is the linchpin of the cognitive nature. The leader must decide, control, and inspire. He or she must decide what to do and issue the instructions necessary to carry out his decision. A leader must control the actions of his/her subordinates to ensure they take proper action. Leading requires inspiring subordinates to overcome the difficulties they face including risking physical harm if accomplishing the mission requires such sacrifice.

COMMAND VS. CONTROL

Command encompasses the authority to make decisions and enforce them. It also includes bearing the responsibility for those decisions and the actions of subordinates. A commander is legally, ethically, and morally responsible for the conduct of his soldiers.

As Lord Moran said, "The art of command is the art of dealing with human nature. The soldier is governed through his heart and not through his head." Commanders must motivate their soldiers to follows their orders. They must convince the soldiers to do this when facing death as a possible consequence. Leaders must have the willpower to persevere when faced with challenges to their authority, their decisions, and their personal endurance.[1]

A challenge to a nation or military force is to select men and women who can be such leaders. Failure to pick the right people as leaders will threaten the existence of the force and success in battle. A military service will only be a success if it can identify leaders, promote them, and assign them where needed.[2]

Control is the process of ensuring that subordinates carry out the commander's decisions. Staffs and standardized reporting and procedures are tools commanders may use to ensure they have adequate control. A leader may use selected subordinates to observe critical events and report directly to the commander outside the standard reporting system.

Span of control refers to the number of subordinate people one person or level of command can adequately supervise to ensure compliance with decisions. Obviously, it is easier to supervise a smaller number of subordinates than a larger number. Selected people or headquarters can supervise more subordinates than others due to their experience, knowledge, and other characteristics.

Communications provide the means to transfer information within an organization and between organizations. Sufficient information must move to provide the basis for decision-making without overwhelming the same process with more information than it can effectively handle. Communications must provide information to alert the leader to success or catastrophe. Both require action. Information flow prevents a commander from becoming isolated from the battlefield. Leaders must guard against demanding more information than that required to make decisions. Every demand for information consumes time, a precious commodity. There is rarely enough time to do everything desired and also rest and reflect. Excessive information requirements waste time.

Maintaining control requires decisions. Time is necessary to transmit decisions to subordinates and for them to execute the decisions. This decision cycle and the time associated with it are important elements of command and control.

DECISION-MAKING

Deciding what to do is not always easy. The leaders must understand the situation they face before they can make a decision. Intelligence becomes important because it should show the commanders what they know and do not know about the enemy. This helps identify the risks associated with the decision. Leaders must be careful not to accept enemy situation predictions as facts to plan against. Plans and decisions must include sufficient flexibility to support changes needed because the enemy does the unexpected or undesired.

Leaders must make decisions based on facts and recommendations provided by their staff and subordinate leaders. In a standard military unit, only those in designated leadership positions have the authority to make decisions. Only such specified leaders bear responsibility for their units' actions. Staffs help such leaders, who are often designated commanders, by providing the information needed to support making a decision. Staffs can also help by supervising decision execution. Unfortunately, these roles sometimes appear reversed in peacetime.

Too often, more senior leaders await staff briefings on recommended courses of action without ever providing guidance. Staffs plan in a vacuum and assume much of the decision-making role because only they know what is happening. Leaders often are not involved in the estimate process except to approve staff actions. This puts the chief of staff in the central decision-making position because he coordinates the staff's actions. If he does not do so, the decision-making process then falls on the shoulders of the principal staff officers and their action officers. This is inefficient and may lead to disaster.

If staffs become too important, bureaucracy grows, and decisions take too much time to make. If leaders, such as senior commanders, are the central component of the estimate and decision-making process, decisions can flow rapidly. No time is lost, while staff officers plan in a vacuum.

The most difficult and often neglected element in the decision-making process is establishing the desired end state. A leader must determine what he or she wants the friendly and enemy situation to be after the operation occurs or as a result of the decision under consideration. This end state provides a clear objective for which all involved can aim and provides a focus for the staff's actions. Without a leader clearly stating what he or she wants to achieve, a staff cannot organize operations to produce the intended outcome.

Decisions and plans must also include desired actions based on changing battlefield conditions. Plans must address actions that follow completion of the operation or action. Plans must also address opportunities that may arise because conditions change during an operation or battle. For example, it is important that the desired end state include requirements such as the restoration of law and order in the opposing land if the goal is to destroy the sitting government. This end state and the subsequent military operations to establish the political leadership's true vision of the opponent after major combat operations are crucial.

The aftermath of Operation Iraqi Freedom major combat operations is a case in point. Regardless of whether the military leadership failed to request sufficient forces to reestablish law and order or the political leadership of the United States refused to provide the resources required, someone made a mistake. Coalition forces were not sufficiently robust to crush an insurgency before it began or to prevent that insurgency from obtaining arms and munitions left over from the Iraqi military. The failure to prevent that insurgency from building combat power inhibited the installation of a new and democratic government in Iraq. Clearly democracy is a good thing, and now is not the time to leave. Planning for subsequent operations is essential.

DECISION CYCLE

The decision cycle is the process of making a decision and passing instructions to those who must act. The time required to do this is critical. Included is the transfer of information to the higher headquarters, so that it can make a decision a part of this continuous cycle.

Since each echelon of command must take time to consider orders from above and information from below to plan and execute a decision, every echelon added increases the time between decision and execution. In other words, each echelon of command included in the process lengthens the decision cycle time.

Reducing the number of echelons of command can shorten the decision cycle time, but it increases the span of control. A span of control that exceeds the capabilities of the headquarters will lengthen the decision cycle time if it does not block the decision cycle because the headquarters has too much to do.

This tension between decision cycle time and span of control requires constant attention by the commanders involved to ensure a proper balance. Modern communications allow commanders to skip echelons if necessary to reduce the decision cycle time. However, that can result in conflicting orders and an intermediate headquarters with no function.

The enemy, of course, interferes with accomplishing the mission and achieving the visualized end state. Intelligence provides the knowledge required about the opponent to eliminate the enemy as a threat. However, the enemy always has a vote on the outcome of battle. A thinking enemy will not necessarily act as expected. Plans must afford sufficient flexibility in order to modify them as the situation changes. Predicting enemy positions and actions through templates is useful in order to provide a means of developing plans and allocating resources initially, but such predictions must also be accepted for what they are—estimates, not certainties.

First and foremost, though, a leader must make decisions. Leaders must also establish an organizational structure that supports their decisions. This structure must facilitate the transfer of decision information to subordinates, so they can act as the leader directs. Feedback to the leaders is essential for them to understand the situation their subordinates face and the results of their decisions.

Decision-making can generally be centralized or decentralized. A centralized system allows the leaders to focus their resources on their priorities. However, it puts a great burden of information flow from subordinates to superiors because the leader must have real-time comprehension of the situation. Otherwise, the time required for information to reach the central point will result in all decisions lagging behind the battlefield events.

Positional, or relatively static, warfare allows for a greater degree of centralization than maneuver or mobile warfare.[3] Events occur at a slower rate when units move little. This time allows for the information flow to occur.

A rapidly changing situation such as with modern armored, or mobile, warfare argues for decentralized decision-making. Events can happen before information can flow through the communication network. A decentralized system pushes the decision-making authority closer to the battlefield. Decisions occur faster in relationship to activities at the point of contact when decision-making is decentralized.

Regardless of which system prevails, the leader must lay out his vision or concept for the operation. This vision serves as a guide for subordinates in the absence of orders or when facing an unanticipated event.

Regardless of whether decision-making is centralized or decentralized, the organizational structure will define interpersonal connections and information flow. Complex tasks require an ordered organization[4] to reduce the confusion and lack of clarity that accompanies complexity. People must know who can make decisions about specific issues, where they send information, and from where they receive information. Organizational structure defines these relationships and the chain of command so crucial to military authority.

INTELLIGENCE

Intelligence is information about an opponent. Intelligence can provide a commander a glimpse (maybe even a panoramic view) of an enemy's plan. Such knowledge provides a commander the chance to exploit enemy weaknesses and to protect friendly vulnerabilities. A prime example of successful intelligence is the now well-known Ultra intelligence of World War II, which enabled the Allied leadership to read a wealth of German communications. This detailed knowledge was of immense value to Allied decision-making. However, intelligence alone cannot guarantee success. The leader must have the tools available to exploit the opportunities provided by intelligence. The leader must also correctly interpret the information provided.

If a leader knows the opponent's tanks have weak armor but there are no tanks or antiarmor systems with which to attack them, this knowledge is of little value. Should the information provided by the intelligence system not be clear as to its meaning because various analysts differ regarding its meaning or because the amount of information obscures the important items amid a mountain of unimportant information, a leader may err in a making a decision. Preconceived notions are another danger. People tend to believe a story that matches what they expect. This can lead to an incorrect interpretation of the meaning of information received.

The Battle of the Bulge in December 1944 is a prime World War II example of intelligence not helping a commander. The Allied leadership was convinced that the difficult Ardennes terrain made that sector of the front a relatively safe one for inexperienced units to gain experience and tired units to rest with little risk of combat. Reports of enemy activity reinforced the belief that action would occur in sectors other than Ardennes.

Intelligence provides the opportunity to wrest the initiative from an enemy. This is normally associated with defending against an attacker. The attacking force generally has the initiative, since it determines where, when, and if combat will occur. Intelligence that discloses the size of the enemy force, technical weaknesses, the timing of the attack, or the point of impact provides a defender the chance to defeat the attack and follow it with a counterattack.

The U.S. Army's recognition of the critical role that intelligence can play has led to a great reliance upon it for decision-making. Intelligence Preparation of the Battlefield (IPB) is the process where the intelligence analyst (regardless of skill, training, and rank) analyzes the battlefield and the enemy to develop possible courses of action. The analyst combines the effects of the terrain and weather on an enemy's doctrinal use of the forces available to determine what the enemy can do. This analysis includes the use of ground and air forces using a series of standard force employment templates as a guide to determine the forces that can traverse avenues of approach or occupy a position. The IPB process should include all staff elements and consider all forces available.

Unfortunately in practice, this process can cede the initiative to the enemy. Portraying an enemy as a stereotype can result in commanders demanding that intelligence officers predict the action an enemy will take. Finally, intelligence products are often the result of the intelligence officer's work rather than the result of the entire staff working in a synchronized effort.

Regardless of the thoroughness of the intelligence work or the precision of the information, the enemy still has a choice to make. Intelligence will rarely be perfect. Intelligence operatives and analysts are human beings. Leaders must weigh intelligence as an input to the decision process and once again make a decision. Leaders must also take care not to let preconceived notions cloud analysis and thought.

INITIATIVE

Focusing analysis on how to counter an enemy action surrenders the initiative in action to an enemy. By reacting to the enemy, a leader allows an enemy the opportunity to act first. By acting first, an enemy can select the time and place of battle.

Reacting to an enemy may be the best course of action if a lack of forces or the area of operations force a decision to concentrate combat power at a critical point after combat begins in order to mass sufficient power to be effective. However, the only way to set the terms of battle where desired is to seize the initiative or wrest the initiative from an opponent. Rather than starting with the enemy course of action a leader should determine a desired course of action (or at least the end state) before analyzing the enemy. Leaders and staffs must analyze the enemy's courses of action that interfere with the desired course of action or attaining the desired end state.

The issue here is the mindset of the decision-maker. Is he or she simply countering enemy actions or judging an enemy's reaction to a given friendly action? Unfortunately, the cookie-cutter approach that the IPB process engenders, especially when time is short, leads into the reaction mode.

PREDICTIVE INTELLIGENCE

Leaders must resist the impulse to demand one enemy course of action to plan against. Intelligence planning does require that, but designing an operation plan to counter one enemy plan is easier than designing one with the flexibility to react to numerous enemy decisions as well as forcing an enemy to make decisions to react to the opponent's plan. Anytime commanders require intelligence officers to specify the "likeliest course of action," they force the intelligence analyst to gaze into a nonexistent crystal ball and foresee the future. This predictive intelligence is very dangerous.

Focusing on one enemy course of action can easily lead to being surprised. Predicting the likeliest enemy course of action and then using that as the course of action to plan against results in a plan that counters one possible enemy plan. It provides an enemy the chance to achieve surprise as well as to seize and retain the initiative. If the enemy selects an option that is not the one predicted, the plan may not be appropriate.

Relying on a prediction as the basis for planning a course of action forces all action down a narrow path that can lead to disaster. Planning must begin with a statement of the friendly commander's desired end state. Some call this the commander's intent. Others may call it vision. The term applied is immaterial, except it must match the doctrine of the organization to which the leader and staff belong. The point is to begin planning with an understanding of the desired friendly situation after the battle and the path to achieve it. Force the enemy to react to the friendly plan. Build in flexibility to defeat all enemy reactions.

Requiring the supporting intelligence agency to make a prediction may also result in its performing limited analysis of enemy capabilities, especially after planning is initiated. If the intelligence analysts must state the enemy's planned action, they will tend to fit subsequent data to the mold that proves the prediction correct. This is a natural human tendency because no one wants to be wrong. Such a tendency can lead to disaster because no one may realize the plan is based on a flawed assumption. Reinforcing preconceived notions will result in people dying, when there is no call for it.

Intelligence officers and analysts must state facts. Making a variety of estimates to accompany the facts is fine as long as all analyses and estimates begin with the facts as the baseline. Predicting a course of action tends to turn the prediction into a fact because all planning uses the prediction as the baseline rather than the facts that are the baseline of the prediction. Explaining a range of possible actions is worthwhile because it encourages flexible planning for operations.

UNCERTAINTY AND FRICTION

The battlefield is also characterized by uncertainty and friction. Both exist to a degree in any conflict but are particularly relevant to a discussion of war. Clausewitz laid the foundation for the discussion of these in On War.[5] Uncertainty and friction make a commander's duties difficult to execute by complicating the decision process.

The information available to a leader is never perfect. A leader must recognize this and make decisions based on the information available tempered by judgment born of experience. This fog[6] that obscures reality affects friendly and enemy information. It magnifies fears and hides capabilities and problems.

Commanders use their staffs to gather information. However, they must recognize that perfection is not possible. The thirst for knowledge must be tempered by that fact. Commanders must be able to visualize the battlefield with this limited picture and make decisions with the information at hand.

The same uncertainty also exists with regard to intelligence or information about the enemy. Obviously obtaining information about enemy capabilities and intentions is more difficult than about friendly units. A thinking enemy will not cooperate. Again commanders must use their judgment to select the proper course.

As Clausewitz said, "Everything in war is very simple, but the simplest thing is difficult."[7] These difficulties whether enemy actions, a lack of resources, a lack of understanding by subordinates, or some other problem combine to impede action. This friction, which is a result of many people doing many things simultaneously, is inherent in any human endeavor. Every time something goes wrong; friction occurs.

The number of people and the multitude of different types of equipment they operate guarantee that some events will not occur as desired or planned. Soldiers make mistakes for a variety of reasons. They may lack training or be tired or exercise poor judgment. Regardless of why, errors will occur when people are involved.

Equipment will also fail. It does not matter how it is designed or how much it costs. Anything made by a human will eventually wear out or break. These equipment failures combined with natural human error guarantee friction, which will accumulate to make military operations difficult.

Uncertainty and friction place a premium on leaders' strength of will and ability to visualize the battlefield. They must conceptualize opportunities and translate them into orders for others to execute. A leader must be perceptive, so that limited information can be used as the basis for making decisions. Leaders must recognize these challenges and train themselves and their staffs to overcome them. Regardless of whether a leader uses intelligence to support a decision or determine a reaction to an enemy, the leader must ensure action occurs. He or she does this through leading people and managing resources.

LEADERSHIP VS. MANAGEMENT

People often make a big issue of leadership versus management. Both concepts are contained within the other. Leadership is the act of inspiring people to accomplish some task. Management involves the allocation of resources to accomplish a task. Both concepts are inherently part of the military decision-making process. However, one—leadership—focuses on people; the other—management—focuses on things.

Leadership will always hold the central role in the cognitive nature of military operations. The danger of the battlefield makes leadership the linchpin of military combat action. Leaders make the decisions that determine who lives and who dies. They focus the actions of the unit. Their character is reflected in the spirit, determination, and will of the soldiers they command. An effective leader's presence is felt whether he or she is physically present or not. He or she must ensure there is an effective mechanism to control his or her subordinates' actions to ensure they accomplish the mission assigned.

The previous discussion dealt with the cognitive process. The impact of the leader on this process determines the effectiveness of the command and control system. Units come to reflect their leaders' characteristics over time, as they make the units act as they see fit. Some leaders are more successful than others. Regardless of circumstances, there are factors or characteristics that mark a successful leader.

MARKS OF A LEADER

Another way to look at leadership is to review several factors that have provided the basis for success in the past. These factors, or marks of a great leader, include a philosophy of war, intuition, tactical and technical expertise, courage, a social contract between the leader and the led, and the ability to make advantageous use of time. All leaders possess these to a certain degree. The leader's and subordinates' personalities and the situation they face will affect the influence these factors have on the ability of one person to lead others.

Leaders must have a philosophy of war that provides a framework for their plans and operations. They must ingrain this philosophy in their subordinates and motivate them through national pride, glory, religion, plunder, or other means. The same factors in addition to ambition, glory, or the desire for some prize may be the motivation for a leader. Personalizing the struggle for all ensures that leaders and subordinates give their best effort toward accomplishing the mission.

A good leader has intuition, a combination of education, experience, and chance. He or she must analyze a situation, select a successful course of action, and have the determination to carry out his or her decision. Intuition, or the ability to make a decision without perfect information, helps a leader make timely, rapid decisions. The leader must be flexible, so the plan can be changed to take advantage of an unforeseen opportunity without losing the opportunity with a detailed (but time-consuming) analysis of the situation. A leader must be able to automatically sense battlefield opportunities.

Good leaders master the instrument they will use. They must understand their unit's capabilities and limitations. Such knowledge ensures a leader will select objectives that can be achieved. The leaders must possess physical courage to inspire their soldiers combined with the wisdom to refrain from taking unnecessary risks. They must have the moral courage to make difficult decisions and stand by them in the face of adversity. A great leader must understand the enemy's capabilities and weaknesses, so they can be exploited. Great leaders build a tradition of victory. Success breeds confidence between the leaders and their troops.

Leaders develop a social contract with their subordinates. Each supports the other. Leaders must not waste their subordinates on pointless operations and must care for their physical, spiritual, and emotional needs. Subordinates must obey their leaders. Disciplined subordinates follow a leader's will whether spoken or not.

Competent subordinates are essential. They must have the expertise to accomplish assigned tasks. They also must understand a leader's intent, so that in the absence of direct contact they can make a decision to change a previously directed course of action and remain within the leader's true concept of operation.

This social contract is related to the moral nature of war because of the obvious impact on the soldiers in the force. The strength of this contract will determine the unit's ability to withstand the stress of combat, especially if defeat or large numbers of casualties are involved. Subordinates must trust their leaders to make good decisions and to not waste their efforts. If they ever feel their leaders are incompetent or insensitive to their needs, this social contract will break.

The idea of a social contract implies a very personal relationship between leader and led. The leaders can initially build this relationship by proving their worthiness to lead. Tactical and technical skills are the foundation. Soldiers will not follow someone they view as incompetent. A skilled leader brings battlefield success. Victory usually means fewer casualties. Victory is always better than defeat.

Great leaders further the building of this contract by showing that they care for their subordinates' personal welfare and that of their families. They do this first by training their subordinates to a level of competence where the subordinates can accomplish the missions assigned. The leaders demand excellence and set challenging goals. Training must demand a tremendous effort, at times even one that soldiers will think they cannot achieve. Soldiers feel confident about their skills when they have met and overcome a difficult challenge. Simple, easy activities are worthless because they are boring, and meeting such goals proves nothing.

On the other hand, training must not demand such a supreme effort that success is consistently impossible. An occasional training failure is not catastrophic; but repeated failures can be if they cause a unit's leaders and soldiers to lose confidence in their ability to fight and win. No unit going into battle already convinced that it will lose has a chance, unless its opponent is in even worse psychological condition. Overconfidence invites folly, but a lack of confidence destroys the moral fiber of a unit.

Leaders must care for their soldiers' families. Human beings feel strongly about familial commitments. Soldiers will always be concerned about their families' welfare. This runs the gamut from such basics as food and shelter and safety. Leaders must provide the best care possible within the limits of their command responsibilities. Leaders must also recognize the impact on the morale of soldiers with unhappy (or worse, physically threatened) families. Soldiers will not concentrate fully on military actions if they face severe problems at home.

As with all things dealing with people, a pure quantification of the impact of various levels of home conditions is difficult. Budget priorities drive resource allocations, which in turn affect family issues. Leaders at all levels must recognize the concern and work within the situational limits.

Leaders must also show they care for their soldiers by not wasting the soldiers' time, effort, and lives. This applies to training and battle. Soldiers will strive to do their best as long as the goal is worthy and their sacrifices necessary to reach the goal. However, they will not willingly sacrifice themselves if they view their efforts as futile.

Time and timing are crucial. Leaders must use time as a resource and plan operations within the time available. They must know when to initiate and stop action. Leaders must understand the relationship between time and space to ensure operations include a balance of both requirements and resources. Deception and surprise depend on this relationship.

All events occur within a period of time. All activities require time in which to occur. Leaders must allocate time to allow staffs and subordinates to prepare to conduct the operations envisioned. Various percentages of time leap to mind including the 1/3–2/3 and 1/5–4/5 rules. Both indicate the amount of available time the higher headquarters takes (the first number, 1/3 or 1/5) compared to the time allocated for the subordinate unit. These rules are rough. The important point is that a leader must provide the time for a subordinate to plan and execute orders or failure is guaranteed.

Time affects the importance of a physical point as well as any event. A physical space is only important or decisive within the parameter of time that the presence or absence of a unit makes the space valuable. No physical space has military value if military operations cannot occur there. Military operations can occur only if military forces are present. Unless a physical space is permanently occupied, the presence of any force is temporary. This period of time when forces are present gives value to the space.

Leaders must ensure that they relate these two factors, time and space, in a productive way. Plans and actions must ensure that sufficient time exists to marshal the resources required and to conduct the operation before battlefield conditions change to invalidate decisions made.

Deception requires an opponent to believe something that is not real is in fact real. A leader must devote sufficient resources to a deception story for it to be believed. The timing of activities that are part of a deception effort must divert attention from the timing of the actual operation. As with actual operations, deception activities occur within a given physical space. These deception actions must deceive an opponent regarding the space used by the actual operation.

NATIONAL WILL

The strength of national will determines the ability of a nation to sustain any struggle. Whether physically destroyed or not, a nation's determination to continue will decide when the struggle ceases. As long as the government and its citizenry are willing to continue, the fight will go on.

This battlefield is by necessity a mental one. Physical conditions certainly affect the outcome, but the state of mind is the key. Physical conditions only matter in the effect on the collective mind of a nation. If physical conditions are so severe or promise to be so severe that continued opposition appears pointless, the struggle is over. Therefore, the battlefield is in the mind.

This struggle is largely one of communication. Here the media, whether broadcast or print, has a very potent role to play, since people generally receive information through their eyes and ears. For this discussion, broadcast media means television and radio, and print media means newspapers, magazines, books, pamphlets, and posters.

Media can be that of a free press, such as in the United States, or of a government-controlled press, such as in the now defunct Soviet Union. Even in a country with a free press, a government may control, or at least use, one or more information dissemination means.

Broadcast media provide information by image. Television does this by picture and word. Radio uses words to evoke images in the mind of the listener. Any speaker does the same. These images tell a story that may be purely informational or designed to convince the listener to do something or that one course of action is better than another.

Print media performs the same functions by using words and pictures for a reader to absorb. Just as the person watching the television or listening to a radio or speaker, the reader must translate the printed words and pictures into mental images. These images may only provide information or provoke some type of reaction.

The images from these media provide the basis for much of a nation's will. Citizens develop opinions based on the information they receive. They can receive information through their experiences or the experiences of others. Media act as the conduit for experiences of others to provide information to the public domain.

The opinions of a nation's citizenry determine their willingness to support their government. In an autocracy, the citizenry's collective opinion may not be as important as the opinion of the ruler. However, the people's opinion remains important because there is always a limit as to what citizens will allow their government to demand. Revolution is always an option. It may be painful, but it remains a course of action.

In a democracy, the citizenry's opinion is paramount. No program, decision, or governmental course of action can survive if a democracy's citizens reject it. Political leaders in a democracy must obey the voters, or they will not remain in power. Marshalling support for any action is essential.

This brings us back to the importance of national will and the media. The battlefield of the struggle for developing and determining national will is in the citizens' minds. They show their will by their approval or disapproval of governmental actions.

The various media then become the weapons used on this battlefield. Broadcast and print media provide the information that determines the opinions in the citizens' minds. These opinions determine the citizenry's support of their government. This support, or lack of it, decides the degree of a government's determination to take or continue a course of action.

The power of the information media can be enormous. If government-controlled, a government can ensure that its citizens only know information that will cause them to see the government in a good light. Propaganda comes to mind as a description of information used to slant opinions to match a certain viewpoint.

In a free press, the power remains immense but more difficult to control. Governments use censorship to limit information dissemination injurious to the country. Censorship is not all bad. It may be essential to protect operational plans or individual privacy (such as with casualty reports). However, censorship can lead to accusations of a government trying to hide the truth. The line is a thin one at times, but censorship is a government obligation when it is necessary to protect the lives of those who defend it.

Regardless of the degree of government control exercised, the media are weapons on this battlefield of the mind. Opinions determine the victor, the stronger will. Information feeds these opinions.

POLITICAL BATTLEFIELD

Political power is the power of government, the ruling or controlling of states and people. The political battlefield is the contest for who (individual or group) will rule. Military power remains a tool of government and so can be considered a component or subset of political power or the political battlefield. However, this discussion will focus on governmental actions not associated with the other types of power discussed here.

All political power includes the struggle of individuals or groups to become the ruling class. This is true whether at the local, national, or international level. This direct struggle for personal power is always part of the political process, whether in a democracy or autocracy.

In a democracy, the struggle is obvious because the politician must convince voting citizens to vote for him. Since this is again a contest for opinion, the politician must use broadcast and print media to convey information to voters to convince them to select him or her as their leader. This battlefield for voter opinion is obvious during any election year.

In autocracies, the rulers must still battle for their subjects' support. Voting is not an issue, but the rulers must ensure that citizens are sufficiently satisfied not to revolt and overthrow them. This battle may again include broadcast and print media. It may also include threats of physical violence.

Regardless of the type of government or technique of influence used, this aspect of the political battlefield is in the mind of the nation's citizens. The ruler or person who wants to be ruler must convince its citizens to allow him or her to rule.

The other component of the political battlefield is the interaction among political entities. At the local level, cities, counties, and states interact with each other to gain advantages for their citizens. This struggle generally orients on the personal welfare and standard of living of the citizens concerned.

The political battlefield at the national level concerns the contest to determine the actions a nation will take. Power here evolves from the ruler(s) and from the governmental bureaucracy that directs everyday affairs. Once two or more nations interact, the international political power struggle is joined. Though the impact is widespread, decisions and actions here remain conceptually the same as at lower levels of political power. The struggle is for influence and independence. Nations want to influence other nations to act in accordance with their desires. Nations strive to be independent of others. They want freedom of action.

All political entities ultimately strive for this freedom to act as they desire in order to protect the nation's citizenry—though the needs of one citizen may take precedence over others such as in an autocracy. This freedom is the core of every struggle for power regardless of type.

The political battlefield then resides in two places. First, it is in the minds of the citizens of the political entity. They must support (or at least not sufficiently object to) the ruler(s). Second, the political battlefield is any forum where two or more political entities vie for the freedom to do as they wish. This struggle occurs in the international media, conferences, government buildings, and the minds of the rulers or leaders. The success or failure of these two contests determines the course a government takes.

ECONOMIC BATTLEFIELD

The economic battlefield is trade. Trade brings wealth or at least the satisfaction of needs. Any organized group like a nation must be concerned about economic activity because it will define the standard of living and technological capabilities of the group. The exchange of goods provides the means for people to at least physically survive and preferably enjoy living by satisfying needs and desires.

Nations want to export excess production and import goods not readily available. This exchange of goods is trade. Nations who export more than they import make money, which allows the citizenry to purchase more of the items they need or want.

A component of economic activity particularly relevant to military operations is that of technology. Technological capability supports a nation's ability to build weapons and other equipment that provide military power. This linkage exists whether discussing a better truck, faster airplane, more powerful computer, or a weapon that requires precise manufacturing skills.

The economic base of a nation must support military needs within the possibilities of conflict a nation faces. Military forces do not produce goods. They buy equipment from industrial companies. If no company produces military equipment, the military forces will be incapable of fighting. Of course, a way around this is for the state to own all industry (such as in a Communist country). Then the government can dictate the production of military hardware. However, doing this precludes other economic activity by the factories concerned because they are devoted to military support. Economic activity still supports the military requirement because the government sacrifices some potential civilian economic activity to ensure an acceptable level of military support.

Failing to prepare for war while at peace puts a nation at great risk. War requires some level of economic mobilization. Soldiers use equipment and supplies. Firepower destroys the same. Expenditures and losses require replacement. If the citizenry also mobilizes to expand the military forces, more equipment and supplies will be needed to field the new units. The degree of preparation before war will determine the time required to prepare once war begins. It will also determine the financial expenditures necessary to provide the industrial support needed.

Therefore, the economic battlefield involves decisions that affect a nation's wealth derived from trade and the decisions to allocate limited industrial capacity to civilian and military support before and after war. This shows the relationships of different types of power. Economic power provides support to military power by providing the tools needed for war. Military power protects economic activity from outside physical interference and can be used to attack another nation's economic capability.

CONCLUSION

The cognitive nature is the mental aspect of war. The military command and control structure is a major component. This structure defines the communications required. Knowledge of the enemy reduces the likelihood of surprise and helps leaders effectively and efficiently allocate resources.

The bottom line of this process is the leaders' ability to use their subordinates. Their decisions must correctly focus the subordinates' efforts to defeat an enemy. Their actions must inspire the subordinates to overcome all obstacles to achieve their common goal. These subordinate soldiers man the equipment and occupy the positions on the battlefield. They compose the fighting force. Without them, there is no war.

The cognitive nature of war also involves the contest for the thoughts dominating the minds of a nation's leaders and citizenry. A battlefield is the place of struggle, where the belligerents vie with one another to resolve the issues that put them in conflict. This "place" may be a physical one such as that where military forces fight. It may also be in the minds of others such as the struggle for ideas associated with national will and political power.

Victory in war comes through convincing an opponent that they have lost. In essence, this is a cognitive change that results from the application of violence at a level that achieves this effect. Whether one nation or group imposes this violence on a civilian population or military forces, the leadership of the opponent nation or group must perceive that continuing the struggle is pointless. This struggle may require many years or it may come through a single action that shocks an opponent into the realization that they have lost. Even a long war could end through the use of an act to shock an opponent. Regardless of whether through one single event or a series of events culminating in a cumulative level of shock occurring, winning a war is a cognitive action supported by physical violence.

Regardless of the form taken, the battlefield remains the point of struggle; the place where conflicts are resolved. Conflict requires resolution. The battlefield varies by the type or types of power involved.

This human element, or the moral nature, is the third basic element of war. The physical nature describes the physical area of interaction, the battlefield, and the tools used to fight. The cognitive nature focuses the actions of the force. The moral nature provides the force necessary to prosecute a war, since war is ultimately a human endeavor.

7

The Moral Nature of War

People fight wars. That is a simple and rather obvious statement, but our fascination with the machines of war often obscures the human element of combat. Tanks, trucks, rifles, and other machines are tools, nothing more. We cannot begin to understand war without considering how people act in war and how war affects them.

PEOPLE AND WAR

Warfare is a human act. Military leaders must understand the relationship between people and warfare if they are to match human capabilities with the missions to be preformed. The leader who can best use and protect this indispensable resource, people, has an advantage over his enemy.

The numerous types of operations that compose the spectrum of conflict place different demands on the moral nature. Doctrine, training, and organization requirements may differ for these types of operations depending on the mission, enemy, terrain and weather, troops, and time available—basically the situation and factors affecting it.

This chapter addresses the human component of conflict. This human side is the moral nature and includes the role of people in military operations as well as the effect of such operations on people.[1]

People affect military operations because people compose military forces. Soldiers operate weapons and equipment. Commanders set goals and priorities. Clausewitz stated that moral factors "constitute the spirit that permeates war as a whole." He described the principal moral elements as "the skill of the commanders, the experience and courage of the troops, and their patriotic spirit."[2] People affect all military operations.

Military operations stress soldiers in many ways. Anthony Kellett included fatigue, sustained operations, climate and terrain, food and recreation shortages, tactics employed, a sense of purpose felt or not felt, enemy firepower, battle outcomes (victory or defeat), and casualties as characteristics of combat that cause such stress on soldiers.[3] Samuel Stouffer's detailed study of World War II soldiers identified a number of combat stresses: fear of death and injury, physical discomfort, lack of sexual and social satisfaction, isolation from affection, loss of friends, having visions of dead and dying soldiers, restriction of personal movement, uncertainty, the lack of value as an individual, lack of privacy, boredom mixed with anxiety, and a lack of terminal individual goals.[4]

The 1986 U.S. Army *FM 26-2: Management of Stress in Army Operations* also provided a list of factors that cause stress in soldiers. The list of factors included fatigue, the requirement to be alert and make decisions, poor visibility at night and in bad weather, isolation, continuous operations, separation from family, loss of leisure time, difficult training, unfamiliar cultures, integration of males and females, climate, terrain, and poor living conditions.[5] Doctrinal updates change such lists, but this one forms the basis for the discussion that will follow.

In order to provide a reference point, this chapter will use the factors below to describe how military operations affect soldiers:

- Fear of death and injury to self and comrades
- Fatigue
- Physical discomfort
- Isolation
- Uncertainty
- Value conflicts
- Boredom
- Separation from family
- Climate, terrain, and culture
- Special skills and tactics
- Lack of privacy

FEAR OF DEATH AND INJURY

Combat means bloodshed. Stress results. Death and injury surround soldiers in war. Richard Holmes noted that "the smell of death is almost as disturbing as the sight of it."[6] Soldiers do not want to be killed or injured but know all will not be able to avoid that fate. Medical support to care for the injured reduces the fear of death due to injury but cannot eliminate it.

Training can enhance a soldier's ability and confidence in his ability to avoid death or injury. Any protection from enemy weapons reduces this stress.

Soldiers also fear the death or injury of comrades. The sight of dead and wounded soldiers reminds soldiers of their own vulnerability. Battle tempo may result in the dead remaining unburied for long periods of time.[7] Loss of comrades reduces social contacts and the social support they provide. Medical support, training, and protection are important factors to reduce the likelihood of death and injury to comrades.

Combat involving large units such as in World War II, the Korean Conflict, Operation Desert Storm, and Operation Iraqi Freedom are the traditional image of war. There the machines of war destroy other machines and the people who man them and support their operation. Obviously soldiers die and are injured in such an environment. Victory is impossible without employing force.

Desert Storm and Iraqi Freedom were unique compared to previous traditional wars, in that the conflict outcome between large units was dramatically lopsided and the technology employed at times made combat seem like a video arcade. Long-range ground direct and indirect fire systems and precision guided munitions from air and naval forces contributed to this appearance by focusing on engagements of machine to machine. The distances at which engagements occurred also obscured the actual participation of soldiers in the fight. Soldiers were physically difficult to see. Nonetheless, they were there as the soldiers who later overran the Iraqi positions discovered. Modern technology kills with great efficiency. Combat in urban areas such as Baghdad during Iraqi Freedom was much more personal than operations in the desert.

The ease with which the coalition forces killed Iraqi soldiers and destroyed their equipment combined with the effects of poor leadership, training, and provisioning broke the will of much of the Iraqi Army. Though certain Iraqi units fought fiercely, most crumbled under the weight of the coalition firepower. The weakened moral state of the Iraqis gave the U.S.-led coalition forces a great victory in both of the Persian Gulf area conflicts.

Chemical and nuclear munitions add the dimension of even greater physical horror to the possibility of death and injury. Chemical weapons can kill without being seen and add the burden of uncomfortable chemical protective suits and masks to avoid such injury. The concern of becoming a casualty with no warning increases the mental pressure on soldiers to stand fast and endure the danger of the battlefield. Training in using protective equipment and good leadership can help soldiers overcome this fear. However, wearing the protective equipment is uncomfortable, especially in warm weather. The threat of dying in your sleep makes rest difficult, but the discomfort of the protective equipment makes sleeping while wearing it difficult. It is frightening to have a soldier wearing a protective mask wake you in the middle of the night yelling, "Gas! Gas!" when you are not wearing a mask.

Nuclear weapons bring the fear of massive destruction. Any concentration of units becomes an inviting target. Nukes also kill through radiation, another unseen threat. The soldier on the battlefield knows he can defeat chemical weapons with his mask and chemical protective suit. He has little chance against radiation because he has no equivalent personal protective equipment.

Nuclear weapons also expand the battlefield when intercontinental ballistic missiles (ICBMs) and long-range bombers are included in the force array. The battlefield then includes home. Fear of death and injury quickly expands to include families because they are now on a potential battlefield. Of course, this fear can exist anytime a soldier is fighting within his country; however, nuclear weapons provide such an immediate expansion of the battlefield and increased likelihood of large-scale death and destruction that they dramatically increase the mental effect of combat on the soldier.

Combat against insurgent forces results in a different stress relating to the fear of death and injury. Insurgents, or guerrillas, attempt to blend in with the population. Soldiers have difficulty separating enemy and friends. Rules of engagement limit soldiers' application of force to destroy the enemy. This limits soldiers' ability to protect themselves. Recent events in Iraq make it clear that fighting insurgents who adopt a terrorist outlook or who do not follow humane treatment of prisoners means that any soldiers captured cannot expect fair treatment or reasonable care. Insurgents who make it clear that they will behead or at least execute prisoners cannot help but engender a level of animosity from opposing soldiers that is not desired by civilized nations. Implementing rules to limit the inherent violence and horror of war may seem pointless. The rules are not pointless, of course, but at the point of the spear it cannot but be difficult to implement restraint.

Failure to restrict the use of force can result in the death or injury of innocent civilians. One of the reasons for posttraumatic stress in Vietnam veterans was guilt over the killing of women and children.[8] Civilian casualties resulting from government and guerrilla land mines hurt government and insurgent attempts to secure popular support in El Salvador.[9]

Other missions can result in unique death and injury stress. The situation faced by U.S. naval commanders in the Persian Gulf while escorting oil tankers in the late 1980s posed special concerns with regard to identifying friendly and neutral aircraft and ships. Concern over the possible loss of his ship influenced the decision of the captain of the USS *Vincennes* who mistakenly downed an Iranian civilian airliner in July 1988.[10] This mixture of friend and foe within the battlefield or area of operations characterizes many types of military operations today.

Certain operations may not involve a threat to a nation's survival. In such a case, the government may not feel compelled to continue the war to achieve a successful conclusion. Success may also be difficult to define. Combat and the subsequent losses may seem to have no purpose. Some

Vietnam veterans experienced significant posttraumatic stress due to the government not prosecuting the war toward an ultimate goal of victory. Veterans' sacrifices appeared meaningless.[11]

Even though one nation may not view survival as a risk, the nation where the fighting is occurring may consider the conflict a threat to its existence. Insurgencies involve an attempt by a group not in power to seize power. Therefore, the political survival of the host government is at stake. This can pose a unique stress for soldiers from an outside power and the host nation forces facing death or injury for an unclear benefit. The host nation may face a situation where it must use all its power to try to survive. The soldiers fighting for their homes and livelihood know that failure is not an option. However, the interests of the outside power may limit its assets committed to support that effort. The nation providing assistance may limit its support, since its survival is not at risk. Soldiers from the outside power may not be as willing to sacrifice themselves for a war that does not threaten their home or their families. Soldiers may hesitate and feel great fear because they do not want to die for a seemingly less important cause.

Soldiers must overcome their fear of death and injury in order to act and survive on the battlefield. This does not mean that they must not fear death and injury. Rational people will fear the potential for death and injury in a dangerous situation. It is a natural response resulting from the instinct for self-preservation.[12] Only a fool would face combat unconcerned for his safety.

However, soldiers must control their fears. They must not let fear prevent them from taking action while facing danger. Overcoming the debilitating nature of fear is the essence of courage. With courage a soldier can overcome the danger of the battlefield.

Fear is not new to battle. As Ardant du Picq said in his classic *Battle Studies*, "Nothing is changed in the heart of man."[13] Fear has always accompanied the soldier. Leaders must consider human weakness as well as human strength. Fear is a weakness or vulnerability that everyone possesses. However, soldiers can control their fear.

Discipline provides the foundation for overcoming fear. Disciplined soldiers know safety comes from a unit in action, not the uncoordinated actions of soldiers acting as individuals. Leaders must enforce discipline. Failure to do so allows panic to begin with defeat to follow.

Success also helps soldiers overcome their fear. Success breeds confidence. Soldiers do not quit if they are confident that the cause is right and they have the ability to win. Success reinforces discipline. By reinforcing discipline, success reinforces unity of action and unit cohesion.

A leader's presence also helps soldiers master fear. Soldiers are calmed by seeing their leaders because they know they are not facing danger alone. Leaders provide a purpose, a direction by making decisions and giving orders. Even if leaders are not actively providing instructions, their presence implies that they are. Leaders' presnce make soldiers believe a direction exists even if it does not.[14]

Ideology can also motivate soldiers to overcome their fear. The exploits of the Nazi SS units on the Eastern Front in World War II are well known. Their hatred and contempt for the Soviet Union combined with the expectation of poor treatment as a prisoner of war made the SS units formidable opponents.

Physical objects can serve as a solidifying force in any military operations. Field artillerymen have always identified closely with their cannons. Sailors are bound by their duty to preserve their ship. Such cohesive force helps the crew of any machine whether on land, on sea, or in air endure the danger of battle.

There is also a limit on the violence and terror soldiers can face before their courage breaks. Lord Moran wrote that months of combat will sap a soldier's reservoir of courage. Then true fear sets in and incapacitates a soldier who was once effective. The constant pounding of high explosive shells for days, weeks, and months on end used up the courage of soldiers in the trenches of World War I.[15]

Memories of previous danger enhance the effect of present danger. Experiences can lead to apprehension which breeds fear. This buildup of tension can destroy a unit.[16] Some means of rest after prolonged periods in combat can reduce this tension.

FATIGUE

Combat is physically demanding. The pace of operations often precludes adequate rest. Fatigue can incapacitate soldiers. Even assault troops may fall asleep due to the physical demands of war.[17] Units need more than one soldier with any particular skill to provide a continuous operation capability. Cross-training ensures that soldiers with critical skills have the time to rest without a unit being penalized for their absence.

All military operations can result in fatigue if the soldiers have inadequate rest. Therefore, this aspect of the moral nature is not inherently different in the various types of military actions. However, if political considerations limit the number of troops committed, fatigue could result because requirements might then exceed capabilities. Since a lack of trained and equipped troops could lead to the same problem, fatigue as a component of the moral nature is a constant throughout the spectrum of conflict.

PHYSICAL DISCOMFORT

Soldiers experience physical discomfort. They must fight in all types of weather on all types of terrain. Rest periods may occur infrequently. Protective measures to save soldiers from the effects of nuclear, biological, and chemical weapons increase soldiers' physical discomfort. If available, proper clothing and equipment reduce discomfort. Combat service support units providing clothing exchange, bath facilities, laundry, bakery, and other personal services also reduce soldier discomfort. Training soldiers to live in field conditions helps them reduce their discomfort due to life outdoors because they learn how to enhance their comfort in difficult situations.

Physical discomfort saps soldiers' strength. It robs them of sleep. It diverts their attention from their mission because they seek more comfortable surroundings. When the body is weak, the mind will not focus. The soldiers' feeling of having a purpose for their actions will decrease.[18] Any distraction that diverts soldiers' focus from their duties through their own neglect or inability to continue is a danger.

Physical discomfort may or may not differ throughout the spectrum of conflict. Living in the field will result in some physical discomfort regardless of the type operations concerned. However, certain types of operations may provide soldiers a better chance to reduce their physical discomfort between periods of combat. Some soldiers in Vietnam occupied bases that had bunkers and buildings equipped with televisions, stereos, air conditioners, refrigerators and soft drink machines.[19] These additions to normal field conditions certainly reduced the physical discomfort of the people who enjoyed them.

Relatively short-term operations like strikes and raids provide soldiers the chance to return rapidly to peacetime conditions. Operations such as peacekeeping, shows of force, and demonstrations try to avoid combat. If avoiding combat provides more time for soldiers and supporting units, then there is more time available to work to reduce physical discomfort. Efforts to reduce discomfort enable soldiers to recover from the tension due to the threat of death and injury, since it is much easier to rest when comfortable rather than uncomfortable.

ISOLATION

S. L. A. Marshall describes the battlefield as "the lonesomest place which men may share together."[20] Modern weapons' lethality has increased the dispersion of units and soldiers in order to reduce the impact of the employment of modern weapons. The threat of nuclear weapons forces units to disperse to avoid presenting a worthwhile target. Dispersion reduces soldier to soldier and unit to unit contact. This lack of contact, visual and physical, makes the battlefield a lonely place.[21]

Social support from peers provides the cohesion that binds soldiers together as a unit in combat. Once soldiers view themselves purely as individuals instead of a group, their unit begins to disintegrate. Soldiers must be ready to risk themselves for their friends and the good of the group—or unit. If they are only concerned with their personal welfare, it becomes very difficult to motivate them to win in battle. They withdraw from it in order to preserve themselves. If soldiers feel alone, they constantly worry about their fate. This is one danger of placing a soldier in an isolated outpost. It will sap his or her will and cloud his or her mind with worry.[22]

Soldiers today may experience a different type of isolation. Weapon lethality with the associated impact on dispersion remains a concern or potential cause for a sense of isolation. However, isolation involves more than soldier and unit dispersion.

Peacekeeping operations provide an example. Peacekeeping forces must maintain neutrality between warring elements. Mutual consent from the belligerents is essential. Should the peacekeeping force lose its neutral status, the belligerents will demand the peacekeeping force leave.

Neutrality protects the peacekeepers. Loss of neutrality may force them to fight.[23] Peacekeeping is more like police work than like combat.[24] Therefore, peacekeepers must isolate themselves from the dispute that required their presence if they are to maintain their neutrality. Soldiers in large unit combat operations do not have to remain neutral.

Soldiers performing security assistance missions must also isolate themselves from any conflict in the host country. Their purpose is to assist a friendly nation facing a threat such as when U.S. forces provided logistical support to Israel in the 1973 Yom Kippur War.[25] Military personnel performing security assistance missions want to avoid, not seek, combat.

Political support may isolate soldiers in other ways. If the survival of a nation is not at stake, segments of domestic and international society may not support military operations. Israel's 1982 invasion of Lebanon was the first time Israel experienced significant domestic opposition to a war. The purpose of the war was unclear. Domestic opposition led to open protests of the war. The refusal of 143 reserve soldiers to fight was indicative of the discontent.[26] Domestic resistance to using military force isolates soldiers from those who oppose such action.

International relations also affect military operations. British soldiers continue to patrol Northern Ireland to enforce peace. The United States and Great Britain are allies, yet American citizens have sent money and weapons to the Irish Republican Army (IRA).[27] Support by an ally to an enemy isolates soldiers from an expected agent of support, when the expected support helps the enemy instead of the ally.

Media coverage also affects the feelings of isolation a soldier may have. Regardless of the spectrum of conflict level, media coverage may bring soldiers' actions into home front living rooms. This can reduce the isolation of the domestic front from the soldiers. Terrorists have become particularly adept at using the media to further a cause. They use terror to influence a large group and attract world attention. Media coverage subjects soldier actions to scrutiny by all those watching.

Media disclosures of antiterrorist actions can jeopardize operations and hostages. Media reporting of a hijacked Lufthansa aircraft captain's contact with authorities in October 1977 resulted in the terrorists murdering the captain.[28] However, in a society where freedom of the press is important, military personnel cannot avoid the media. Soldiers must learn to work with the media's presence.

UNCERTAINTY

Soldiers cannot avoid uncertainty. The threat of death and injury makes survival uncertain. Poor communications foster uncertainty by clouding the information flow among leaders and soldiers. Soldiers do not have control over their destinies. Commanders must often make decisions without the soldiers' input. A thinking enemy opposes soldiers and tries to ensure their uncertainty to enhance his opportunities for success. Eliminating all uncertainty is impossible as long as people are involved.

The lethality of the battlefield has caused an increase in uncertainty by reducing a soldier's ability to rest. This was evident in World War I. Field artillery fires made rest difficult. There were few safe moments.[29] Soldiers constantly feared the unseen high explosive rounds. This heightened their uncertainty and at times crushed their will to continue.

Uncertainty forces decisions based on estimates rather than facts. This drives intelligence operations that attempt to reduce uncertainty by determining ground truth. This need to eliminate uncertainty results in a constant desire for information to flow up and down the chain of command.

Uncertainty about conditions at home affects a soldier's mental state. Mail and visits from home by political and entertainment celebrities reduce this anxiety by providing a link to the "real world." In this day of instant communications, telephone and e-mail contact are other ways to ensure the soldiers deployed know what the conditions at home are. The commonplace telephone was a critical morale booster during Operation Desert Shield.

The difficulty of separating friends and enemy in a guerilla war adds uncertainty. Terrorists bring even more uncertainty to military operations. Distinguishing violent criminal acts from terrorist actions may be difficult.[30]

Terrorist actions may be designed to produce an overreaction by government forces.[31] Overreaction may alienate the government from the population, the focus of the power struggle. Guerrilla warfare in World War II Russia and Yugoslavia was characterized by brutality and atrocities on both sides. German atrocities in response to partisan brutality alienated the local population.[32]

Foreign support to terrorist groups can bring further uncertainty in trying to determine who the enemy is and how to eliminate the threat. Libya's support of terrorists in the Philippines, Northern Ireland, and the Middle East was an example of such foreign aid.[33]

Peacekeeping, shows of force, and demonstrations involve their own special kind of uncertainty. Uncertainty exists due to the threat of combat always being present. Military forces with such missions try to avoid combat but must always be prepared to defend themselves. Failure to do so can result in disaster. The consequences of such a self-defense failure were demonstrated by the 1983 bombing of the U.S. Marine Corps barracks in Beirut, Lebanon, where over 240 U.S. military personnel died.

VALUE CONFLICTS

Value conflicts stress soldiers. Society does not sanction taking someone's life. However, soldiers must kill their enemies even though society prohibits aggression.[34] Society's condemnation of killing another person conflicts with a soldier's duty. Soldiers must also deal with the conflict between the duty to function in a threatening environment and the desire to stay alive and uninjured. Leaders must weigh the requirement to accomplish missions that will result in the death or injury of their soldiers.

Certain operations today include different value conflicts from those generally thought applicable in war. Soldiers train to use their weapons in combat. However, many missions require restraint when using lethal force. Fighting guerrillas, peacekeeping, shows of force, and demonstrations may require soldiers to shoot only to protect themselves or to use their weapons carefully to avoid injuring innocent people. The requirement to consider rules of engagement that inhibit the use of deadly force results in conflict within the soldier to determine when to fire or not. The soldier knows that failing to fire can result in his or her comrades' death or injury. Firing at the wrong time may hurt the wrong target and work against his or her mission. The dilemma of the captain of the USS *Vincennes* again comes to mind.

Special legal concerns also may arise. Governments may want to treat captured insurgents as criminals. Treating them as prisoners of war may confer upon them a legitimate opposition status that could enhance the insurgents' popular standing. However, interpretation of the 1977 Geneva Protocol recognizing armed forces as all organized forces with an internal disciplinary system to enforce compliance with international law may confer such a status on an insurgent group.[35] As Lieutenant General (Retired) L.D. Holder, former director of the U.S. Army's School of Advanced Military Studies at Fort Leavenworth, Kansas, has noted, treating an insurgency as a civil operation may make soldiers subject to civil authority in addition to the normal military chain of command.

Using military forces to defeat terrorists may make them appear stronger than if nonmilitary security forces are used. If terrorists want political legitimacy by being viewed as an army, a government using its army against them may confer this status on them. Great Britain faced this problem in Northern Ireland.[36] While a nation may not want to escalate the violence or appear to confer such legitimacy, there may be no choice because military forces may be the best equipped resource to employ.

Military personnel must be prepared to conduct operations viewed as legal by their government that another may consider illegal. Egyptian commandos discovered the danger with such a mission when they attempted to liberate hostages aboard a hijacked DC-8 at Lanarca, Cyprus, in 1978. When the Egyptians attacked the plane, Cypriot soldiers returned their fire and stopped them. The Cypriots arrested the Egyptians. The hijackers later surrendered.[37]

BOREDOM

Lord Moran noted in World War I that the desire for change resulting from boredom could lead to rebellion and discontent.[38] Boredom broken by periods of great anxiety characterizes warfare. Rapid, continuous operations result in fear and anxiety; however, logistics or the limits of soldier endurance will eventually force a pause in operations. These pauses provide time for rest and reconstitution but can result in boredom.

Any military operation will include periods of boredom broken by periods of anxiety. Missions that seek to avoid combat may result in longer periods of boredom.

Imagine the impact of small units occupying observation posts and checkpoints for extended periods of time. As long as diplomacy maintains peace between the belligerents and the peacekeeping force maintains its neutrality, no combat occurs. U.S. peacekeeping elements in the Sinai have experienced boredom because the lack of combat results in little activity for the soldiers. The troops have felt isolated due to cultural differences, which further limits available activities to reduce boredom.[39]

There is a similarity between the cycle of boredom interrupted by anxiety and the life of a combat pilot. Lord Moran noted how World War II pilots in Great Britain experienced stress due to the sharp contrast between combat and life at the air base. Pilots lived in general safety in a civilian environment in Great Britain. However, they flew missions over Europe in great danger. These swings between safety and great danger were a significant strain for the pilots.[40]

Today's soldiers face similar stress. Anytime military personnel establish a secure base from which to operate against an enemy, they experience this contrast of safe versus hostile environments. Firebases and air bases in Vietnam were examples. The strain comes from the thought expressed by Moran as "keeping alive the idea of another way of life—the chronic danger of an alternative in war."[41]

SEPARATION FROM FAMILY

Modern armies do not intentionally deploy service personnel's families into combat. Soldiers do not need to be concerned for their families' safety while fighting. However, this separation deprives soldiers of their usual social support. This can make soldiers feel isolated from home and safety.

No government should intentionally subject families to physical danger because they are not prepared to defend themselves. Soldiers will not give full attention to their duties if they are concerned about their families. Unfortunately, operations may occur in places expected to be safe. Consequently, if the situation becomes dangerous and a soldier's family is present, then the presence of the family, or the lack of separation from family, can be a stress factor.

Terrorism is a threat everywhere. Certain places are obviously more dangerous than others. Traveling in the Middle East involves a certain risk. After September 11, 2001, Americans and anyone who associates themselves with Western civilization must be concerned about a terrorist attack when least expected.

American soldiers are by no means the only soldiers who have faced the dilemma of accepting separation from their families. The early stage of the revolution in Algeria against French rule included the murder, wounding, and rape of more than 200 Europeans, resulting from Muslim demonstrations in May 1945. French security forces responded by killing thousands of Algerians.[42] IRA terrorists killed two Irish soldiers at home on leave in August 1971.[43] IRA gunmen killed a prison officer as he walked away from a wedding while holding hands with his wife and six-year-old daughter in April 1979.[44] American soldiers with their families in Panama faced that stress due to concern for their safety when Manuel Noriega headed the Panamanian government.[45]

As long as military service separates soldiers and families, the stress will be similar to that normally associated with war. However, failing to anticipate a threat and not separating soldiers from their families when a danger exists then adds stress by placing families in harm's way. There is always a danger that certain situations may not appear to be a real threat, which can result in military families being in danger without realizing it and taking precautions to remain safe.

CLIMATE, TERRAIN, AND CULTURE

The climate, terrain, and local culture of the battlefield affect the soldier. Climate and terrain may add to a soldier's physical discomfort if different from those of where the soldier was stationed. Soldiers may have to adjust to an unfamiliar culture characterized by different customs and language.

These factors pose virtually no inherent difference in the war's moral nature regardless of the type of conflict. Soldiers should train and be equipped for the climate and terrain where they will operate. Soldiers should be acquainted with the culture where they will be stationed or fighting. However, operations mandating a restraint of force and depending on legitimacy in the eyes of the host population require more consideration of the local culture than others. The Soviet Union's antireligious program during its operations in Afghanistan failed to appreciate the population's feelings. This program provided the Afghan resistance the solidifying force for an Islamic holy war.[46]

SPECIAL SKILLS AND TACTICS

Training attempts to prepare soldiers for combat by providing them with the special skills necessary to ensure their success and survival. Proper training supports the tactics used in combat. If expectations match reality, soldiers will experience less stress due to uncertainty and the effects of climate, terrain, and culture. Experience in combat provides the basis for modifying tactics when training fails to adequately prepare soldiers. The battlefield is very different from soldiers' civilian experiences.[47] Training attempts to reduce the surprise that results from such differences.

The wide variety of missions faced by a modern day soldier requires special skills not needed in the civilian world. Failure to prepare soldiers to use the skills necessary in their duties will have disastrous results. Soldiers will lose confidence in their ability to defeat the enemy because they will lack the ability to do so. They will not be able to employ tactics that will win. Morale will suffer. The force will fail.

French forces responding to the 1954 revolution in Algeria were trained and equipped for combat in Europe. They were capable of controlling roads, not chasing guerrillas over rough terrain. Ambushes took a toll on the French mechanized forces without them being able to respond decisively. Civil authorities wanted a pacification program but had difficulty providing clear guidance. Security forces were unsure if they were to "regain the confidence of the inhabitants" or crush the rebellion with force.[48]

Due to the necessity for restraint in certain situations, tactics can have a marked impact on the success or failure of the operation. Tactics allowed in combat may be illegal in certain special operations. British Special Air Service (SAS) soldiers killed three IRA terrorists in Gibraltar in March 1988. The terrorists were unarmed. Witnesses claimed the soldiers murdered the terrorists. An inquiry deemed the shootings lawful.[49]

Sometimes people expect soldiers trained to kill enemies to also act like policemen. Soldiers in such a situation face a real problem. Questions regarding the authority to make an arrest and provocations warranting the use of deadly force are issues with which soldiers must contend in certain missions. Training and clear instructions are crucial.

Governments may require their military forces to perform missions not related to combat roles. Civil action programs are an example and are not new. Civil support missions are not just the purview of American forces. Chinese Communist soldiers have harvested crops and British engineers have built railways, docks, and roads in the Sudan as examples.[50]

LACK OF PRIVACY

Soldiers lose privacy due to the requirements of communal living in military forces. This is true in peace and war. Since units are composed of numbers of soldiers, this stress is unavoidable.

Lack of privacy will be a problem in peace and war. The spectrum of conflict is immaterial. Soldiers will function in close proximity to other soldiers in all conflicts. Military life means a sacrifice of absolute personal privacy.

In operations today men and women are constantly working together in field conditions. The difficulty of maintaining privacy to completely separate the sexes is virtually impossible if efficient and effective operations are the principal focus. Consequently a loss of privacy occurs. There is no way to prevent it.

DOCTRINE, TRAINING, AND ORGANIZATION

Combat means bloodshed. The fear of death and injury will be the same when soldiers fight. All military operations involve fatigue if soldiers do not get adequate rest. Physical discomfort will characterize field conditions. Soldiers will experience battlefield isolation when facing modern weapons. The value conflicts of murder versus duty, mission versus people, and self-preservation versus duty will stress soldiers in all forms of combat. Boredom will continue to be broken by periods of anxiety. Soldiers may be separated from their families. Climate, terrain, and culture will affect operations and soldiers. All military operations involve a lack of privacy.

However, the considerations in the moral nature of military operations differ just as the types of operations differ. The fear of death and injury is different between large unit combat and other operations where it is difficult to identify the enemy and more restraint is required in the use of force.[51]

Physical discomfort may have less impact on soldiers if they have the opportunity to build comfortable facilities. Isolation may affect soldiers differently due to the heavy impact of domestic and international politics, media coverage, and the need to consider the local culture. Uncertainty is different when it is difficult to identify threats. Value conflicts are heightened by the added requirement to use force with restraint and special legal considerations. Boredom is a special problem when there is a lack of combat action. Family separations can pose unique problems when the possibility exists for soldiers and families not to be separated in certain dangerous situations. Training and tactics differ among types of operations, but the impact of having the wrong training and tactics is generally the same.

Simply knowing the moral nature of war exists is not enough. The important issues are the implications for doctrine, training, and organization that can help soldiers overcome the negative characteristics of the moral nature. Doctrine provides the foundation for the Army's training and organization. Training must provide the capability to perform the tactics, techniques, and procedures that are contained in doctrine. The Army's organization must provide the units and skills necessary to operate in accordance with the doctrine.

Doctrine

Soldiers must use their weapons to succeed in large unit operations or any direct combat. However, restraint is extremely important in many operations today that require the avoidance of innocent casualties. The dilemma is that these two requirements work against each other. If Marshall's observation that few soldiers fire their weapons[52] is true, then, today, training for restraint may exacerbate the problem. If Marshall's contention is not true, teaching restraint will be difficult. Should doctrine fail to highlight this issue, leaders may not appreciate the dichotomy and fail to deal with the contrasting requirements.

Tactics for military operations vary widely due to the multitude of missions possible. Individuals and units must always be prepared to perform the combat tasks. However, they also must be able to function in roles more police-oriented than combat-oriented. In underdeveloped countries, combat support and combat service support operations may be more important than combat operations.

Underdeveloped countries may need roads, schools, and medical support more than weapons to cure the social ills that form the basis for discontent and revolution. Disaster relief does not involve combat but will require combat support and combat service support. Combat units may support combat support and combat service support units rather than the other way around, as combat units are a source of disciplined manpower available to supplement the manpower in support units.

Doctrine must provide for tactics to defeat the many types of threats in all types of conflicts. For example, fighting drug traffickers poses unique problems for all military services. Doctrine must provide the conceptual basis for the integration of civilian law enforcement and military services. Operations will be joint and may be combined. They may also include jurisdictional considerations between the multitude of federal and local law enforcement agencies. Deciding who is in charge will be difficult and is crucial as in all military operations.

Doctrine must focus force design and structure initiatives to ensure proper organizations exist to meet the required military capabilities. The mix of combat, combat support, and combat service support elements is important and will differ among the different types of military operations. Doctrine must identify any special skills required for inclusion in Army force designs. Doctrine must identify the mix of the various force design types. This mix combined with requirements based on national policy allows the Army to produce the appropriate force structure. Soldiers must learn how to implement this doctrine through training programs structured to simulate combat conditions and to highlight these doctrinal concepts.

Training

Soldiers must prepare themselves to confront moral nature issues. Mental toughness is necessary for soldiers to withstand the stress of military operations. Mental agility is necessary to confront the wide range of missions and threats. Soldiers must be prepared for a multitude of combat and noncombat roles regardless of the type unit to which they belong.

Soldiers must maintain the initiative in setting the tempo of operations (or social reforms in underdeveloped nations) as in all military operations. Physical fitness is important, so that soldiers have the stamina to endure the harsh climate and difficult terrain in many underdeveloped nations where combat operations occur. Individuals must study the culture of the areas where they will operate to reduce stress from a strange environment. Soldiers must always strive to master the skills associated with their rank and duties. Failure to do so reduces their value in any situation.

Military schools must prepare soldiers to deal with the moral nature of war. Schools must point out the differences in the moral nature in the various levels of the spectrum of conflict, so that leaders recognize specific training needs. Unit training programs must reinforce school training through refresher classes and training for tasks not covered by schools.

Units must train soldiers to expect family separations. They must also train soldiers in methods to protect their families if a threat to them exists. A nation's government has a moral obligation to protect military families. Family support groups are an important piece of the U.S. Army's plan to provide this care for families.

Training must prepare soldiers to show restraint in using force if restraint is needed but also ensure that soldiers are able to be sufficiently violent when called upon to physically combat an enemy. They must understand the need for rules of engagement to protect innocent parties and limit conflict escalation. Soldiers must understand the need to be neutral when the situation requires it. Soldiers may have to suppress the desire to favor one side over another when one belligerent's actions appear to warrant support or retaliation.

Training must identify the threats expected and ways to recognize them. Leaders must expect high visibility due to media and political interest. Soldiers must expect close scrutiny of their actions by individuals and groups at home and abroad.

Training must be joint and combined because military operations will be. Exercises must include the same types of forces expected to be in the theater. Only repeated training exercises can ensure that the different services and allies develop the tactics, techniques, and procedures necessary for success.

Units must focus on wartime missions and be theater-oriented. In addition to individual training, unit training must prepare soldiers for the physical demands of the theater where they will deploy. Unit training should address cultural concerns because of the battle for the minds of the host population. Respect for the local culture is a key ingredient if the military force is to earn the respect and support of the people. Focusing training on the theater where soldiers will operate reduces the negative impact of changes in climate, terrain, and culture. Soldiers must understand the people living in the area, so that the methods used do not unnecessarily alienate the population.

Units must ensure soldiers understand the consequences of their actions. They must know the limits of legal force. The SAS soldiers who killed the IRA terrorists in Gibraltar provide an example of the potential consequences of illegal action. Obviously, close scrutiny by agencies and individuals not conducting operations means soldiers must understand exactly what they can and cannot do. Failure to understand such limits could result in the soldiers facing criminal charges for using the weapons they are trained to use. British Private Ian Thain discovered what can happen when such limits are overstepped. In December 1984, he was convicted of murder for killing a civilian in Northern Ireland. Private Thain received a life sentence.[53]

Units must develop training programs to build small unit cohesion. Cohesion will help the soldiers cope with the stresses of isolation due to physical location or cultural differences. Cohesion will keep the units intact when uncertainty threatens to destroy morale. It provides social contact when families are not around to do so. Cohesion also reduces the invasion of privacy soldiers experience in military life. Small unit cohesion provides the social support structure soldiers need when they grapple with value conflicts.

Cross-training of unit personnel can reduce the problems of fatigue and boredom. Cross-training provides more soldiers with the skills required to perform a task. Taking the time to cross-train soldiers during rest periods reduces the problem of rest periods leading to boredom. Cross-training also decreases the problems in a unit when death or injury incapacitates key individuals.

Training exercises must include scenarios matching the wide range of possible combat operations if soldiers are to learn to cope with the human side of such use of military force. However, a problem with such exercises is the time required. Deployments help units prepare to move. Units can conduct combat training exercises of all types; however, the time required to conduct a successful counterinsurgency program is so great that it is difficult for units to devote all the resources necessary in training that can replicate the time factor. Soldiers in peacetime know exercises will end. Making soldiers feel to the degree necessary the stresses of isolation, uncertainty, value conflicts, boredom, and separation of family is very difficult.

To better simulate the moral nature of the range of operational requirements, exercises should be at installations other than where a unit is based. The exercise location should have a different climate and terrain than the unit's home station. People to play host nation civilians with a different language and culture should be in the training area. Soldiers should not know when the exercise will end in order to stress them with regard to feelings of isolation, uncertainty, boredom, and separation from family. The U.S. Army's combat training centers in California, Louisiana, and Germany have provided challenging and worthwhile training environments and been mainstays in ensuring the success of U.S. Army units in combat and other operations.

Scenarios must provide situations where soldiers experience value conflicts and uncertainty such as ambiguous target sightings and enemy soldiers mixed with civilians. Exercises should include casualty play to force units to rely on personnel redundancy and cross-training to continue to function.

Organization

Military organizations must contain the trained personnel and elements to perform their missions. Personnel redundancy reduces fatigue problems. Combat service support units reduce physical discomfort through the services provided. Medical support reduces the fear of death and injury. Morale support activities can help reduce boredom.

Specialists concerning the threat and host nation take on increased importance when it is difficult to separate enemy forces from civilians. Such specialists can aid in determining who is friendly by gathering human intelligence through the local population. These specialists can also help soldiers respect the local culture, which is important to avoid alienating the population. The same cultural respect is necessary for medical, civil affairs, and other combat support and combat service support teams to improve living conditions in the host nation without turning the supported country into a miniature America overnight. Progress takes time.

The mix of combat, combat support, and combat service support units required differs throughout the spectrum of conflict. Support to host nation governments often involves noncombat actions. Roads, schools, water treatment plants, and bridges are a few of the facilities a government may need to reduce the population's discontent. Making the host nation sufficiently strong to survive without outside help reduces the need for troops to be deployed.

This strength is in part military; however, the population will view its government more favorably if the government can provide a decent life. Using combat support and combat service support units instead of combat units has domestic and international political benefits as well. Casualties suffered by the nation helping the host government should be lower since its in-country forces would not be trying to fight. The assisting nation would be helping the host government better itself and support its people. Outsider military units would not be killing people opposed to its policies. However, the host nation's security forces must be capable of securing the nation. If they are not, then the outside power must be prepared to deploy combat units or other security forces to supplement those forces of the host.

The value conflicts discussed earlier that distinguish the moral nature of different types of operations will also increase the importance of legal counseling activities. Legal guidance will be particularly important to help leaders deal with the use of force in operations not part of a declared war. Legal advisors who are experts in local law must be available to ensure soldiers do not run afoul of local restrictions.

When facing a lack of clear guidelines for defining success and isolated from home, counselors are particularly important. If the military action is an unpopular one, counselors (chaplains, psychologists, and the like) to help soldiers deal with the added stress will be important. Organizations with counselors to help families cope with the stress they feel are also valuable.

Teams of mental health experts to treat stress problems are useful in military operations. The pace of operations will determine if time is available for such teams to reduce the effects of stress. The military services deployed such teams to help the crew of the frigate USS *Stark* after the Iraqi aircraft attack in May 1987 and to help hostage victims five times in the Middle East from 1985 to 1986.[54]

Army force structure must address the specific demands of all types of operations. Teams of the specialists discussed previously should be components of the structure. These teams should be theater-oriented to provide the focus and skills necessary. Force developers must give special consideration to the combat support and combat service support skills needed. This mix will depend on the economic, transportation, communication, legal, religious, and political infrastructures that exist in the theater.[55]

Having sufficient troops on hand to provide for personnel redundancy and rest periods is not unique to any type of military operation. However, the deployability of the forces necessary is an issue. This does not refer to the capability of a certain number of aircraft to deploy a certain size unit.

SUMMARY

The moral nature requires consideration in military doctrine, training, and organization to maximize the ability to conduct operations. Failure to recognize this impact will degrade the military unit's ability to accomplish missions assigned. There is no need for that to happen. The impact is apparent.

The problem does not stop there, however. Soldiers and units conducting different types of operations require different mental outlooks. Time and other resource limitations make preparation for all conceivable missions within the spectrum of conflict difficult for traditional units to accomplish. Military personnel and units must focus their efforts if they are to perform at their best.

This leads to a strategic or policy dilemma. A nation's military and political leadership must decide how to use military forces. Do they want to conduct operations throughout the spectrum of conflict (a balanced approach)? Do they concentrate on one type of operation? Do they focus active component forces at certain types of operations and reserve component forces at others?

The answers to these questions will ultimately determine unit tactical capabilities to cope with the moral nature of military operations regardless of the type of conflict. Failure to consider the moral nature differences in the spectrum of conflict will lead to the fielding of a military force that will at least not perform as well as it could and may fail. That would be a tragedy for the soldiers sent to fight in a manner for which they are not prepared. It would be a disservice to the country.

People conduct military operations. Leaders must consider them in every action. They are the most precious and responsive resource in a military force. The moral nature can never receive too much emphasis.

Whether considering one of the natures of war as a focus for study or some aspect of the desire for power or control, anyone examining military actions must also investigate how military forces change over time to adapt to new ideas and new technology. Subsequent chapters will examine how organizations and especially military organizations institute change. Key factors in the distinction between evolutionary and revolutionary change will be discussed. The present transformation program within the U.S. Department of Defense is very instructive in providing a foundation for this review of how to change.

8

The Need for Change

The U.S. Department of Defense has been undergoing a major change in all of the services categorized as transformation. However, major change is not a new phenomenon in the military services; nor is it new in civilian industry. In order to understand the meaning of transformation, a definition of evolutionary and revolutionary change is necessary. A review of change in industry and in the military services will then help explain transformation and the important elements of a major program of change.

EVOLUTIONARY AND REVOLUTIONARY CHANGE

Evolutionary change and revolutionary change are evident in industry and government. However, terminology sometimes differs in the description of the two types of change. Profound change is a term used in descriptions of major changes in industry. Military discussions of present efforts to change involve the revolution in military affairs and transformation.

Change in Industry and Government

People and social systems often resist change. However, the desire to experience something new often offsets the resistance caused by the fear of change. Resistance to change can be emotional or based on some sort of rational analysis. An emotional resistance to change can result from economic, personal, or social concerns. Three factors that can be considered for alteration to overcome people's resistance to change are the environment, a person's perception of the forces surrounding him or her, and the basic value system of the people involved in the change process.[1]

Rapidly growing companies owe their success to their marketing of new goods and services. However, the speed of decision-making required in such companies is very difficult for leaders and organizations to cope with. People often cannot cope with rapid change because of the emotion associated with delegating tasks, unmet career expectations, and recruiting and training challenges. Rapid growth also brings uncertainty and ambiguity and can cause even more change in order to keep an organization in balance. Possible solutions include careful recruiting and training, team structures and team building, managing an informal culture, human resource planning, staffing personnel functions with qualified people, and senior leaders being sensitive and tough.[2]

Companies with strong management teams develop future leaders by focusing their limited leader development resources on developing those junior personnel who have leadership potential. Compensation, promotion, development, and training are all part of successful leader development programs. John Kotter pointed out several practices that are important in growing this leadership pool. One is to have line management drive recruitment. A second practice is to focus recruiting a few universities. Hiring standards must remain high. Recruitment must also focus on finding leadership potential and developing a system to close the deal when finding new people.[3]

Efforts to change fail for several reasons. The first error is allowing too much complacency. A second error is to fail to create a coalition to guide the change effort. A vision is a powerful tool in implementing change; however, when a vision exists, managers sometimes fail to communicate the vision. Obstacles sometimes interfere with employees understanding the vision. Short-term victories are important to maintain momentum. Declaring victory too soon could inhibit change. Corporate culture must provide an anchor for change.[4]

Complacency often defeats efforts to change organizations. People who try to change organizations fail to overcome this complacency because they overestimate their ability to force change on the organization, fail to recognize how their actions may reinforce the status quo, lack patience, and become paralyzed by the risks that accompany reducing complacency. Reasons for complacency include the lack of a visible crisis, the indication of success by the environment, standards being low, people seeing functional goals and not overall business goals, internal controls being set up to ensure success, and feedback only coming from these faulty evaluation systems. Overcoming these obstacles requires implementing signs of success, higher standards, new internal control systems, increased feedback, and rewarding honest comments.[5]

Programs can fail for a number of reasons including complacency, no guiding coalition, a lack of vision, allowing obstacles to block a vision, no short-term victories, declaring success too soon, and failing to ensure that the corporate culture changes. Kotter describes eight stages that all successful changes must go through: (a) establishing a sense of urgency, (b) creating a guiding coalition, (c) developing a strategy and vision, (d) communicating the vision, (e) empowering broad-based action, (f) generating short-term wins, (g) consolidating gains and produce additional change, and (h) institutionalizing the change in the culture.[6]

David Nadler and Michael Tushman consider organization leadership to be a critical component of implementing organizational change. Strategic change has an impact on the entire organization system and incremental change as aimed at enhancing effectiveness but not affecting the basic organization structure. Reactive change occurs in response to an event outside the organization. Anticipatory change occurs in preparation for the future. The degree of change will vary from tuning to adaptation, reorientation, or recreation. The role of leadership is most important when reorientation is required. Reorientation is a change needed in anticipation of a future situation, and strategic change is required. Leadership is crucial here due to the need to anticipate the need for strategic change, the necessity to "create a sense of urgency," and the requirement to manage the pain associated with the change. Nadler and Tushman refer to the "magic leader" as a charismatic leader who can envision, enable, and energize change. However, the authors also point out that there are limitations to what a magic leader can accomplish, and a leadership team may be required in order to institute change.[7]

Yvan Allaire and Mihaela Firsirotu have discussed four strategies for organizations to use in making radical changes. Reorientation involves ridding a company of its current business and moving into a new field. Turnaround requires action to prevent bankruptcy and time to implement a new business strategy. Revitalization describes a situation where survival of the company is not at stake and poor performance is due to external factors. Transformation is where current performance is satisfactory, but a change to meet the future is needed. This is the most challenging requirement for a leader and requires vision and will to carry through. Allaire and Firsirotu laid out six steps to implement a radical strategy: The first step is to make a correct diagnosis. The next is to produce a strategy for change. The third step is to assess the company's culture and structure. The fourth step is to define goals. The fifth step is to propose a broad agenda for the change. The final step is to stabilize the company.[8]

The degree of change is also an important consideration. Peter Senge described profound change as "change that combines inner shifts in people's values, aspirations, and behaviors with 'outer' shifts in processes, strategies, practices, and systems." He emphasized that such a level of change requires that a learning organization develop an attitude of open discussion and establish a free exchange of ideas. Senior leaders must establish an environment for such open dialogue that includes local line managers and informal network leaders.[9]

Businesses face a different world today, where the prime challenge is to manage complexity and deliver capability simultaneously. Hypercompetition, increasing organizational complexity, rising external stakeholder power, and electronic business technology are four major reasons for the turmoil that businesses face. Roger Burlton encourages businesses to adopt a customer focus, design products so they are modular and can evolve, make use of technologies that are adaptable, continually strive to improve worker knowledge, and ensure their processes are flexible and responsive.[10]

Military Change

The U.S. Department of Defense Command and Control Research Program has produced a number of texts aimed at enhancing the understanding of the impact of information technologies on national security. David Albert and Richard Hayes in *Campaigns of Experimentation* stated that the first step in transforming an organization is to recognize the difference between incremental and disruptive innovation. Organizations must also reward people who propose innovation. Disruptive innovation is revolutionary change. Incremental innovation is evolutionary change.[11]

The U.S. military experienced a period of isolation from society after the civil war. The withdrawal of the military from society produced reforms in the professionalism of the military services, which laid the foundation for success in World War I and World War II. The changing security requirements of the United States affected how its officers' roles in the nation's defense and in American culture changed. Samuel Huntington considered the return of the military services from concentrating on frontier patrolling to participating in international affairs as World War I approached marked the beginning of conflict between the ideals of the conservative military officer and liberal society. The end of World War II and the beginning of the Cold War resulted in the military officer corps more closely aligning with the interests of large defense industries.[12]

The debate over how to change also affected Great Britain's readiness for World War II. The conservative nature of British military leaders combined with a lack of political support and limited resources slowed the development of British armored warfare doctrine. However, the British Army made more progress than the Soviet and American Armies made in developing armor doctrine. The requirements of the many theaters where the British Army stationed soldiers complicated the development of advanced equipment because the needs of warfare and mobility in places such as India and the

British Isles were so different. The debate over whether Great Britain should be prepared to fight on the European continent also retarded progress. The defense of the empire was the single most significant factor in preventing British armor doctrine from reaching its full potential.[13]

Stephen Rosen has discussed the difficulty that bureaucracies have in trying to implement change. By their nature, bureaucracies maintain a steady state and do not change. Military innovation includes changes in organization behavior and changes in warfare concepts and organization design. Rosen suggested that military innovation in peacetime occurs when senior leaders conclude that a change is required and set a strategy in motion that has "intellectual and organizational components." Civilian leaders help by supporting and protecting these officers from interference. Wartime innovation is possible but only within an established chain of command. Rosen separated technological innovation from other military innovation because of the impact of scientists affecting the change. Managing uncertainty is also a characteristic of technological innovation.[14]

Well-known futurist writers Alvin and Heidi Toffler described three waves of economic development, which brought with them revolutionary changes in warfare. The first wave was the agricultural revolution. This provided communities the ability to store economic resources that were then worth fighting for and led to the development of political entities. The Industrial Revolution brought standardization as well as mass production and mass destruction to warfare. However, this second wave has reached its limits in lethality, speed, and range. Third wave economic development produces wealth based on knowledge, defined as information, data, images, symbols, culture, ideology, and values. The Army's AirLand Battle doctrine developed to defeat the Soviet Union was the first step toward this revolution in war. A military revolution only occurs when society changes to a degree that its armed forces then experience a change in technology, culture, organization, strategy, tactics, training, doctrine, and logistics.[15]

A very useful definition of military revolutionary change can be found in an article by Andrew Krepinevich, where he defined a military revolution as a combination of technological change, weapon system development, new operational concepts, and organizational changes to make a fundamental change in the manner of the conduct of warfare. Change usually takes years to implement. If military organizations fail to adapt to changes in technology and concepts, then they will be at a distinct disadvantage in any conflict. The author also made several general observations about military revolutions. Technological change makes revolution possible, but it will not ensure that a revolution occurs. The advantages provided by a revolution are temporary. Asymmetric objectives, cultures, and resources may lead to specialized competitors. Technologies that form the basis for a military revolution often begin development outside of the military environment.[16]

Larry Addington has noted changes affecting warfare from the eighteenth century through Operation Desert Storm ranged from organizational and societal to technological. He also stated that the "most encouraging pattern that seems to be emerging in the post–Cold War era is a willingness of the great powers to seek accommodation." War in the present and near future will include conflict with states of lesser size with occasional U.N.–sponsored interventions.[17]

Changes in the business community due to information technology provided the impetus to the U.S. military to look to information for the next improvement in military capability, according to Carl Builder. Computers, worldwide information systems, and precision weapons resulted. Technology must combine with changes in concepts and doctrine if a true revolution in military capability is to occur. Rather than nation-to-nation conflict, smaller groups fed by ethnic and religious disagreements will challenge the United States militarily in the future. This change in the operational environment may be the true revolution.[18]

Cycles of war, rather than revolutions, provide another way to discuss how technological change has affected military operations over time. Major General (Retired) Robert Scales wrote that since the industrial age began, technological change has dominated military change rather than other factors such as demographics and politics. The power of defensive weaponry dominated operations during the industrial age; however, the combination of information and speed of maneuver may now allow the offense to dominate. Information technology will bring an unprecedented level of battlefield awareness. Speed of maneuver, strategic to tactical, will combine with this new understanding to restore offensive warfare to precedence.[19]

Williamson Murray and Thomas O'Leary also argued that technology was not the important ingredient in sparking the transformation of a nation's military capability. The combination of new ideas or concepts with new technology brings on a transformation of military capability. Implementing new technology in an entire army is not as important as discovering new concepts on employment of military force to exploit the opportunities provided by technological change.[20]

This possible revolution in military affairs now under way did not begin yesterday. William Owens stated the United States has been undergoing a revolution in military affairs for almost two decades. The military services began to seek new ways to counter the threat of the Soviet Union in the aftermath of Vietnam. Desert Storm showed precision weapons, global positioning technology, and communication technology could provide a dramatic increase in military capability. However, budget cuts slowed the pace of revolution and resulted in stagnation of the transformation. Owens stated that the slow period may be ending and that new operational and organizational concepts are combining with technological advances to speed the pace of change.[21]

Robert Killebrew referred to the actual revolution in military affairs as a social revolution that has developed via the information age. Technology is a supporting factor in the revolution. The communication network today makes every citizen a participant in war. This free flow of information makes religion and nationalism into themes that a nation or some other political actor can use to mobilize a population to act. This ability to disseminate information and ideas is an issue affecting the insurgency in Iraq.[22]

Differentiating Evolutionary and Revolutionary Change

Differing degrees of change exist in civilian industry and in the military services. Revolutionary change is not simply the result of the introduction of new technology. Instead, revolutionary change results from the combination of changes in operational concepts, weapon systems, organizational structure, and technologies used in military equipment systems. When change of this magnitude occurs, there is a fundamental shift in how a military force fights.

Many writers today believe we are in a period of revolutionary change with regard to military operations. However, many actually focus on the technological impact of information technology as the foundation for this revolutionary change. Clearly the great strides in information technology afford military leaders an opportunity to fight differently because it enables them to know more about themselves and about their enemies. However, if the organizational designs, operational concepts, and weapon system enhancements do not accompany this information enhancement, there will be no fundamental shift in how warfare is conducted. Warfare may change, but the change will not be revolutionary.

IMPLEMENTING CHANGE

Recognizing the need for change or the opportunity to change does not equate to successful implementation. Any organization desiring to change itself must develop a program to carry out the planned change. There are many ways to look at or explain these programs whether in industry or the government. A review of them provides some indication of the methods that might be used to implement change.

David Nadler and Michael Tushman have written extensively on implementing change in organizations. They proposed a systems model for organizational behavior that described a system of inputs, transformation process, and outputs, with feedback linking output to input. The transformation process is composed of tasks, individuals in the organization, organizational arrangements, and informal organization. Tasks include the jobs performed by people and the organization. The individual component includes the characteristics of the members of the organization.

Organizational arrangements mean the organizational structure including leadership. The informal organization refers to the informal relationships within the organization. The interaction of these elements then determines the resulting outputs from the organization.[23]

In 1988, Nadler and Tushman defined the context surrounding organizational behavior as consisting of the environment, the organization's resources, and the organization's history. Changing these three aspects of the context of organizational behavior is not possible in the near term. An organization implements its strategy through the decision process for allocating resources within the environment that the organization operates. Some form of output or product results from the organization functioning. A high level of congruence among the organization's components (tasks, individuals, and formal and informal organization structures) increases the effectiveness of the organization. Therefore, finding ways to increase congruence among these components will lead to increased organizational effectiveness. Nadler and Tushman also discussed several reasons for redesigning an organization. A major strategic shift or task redefinition may require an organizational change. Cultural or political change may indicate a need for change. Growth and personnel turnover could also indicate that reorganization is necessary. There also may be organizational design problems that come to light and may require a redesign.[24]

Several challenges can inhibit organizational change. Political power structures within the organization may view the change as a threat to that power. Anxiety in moving to a new system retards acceptance of change. Change also threatens to disrupt present management control systems, which can generate resistance to change. Communication is important in order to explain the need for change. Having individuals participate in the change process and rewarding new behaviors can reduce resistance to change. Providing time for employees to disengage from the present system and to adopt the new one is also important in gaining acceptance of change.[25]

After continuing their research for many years, Nadler and Tushman developed a description of an organization as a system of components that interact with one another and the environment outside the organization. All systems, or organizations, seek equilibrium. When the components of an organization are balanced and consistent, they are congruent. Shaping the political power structures as part of managing the transition process such as by winning over key power groups, building political momentum by the actions of leaders, building the perception of change, and building a sense of stability is important.[26]

IMPLEMENTING CHANGE IN THE U.S. ARMY

The Army has executed many programs of change. Change programs have varied in scope and the length of time that the programs remained relevant and in favor. Examples of these U.S. Army programs of change provide a useful foundation for understanding evolutionary and revolutionary change. Introduction of the tank and airpower into the armed forces was a major effort prior to World War II. After World War II, the Army experienced a number of conceptual, organizational, and technological shifts, as it grappled with the advent of nuclear weapons, limited wars in Korea and Vietnam, the demise of the Soviet Union, and the impact of information technology change in the latter twentieth century.

A major effort to implement change in the Army between the two world wars was the integration of the tank and airpower into the U.S. Army. The National Defense Act of 1920 was a key document in the process of change between the world wars because it placed the Tank Corps in the infantry branch and established an air service. This hampered development of tank doctrine and any revolutionary use of armored forces as developed by Germany. On the other hand, the separate air arm allowed proponents of aircraft to develop new ideas. The Army developed tanks to support infantry maneuver. Strategic bombardment dominated air service thinking. Internal dynamics with the Army retarded the exploitation of both systems in World War II. The schools remained very conservative. Powerful branch chiefs undermined new ideas. Resources were tight. The War Department bureaucracy was unable to cope with the needs of modern warfare once war began.[27]

Army doctrine underwent significant change between 1946 and 1976. A number of factors caused the Army's change including new weapon systems, improved tactical mobility, nuclear weapons, military leaders' opinions, wartime requirements, branch disagreements, military service competition, and the evolution of national security policy. The Army's main priority throughout this period was the defense of Europe; however, Army doctrine shifted from conventional operations to counterinsurgency war as the Vietnam War demanded attention and then back to conventional operations in Europe. In the 1950s, the Army made a radical doctrinal and organizational change to try to address land operations on a battlefield including nuclear weapons; however, the Army never fully embraced this concept and reverted to a more conventional view of war.[28]

The requirements of war in Vietnam demanded that the U.S. Army focus on counterinsurgency operations. The end of that war resulted in a refocusing on opposing a Soviet Union attack in Europe. This return to a European focus coupled with a recognition of the lethality of modern weapons led to the development of the active defense and the 1976 *FM 100-5: Operations*. Infantry doctrine experienced the most change during this period with armor and field artillery doctrine remaining relatively stable. Tactical mobility increased substantially, but this also resulted in a loss of strategic mobility, as the Army division became heavier. U.S. Air Force lethality increased, and its doctrine began to react to the Army's needs.

Overall, the Army's doctrine began to rely more and more on firepower, attrition, and the defense instead of offensive maneuver.[29]

The situation in Europe demanded a significant modernization effort by the Army in the 1980s. Division and corps structures received much attention. Several studies examined how best to organize both levels of command and how to stay within the personnel ceiling of 780,000 soldiers. At the same time, Army doctrine was exploring how to fight the Soviet Union in Europe. These studies and events led to a change in the heavy division which shifted assets to the corps level and led to the development of the 10,000-man light infantry division.[30]

The demise of the Soviet Union with lessons learned from the 1991 Persian Gulf War resulted in a relook of Army doctrine. This resulted in a 1993 *FM 100-5: Operations*. The new doctrine emphasized the Army's strategic role in the world and built on the recent success of doctrine. The field manual addressed a broad spectrum of Army operations and emphasized logistical considerations more than it had in the past. Force projection was addressed more so than in the past. The concept of command and control evolved into battle command. The doctrine added versatility to the previous four tenets of AirLand Battle doctrine, which were initiative, agility, depth, and synchronization.[31]

The Combat Studies Institute noted that the Army conducted at least eleven major reviews of its structure during the last century. General Eric Shinseki when Chief of Staff of the Army directed the Training and Doctrine Command to initiate another such review in November 1999. The Combined Arms Center then directed the Combat Studies Institute to conduct a review of previous transformation efforts.[32]

The Army's first such major restructuring effort was a three-brigade division with three infantry regiments in each brigade, which was instituted after the Spanish–American War. The personnel requirements of trench warfare resulted in a two-brigade division with two regiments in each brigade that was larger than its predecessor in order to meet the manpower demands of trench warfare. After World War I, the Army reviewed its divisional structure and adopted a triangular division of three infantry regiments that was designed for open area warfare and that relied on the pooling of equipment at corps and higher command echelons, which endured through World War II. The tank's arrival in the force structure resulted in a new armored division design for World War II. Mountain and light division structures also operated during World War II. Other technologies affecting changes in division structure were mechanization of all kinds, aviation, and electronics. Self-propelled artillery, better voice radios, semiautomatic rifles, and light machineguns contributed to the changes within the Army. Table 8.1 summarizes the characteristics of the change associated with major changes in Army combat developments through World War II in the twentieth century.[33]

Table 8.1 Major Changes in the Twentieth-Century Army through World War II

Combat developments program	Operational concept changes	Weapon system changes	Organization changes	Technological changes	Fundamental change in warfare
Triangular infantry division in 1939	Mobile warfare in open terrain	Tanks, improved radios	Pooling of support at higher command levels	Mechanization, electronics, aviation	No. Operations focused on infantry support
Armored division from 1940 to1943	Mobile warfare with massed tank operations	Tanks, self-propelled artillery, improved radios	Massed formations of tanks; task organized brigades	Mechanization, electronics, aviation	Yes. Armored and infantry forces operating in open warfare

After World War II the Army decided to maintain infantry, airborne, and armored division designs for its 1947–1948 division reorganization. The Army concluded that ground combat had not changed even though nuclear weapons had joined the arsenal of military weaponry. Manning and equipping difficulties resulted in the Army lacking capabilities that the force structure indicated. There was little doctrine change between 1945 and 1950.[34]

The advent of tactical nuclear weapons and the results of the Korean War resulted in the development of the Pentomic Division design, which never achieved true acceptance within the Army. The Pentomic Division focused on ground combat, where nuclear weapons would be used on the tactical battlefield. Five battle groups, each with five companies, formed the principal maneuver elements within the division.[35]

In 1965, the Reorganization Objective Army Divisions (ROAD) structure with three maneuver brigades replaced the Pentomic Division design. The ROAD design included a division base containing headquarters, artillery, engineer, aviation, and support elements. Three brigade headquarters allowed for the task organizing of the nine maneuver battalions and other units as needed. The ROAD division was an outgrowth of the armored division design from World War II. Table 8.2 summarizes Army combat developments major changes from 1947 through the ROAD division and points out that no revolutionary change occurred; however, the Pentomic Division structure might have resulted in revolutionary change if the Army had adopted it.[36]

The mobility of the helicopter provided the impetus for the Army to develop an air assault division design in 1963. The helicopter dramatically increased the range of movement possible for the infantry and supporting units. The increased mobility provided the division with the ability to rapidly change direction and to shift resources to meet unexpected threats. New supporting concepts included aerial artillery, air assault, and airspace control as part of the ground battle. The Army used the air assault concept extensively in Vietnam. The Army focused doctrinal and tactical thought on counterinsurgency operations during the Vietnam War.[37]

In 1971, the Army decided to combine the power of the helicopter and armored forces for warfare in Europe; however, this TRICAP (triple capability) division lacked the necessary tank firepower judged critical for success. This new division design included an armored brigade, an air assault infantry brigade, and an air combat brigade. Synchronization of command and control was difficult. New antitank weapons, improved armored vehicles, and new target acquisition systems added to the division's capabilities. Studies of the TRICAP design and the 1973 Middle East war convinced the Army that the division needed more tanks and less airmobile infantry. The 1976 doctrine of the active defense was a reaction of the Army to the necessity to fight and win even though outnumbered. Table 8.3 summarizes

Table 8.2 Major Changes from 1947 through the ROAD Division

Combat developments program	Operational concept changes	Weapon system changes	Organization changes	Technological changes	Fundamental change in warfare
Division reorganization in 1947	No major change	No major changes	Reduced division types to infantry, airborne, and armored	Nuclear weapons on the battlefield	No
Pentomic Division from 1955 to 1963	Operations on a larger battlefield using of nuclear weapons	No major changes	Five battle group of five companies each in a division	Nuclear weapons on the battlefield	Intended as major change but not accepted
ROAD from 1960 to 1963	A return to a conventional operations focus	No major changes	Common division base	None	No

Table 8.3 Major Changes Associated with the Air Assault and TRICAP Programs

Combat developments program	Operational concept changes	Weapon system changes	Organization changes	Technological changes	Change in warfare
Air assault division	Counterinsurgency operations, air assault operations	Helicopters (transport, fire support, command and control)	Air assault infantry, aerial artillery	Helicopters for tactical mobility	Yes
TRICAP	A return to a conventional operations focus	No major changes	Armored, airmobile infantry, and air attack cavalry	None	No

Table 8.4 Major Changes Associated with the DRS 1976 and Division 86 Programs

Combat developments program	Operational concept changes	Weapon system changes	Organization changes	Technological changes	Change in warfare
DRS 1976	Conventional operations	Modernized equipment; little change	Similar to ROAD	None	No
Division 86	Conventional operations	Forty new weapon systems	Air attack cavalry brigade	None	No

the changes associated with the air assault and TRICAP division programs. The helicopter employed in the air assault division resulted in revolutionary change.[38]

The U.S. Army's next formal effort to examine the division structure was the Division Restructuring Study (DRS) of 1976, which integrated new weapon systems. Improved antitank weapons and fire support techniques and air-delivered munitions required integration into the division fight. The Army decided that the division required greater dispersion as well as greater mobility in order to mass forces to prevent breakthroughs by an attacking enemy. More combat support and combat service support units were essential to maintain the new weapon systems. The new division design was better prepared for defensive operations while the earlier ROAD design was better for offensive operations.[39]

In 1978, the Army began the Division 86 study, which resulted in the inclusion of an aviation brigade and the integration of forty new weapon systems. The division design was oriented on defeating the projected Soviet threat of 1986. The design resembled the ROAD division, but all division aviation was formed under an air cavalry attack brigade. A division support command included all combat service support battalions and the division artillery included three 155-mm artillery battalions, an 8-inch battalion, and a multiple launch rocket system battery. Personnel shortfalls delayed fielding of the division design, which was too heavy to deploy rapidly. Table 8.4 summarizes the major changes associated with the DRS 1976 and Division 86 programs. Both divisional design programs focused on conventional operations, and no technological change occurred.[40]

The Army initiated the high technology test bed in 1980 by modifying the 9th Infantry Division into a high technology light division in order to provide a powerful force that was deployable by C-141 aircraft. The experimenting unit designed and tested itself, which was a departure from normal Army practice. The division used a variety of Army and commercial equipment to develop combined arms, light attack, and air attack cavalry formations.[41]

The need to fight outnumbered against the Soviet Union in Europe and the lethality of modern weaponry resulted in the Army developing a new doctrine summarized in the 1976 version of *FM 100-5: Operations*. However, the doctrine's focus on the active defense and firepower rather than the concepts of maneuver, and the offense resulted in much debate and changes in the early 1980s. The Army leadership eventually concluded that the best way to defeat a Soviet attack was to focus on an integrated (nuclear and nonnuclear) battlefield that included simultaneous close, deep, and rear elements operations. The 1982 version of *FM 100-5* brought this new doctrine into existence and called it "AirLand Battle."[42]

By 1983, it was clear that the Army needed a light infantry division (LID) in order to operate in many of the environments faced by the Army and in order to produce a force that was deployable by C-141 aircraft. The 7th Infantry Division became the Army's first light infantry division. The Army designed the LID such that it could be deployed rapidly and to operate in a low-intensity combat environment for 48 hours without additional support. The light infantry division lacked heavy combat firepower and tactical mobility; however, the Army found uses for the division in several combat operations.[43]

The Combat Studies Institute concluded its review of previous Army efforts to transform itself by discussing the Force XXI program. Improvements in information technology resulted in the initiation of the Force XXI program in 1993. The new technology showed great promise; however, the immaturity of the technology hampered the unit's ability to exploit the potential of the changes in information technology. Table 8.5 summarizes the changes associated with the high technology test bed (HTTB), LID, and Force XXI programs. These three programs did not include revolutionary change. The Army lacked the resources to exploit the concepts and materiel envisioned in the HTTB. The LID included no changes in weapon systems that would qualify for revolutionary change. Force XXI did not include major changes in weapon systems even though the use of information technology was expanded.[44]

Table 8.6 summarizes the conclusions of whether specific combat developments programs resulted in evolutionary or revolutionary change.

When defining revolutionary change as the combination of changes in operational concepts, weapon systems, organization, and technology, the Army experienced a mixture of evolutionary and revolutionary change. Using the criteria established for revolutionary change, the 1939 triangular infantry division, the division reorganization in 1947, the ROAD division, TRICAP, DRS 1976, Division 86, LID, and Force XXI were evolutionary. The Army modernized its weaponry many times. Operational concepts did

Table 8.5 Major Changes Associated with the HTTB, LID, and Force XXI Programs

Combat developments program	Operational concept changes	Weapon system changes	Organization changes	Technological changes	Change in warfare
High technology test bed	Rapidly deployable, mobile, and powerful formations	Light attack motorized systems	Combined arms battalions, light attack battalions	None	No; the Army lacked the resources
Light infantry division	Division deployable in 500 C-141 aircraft sorties	No major changes	Light infantry formations	None	No
Force XXI	Standard operations enhanced with new information technology	No major changes	Heavy division with new command and control systems	New information technology systems for command and control	No; systems not mature

Table 8.6 Summary of Previous Army Combat Developments Programs

Combat developments program	Evolutionary	Revolutionary
Triangular infantry division in 1939	Yes	No
Armored division from 1940 to1943	No	Yes
Division reorganization in 1947	Yes	No
Pentomic Division from 1955 to 1963	Not adopted	Not adopted
ROAD from 1960 to 1963	Yes	No
Air assault division	No	Yes
TRICAP	Yes	No
DRS 1976	Yes	No
Division 86	Yes	No
High technology test bed	Not adopted	Not adopted
Light infantry division	Yes	No
Force XXI	Yes	No

not often change. Technology did not support a major change in many cases. The lack of resources also sometimes precluded executing a revolutionary change in many cases.

Army combat development programs provided revolutionary change only twice as defined by the criteria discussed here. The advent of the tank dramatically changed warfare between the world wars by increasing the scale of operations through enhanced and protected mobility. The helicopter revolutionized warfare by the radical change in mobility that accompanied its use in counterinsurgency operations in Vietnam. The Pentomic Division era might have brought revolutionary change had the Army fully adopted the concept with nuclear weapons being an integral feature of the battlefield.

SUMMARY OF PREVIOUS U.S. ARMY PROGRAMS OF CHANGE

The U.S. Army has conducted numerous programs that included some degree of change for itself. These have met with a range of emotions and levels of support. Senior leadership support has been critical for any successful implementation of change. Technological change alone is insufficient to support a major change in warfare. The U.S. Army cannot change itself without doing so in coordination with other military services because the Army will never fight without one or more additional military services in action alongside.

The United States and its allies around the world face a challenging national security environment. The war against terrorism continues with combat operations in Iraq and Afghanistan daily. Soldiers, civilians, and family members are deployed worldwide, supporting the U.S. national interests and safeguarding its freedom. Preparing for the future in order to continue the history of successful defense of America is the duty of its civilian and military leadership as well as the service personnel who have pledged their lives through their service. The United States must respond to change in the world, and we must capitalize on its soldiers' and civilians' "natural talents and enthusiasms"[45] as the means to meet these challenges.

President George W. Bush highlighted the terrorist threat that we face in his 2002 State of the Union address. Iraq, a member of the axis of evil consisting of Iran, Iraq, and North Korea, has fallen. But we still face Islamic extremists who oppose democracy in Iraq. Iran and North Korea have changed little. President Bush made it clear that the war against terrorism has only just begun and that the resources of the United States are focused on winning it. We must continue to be prepared to win this war.[46]

The Army must prepare for future requirements and to prosecute the war we are now fighting. Cohen and Gooch pointed out that militaries must look at how change on one level of conflict will affect another.[47] It is important for military organizations to think through how an enemy will react to their actions as well as how they might react to an enemy's. We often refer to our enemies today and in the future as seeking an asymmetric method to use to attack us. We must carefully think through the reactions of others to actions we take.

General (Retired) Montgomery Meigs stated that asymmetric war dominates the attention of the public today, as we face this new challenge of terrorism within America's borders and directed against U.S. citizens around the world. Unfortunately, a distinction between asymmetric actions and a terrorist devising an idiosyncratic method of employing his resources is needed. Asymmetry is the absence of a common basis of competition. Idiosyncratic refers to employing an asset in an unusual manner. The combination of American special operations forces, sensors, space-based communications, precision weapons launched by aircraft, and Northern Alliance ground forces was an example of asymmetric force employed against the Taliban. Al Qaeda's use of commercial aircraft as manned weapons was an example of an asymmetric weapon, for which there was no comparable system or countermeasure, used in an idiosyncratic way. The Army must constantly seek new ways to use the technologies available. We must seek an asymmetric way to use our systems, so that we set the pace of change and the tempo of operations. That will give us the initiative that we must have in order to win this war against terrorism.[48]

As we move toward the future, we must continue to seek ways to cope with change. Peter Drucker pointed out that no institution has experienced more change than the U.S. military. Weapons technology, doctrine and concepts, organizational structures, and command structures have changed dramatically throughout the history of the Army. Drucker also emphasized that all organizations must include a way to manage change within their basic structure.[49]

Organizational change is not solely a challenge for the Army or the other services. One way to define the context surrounding organizational behavior is to describe it as consisting of the environment, the organization's resources, and the organization's history. These cannot be changed in the near term. Organization strategy flows from the decision process on how to allocate resources within the environment in which the organization operates. Some form of output or product results from the organization functioning. A high level of congruence among the organization's components (tasks, individuals, and formal and informal organization structures) increases the effectiveness of the organization. Therefore, finding ways to increase congruence among these components will lead to increased organizational effectiveness.[50] Military organizations planning a program of change must find congruence among their missions, soldier and other service personnel capabilities, and force structure.

9

Transformation

After the demise of the Soviet Union, the United States entered a period where the Army leadership expected to be allowed to focus on a future threat and capabilities while saving funding on the maintenance and upgrade of existing equipment in the near term. Even the Iraq invasion of Kuwait with the subsequent operations of Desert Shield and Desert Storm did not convince the leadership that the course that they were following was in error. Clearly the world was not at peace; however, the threat of nuclear annihilation seemed low, and the strength of the current U.S. military was high compared to potential threats around the world. Consequently, the Army focused a great deal of effort on preparing for future operational requirements.

THE BEGINNING OF MAJOR CHANGE

Change has always been present in the U.S. military forces. An example of how the Department of Defense began to grapple with the changes after the demise of the Soviet Union and the improvements in information technology was the 1996 conceptual framework for future warfare titled *Joint Vision 2010*. The vision statement proposed four operational concepts: dominant maneuver, precision engagement, full dimensional protection, and focused logistics. *Joint Vision 2010* emphasized that the primary purpose of the U.S. armed forces was to deter conflict; however, the document also stated that the armed forces would fight and win the nation's wars if deterrence failed. This future vision also stated that future military forces would rely on enhancements in information technologies.[1]

The U.S. Army's Training and Doctrine Command report to the chief of staff of the Army on the "Army After Next" project in 1997 emphasized that knowledge and speed would increase velocity in warfare and characterize the next cycle of change. This report stated that the Army was in a societal change from the industrial age to the information age. It discussed using the lack of a major foreign power competitor as an opportunity to jump to future capabilities while holding present technological capability constant. The report also argued that the Army must restore the balance between firepower and maneuver in order to avoid protracted war and stalemate on a future battlefield.[2]

Major General (Retired) Robert Scales led the Army's "Army After Next" project when it first began. He argued that by 2010, the U.S. Army would be knowledge-based. This knowledge must then be combined with speed of action and decision-making in order to win on future battlefields. Scales also stated that it was unlikely that a true peer competitor would arise to confront the United States in the next twenty years. However, a major competitor composed of one major state or a group of states may become our enemy. The U.S. Army must also find ways to increase the tempo of operations in order to cross the killing zone faster. The Army must seek ways to avoid attrition and to defeat an enemy through inflicting paralysis.[3]

These three examples are not intended an exhaustive list of Army or Department of Defense writings during the late 1990s or during any period in the history of the U.S. armed forces. However, they do point out a few ideas that were growing in importance as the U.S. military approached the latter years of the twentieth century. Clearly information technology changes were moving to the forefront of consideration for supporting change. Writers also viewed speed to be important as a means to maintain the initiative and set the terms of battle.

ARMY TRANSFORMATION BEGINS

On October 12, 1999, Secretary of the Army Louis Caldera and Chief of Staff of the Army Eric K. Shinseki announced their vision of a more strategically responsive Army during the annual meeting of the Association of the United States Army in Washington, D.C. The announced goal for deploying forces was for a brigade to deploy anywhere in the world within 96 hours, a division to do the same within 120 hours, and five divisions to deploy within 30 days. The Army also announced that a smaller logistical footprint was a goal with the potential for the Army transitioning to an all wheeled vehicle force.[4]

General Shinseki also stated that the Army would immediately begin to change itself in order to meet the new goals for strategic responsiveness.

He selected Fort Lewis, Washington, as the first place to begin to change brigade structures because Fort Lewis provided the opportunity to transform a heavy brigade and a light brigade on one installation. The secretary of the Army and the chief of staff agreed that the Army must continue to train to be prepared to win the nation's wars; however, the present geopolitical situation demanded a more deployable force. Shinseki noted that most Army airlift is devoted to logistics, which means that lighter, more fuel efficient vehicles will reduce the logistical burden and decrease the airlift requirement.[5]

Shortly after this initial announcement, Caldera and Shinseki pointed out that soldiers carry out the national security strategy by finding peaceful solutions to problems, relieving human suffering, and winning the nation's wars when called upon. Caldera and Shinseki also stated that the Army must be dominant across the full range of operational missions. They reiterated that the Army was prepared to accomplish any mission demanded by the American people.[6]

Another aspect of transformation clearly linked to the enhancements in information technology. General Shinseki's vision also included the vision that America's soldiers would "see first, understand first, act first, and finish decisively" in a full spectrum capable Army. Technological change and changes in the security environment mandated change in the Army.[7]

The interim brigades sparked a great deal of discussion because of the belief that the chief of staff was determined to field a wheeled but armored force. However, the Army's challenge was to produce a series of combat vehicles with the survivability of the M1 tank and the Bradley infantry fighting vehicle that also had the ease of deployment of light forces. Shinseki stated that the interim brigades would use commercial off-the-shelf equipment rather than new systems. He reportedly described transformation as being science and technology investments that support fielding the Objective Force.[8]

The Army's 2001 posture statement emphasized the Army's broad range of responsibilities to conduct operations across the full spectrum of war. Another phrase often associated with Army transformation stressed that the Army must remain "persuasive in peace, invincible in war." Soldiers were stationed all over the world in a wide variety of missions including being forward deployed for operational requirements and in support of peacekeeping and humanitarian missions.[9]

The 2001 posture statement also stated that the Army was prepared "to fight and win two nearly simultaneous" major theater wars. The Army must be able to deploy rapidly and be versatile and survivable in order to accomplish the wide range of missions it confronts. The Army was to remain a values-based force, as it transformed into the Objective Force. Army transformation included purchasing off-the-shelf equipment for the initial brigades to transform into a more deployable force. These initial brigades were to be part of the Interim Force as the Army transitioned to the

Objective Force.[10] While not a critical issue, there was some confusion, as the Army attempted to clarify whether these brigades were interim or initial. Interim Brigade Combat Teams became the predominant term, until a name for the basic combat vehicle designed for the brigades was settled upon.

Transformation included continuing the process of infusing new information technology capabilities into the Army while emphasizing the development of the Objective Force, which included information technology advances as well as a new vehicle fleet. Only selected elements of the Force XXI modernization package would be fielded. The Comanche helicopter and Crusader artillery system were included as major components of the transformation program. Interoperability with other military services was a key issue.[11]

This initial start at transformation focused on providing an Army ready for all missions. Speed of deployment and using the enhanced speed of information flow were both critical elements of instituting change. Using the posited characteristics of revolutionary change as changes in organization, weapon systems, operational concept, and technology, the Army transformation program including the Future Combat System qualifies as an example of revolutionary change. The demise of the major threat of the Soviet Union provided an apparent window of opportunity for change without undue risk. That window closed on September 11, 2001.

THE IMPACT OF 9/11

The terrorist attacks at the World Trade Center in New York and the Pentagon in Washington, D.C., on September 11, 2001, changed the national security environment—or at least convinced the Army and national senior leadership that a future threat was not the problem requiring immediate attention. The United States now faced a threat that would fight in unexpected ways. This threat also exhibited a hatred that was difficult to understand. The war for which the Army had been preparing now seemed not to be the correct focus for modernization programs. Consequently, the Army leadership made changes in the transformation program.

The beginning of the war against the terrorists who attacked the United States, often referred to as the global war on terrorism, or GWOT, began as soon as the nation's leadership identified appropriate targets for a response. Operations in Afghanistan in cooperation with Afghani groups opposing the Taliban regime crushed the major hostile forces relatively quickly; however, these operations did not eliminate all anti-U.S. terrorist or Islamic fundamentalist groups. Operations continue even at the time of this writing to kill or capture Osama bin Laden and others who instigated the September 11, 2001, attacks. Clearly the focus of the U.S. military leadership had to shift from preparing for a future world dominated by information technology to using the resources available now to fight a war thrust upon us and on U.S. soil.

An example of this impact was the 2002 cancellation of the Crusader program that earlier had been characterized as a component of the future Army. The Army had expected Crusader to be the new field artillery cannon system. The resource requirements of the Army's current operations were too great to sustain all programs, so the Department of Defense and Department of the Army senior leadership concluded that continuation of the program was not possible.[12]

The U.S. military forces also destroyed the Iraqi military and overthrew the dictatorship of Saddam Hussein in Operation Iraqi Freedom in 2003. This operation was conducted rapidly in very difficult circumstances. Clearly the U.S. military once again showed that in a major combat operation, it had no peer. Unfortunately, an insurgency began shortly after the conclusion of the major combat operations in Iraq. That insurgency continues to take American and Iraqi lives and dominate requirements placed on the U.S. Department of Defense. General Shinseki retired, and General Peter Schoomaker, who had previously retired, replaced him as the chief of staff of the Army (CSA).

In his first media roundtable, General Schoomaker announced that he planned to adopt a smaller, brigade-type organization in the Army. The 3rd Infantry Division would reorganize, so that the current three brigades in the division would become five. The CSA also organized task forces within the Army to study fifteen focus areas: the bench; Army aviation; leader development and education; Combat Training Centers/Battle Command Training Program; Current to Future Force; the network; modularity; joint expeditionary mindset; active component–Reserve component balance; unit manning; installations as flagships; resource processes; strategic communications; authorities; responsibilities; and accountability.[13]

The Army had continued to modernize throughout the beginning of combat operations and changing leadership. Continuing such programs while conducting current operations was not a new phenomenon. The vehicle selected for the IBCTs (Interim Brigade Combat Teams) was named the Stryker, so the IBCTs became Stryker Brigade Combat Teams or SBCTs. The first SBCT to deploy to Iraq was the 3rd Brigade, 2nd Infantry Division. While it performed well, the Army concluded that some modifications were in order with regard to aviation, fire support, computer networks, and sensor capabilities. Plans included adding helicopters to the brigade, increasing the number of howitzers in the brigade, providing better communications to support the computer networks, and improving the current sensors.[14]

The major shift in organizational structure to a brigade-oriented force quickly began. The Army leadership's decision to reorganize the current force into more deployable modular brigade size units of action would increase the available maneuver brigades from thirty-three to between forty-three and forty-eight. The intended outcome was to produce increased flexibility in addition to greater interoperability with joint forces, which would make the Army more capable.[15]

Even with the focus on current combat operations, work on the Future Combat System continued. In 2003, The Department of Defense approved the Future Combat System (FCS) program entering the System Development and Demonstration (SDD) phase. The FCS Lead System Integrator team of Boeing and Science Applications International Corporation would develop the FCS program as a networked system of systems that will include eighteen manned and unmanned air and ground vehicles.[16]

While there was no doubt that change was occurring, there was debate over whether transformation was evolutionary or revolutionary. Douglas Macgregor argued that the present transformation program was not revolutionary because the Army leadership was unwilling to change long-standing institutional bias. Transformation relied too much on enhanced battlefield awareness and on striking targets from a distance. Macgregor concluded that the Army needed an organizational structure that was inherently multiservice and a leadership philosophy that encouraged combat leaders to take advantage of opportunities provided by an effect-based operational construct.[17]

Steven Metz and Raymond Millen wrote that the Army had to transform, so that it could perform the wide variety of missions that it then faced. The Army's missions ranged from major combat operations to antiterrorism. Metz and Millen concluded that in order to determine the changes needed, the Army had to determine the shape and characteristics of the future international security environment, develop the characteristics of the future battlefield, determine the potential or probable roles and missions of the Army, decide how the Objective Force should contribute to the successful execution of those roles and missions, and explain why an Army is needed.[18]

The U.S. Army developed a series of transformation roadmaps to describe how it would change to meet the new security environment and capitalize on modernization programs ongoing or planned to start within the construct of multiservice, or joint, operations. One roadmap referred to transformation as "a process that shapes the changing nature of military competition and cooperation through new combinations of concepts, capabilities, people, and organization." Transformation now included a number of initiatives to change the present day Army as well as to develop the future Army. Important capabilities addressed were modular, combined arms units; battle command on the move; and improved force protection capabilities for soldiers and platforms. The Army considered this program to be a process rather than an end state to achieve.[19]

Regardless of the progress made in modernizing the force and changing organizational structures to meet the new demands of operations around the globe, the Army could not sustain every program previously supported zealously. Even though formerly identified as an important element of transformation, the Comanche attack and reconnaissance helicopter program was cancelled. The Army concluded that it was more important to upgrade and maintain the aviation fleet in order to face the present battlefield threat than it was to field a new helicopter designed for another battlefield threat. The Comanche had been under development for 20 years.[20]

In 2004, the U.S. Army leadership emphasized the challenge that the Army faced with the nation being at war while needing to change in order to prepare for the future. The United States faced an enemy who was determined to destroy the American way of life. The same enemy was engaged with the United States in a war of ideas, even if this enemy did not represent a specific nation-state. The Army faced an immediate demand to help soldiers who were fighting. The institutional Army also needed to change. This change needed in the Army included a "rapid evolution to a campaign-quality Army with joint and expeditionary capabilities." Joint operations had to grow from merely being interoperable to being interdependent at strategic to tactical levels. Modular units, modular headquarters, and more force stability were now key aspects of transforming the Army.[21]

The U.S. Army's 2004 transformation roadmap stated that transformation included culture, process, and capability components. The most important element of the campaign plan to transform the Army was the decision to activate up to fifteen additional active duty brigade-sized units through implementing a modular brigade design. Force stabilization, active and reserve component restructuring, and redeploying assets to support modularization complement the fielding of the new brigades. The Army planned to generate a mixture of brigades in different states of readiness to support operations. These phases of the deployment cycle would include reset, modular conversion (if not already accomplished), training, and ready for deployment.[22]

Brigadier General (Retired) Huba Wass de Czege emphasized that the new current force units of action would provide more brigade-sized units for deployment, create standardized forces for regional combatant commanders, and be more integrated into joint forces than current force brigades. Improved reconnaissance and joint linkage for intelligence operations and fire support ensured that the two-battalion units of action are as lethal as the current force three-battalion brigades. However, Wass de Czege stated that if future resources allow, the Army should add the third maneuver battalion. This would improve lethality and increase endurance and lethality of the force.[23]

U.S. Army literature continued to emphasize the need for an expeditionary and joint operation mindset on the part of soldiers and civilians. All Army members had to remember that they were soldiers first and had to live by Army values. A campaign quality Army that also has a joint and expeditionary mindset must accept that the Army is serving a nation at war and that the Army is part of a multicomponent team. The Army leadership also stated that while it must recruit soldiers, it must also retain families.[24]

The initial FCS-based Objective Force had posited a brigade-sized organization referred to as the unit of action (UA). By 2004, design efforts were well under way to develop the structure of the higher level organizations as the unit of employment (UE). The UE would encompass current division, corps, and theater level Army service missions and organizations in two levels, UEx and UEy. Units of employment would be tailored with modular brigade-sized units of action of various types in order to meet strike, intelligence, and logistic requirements.[25]

The Army's *2005 Posture Statement* reported that the Army faced an uncertain and unpredictable environment, where there was little distinction between peace and war. The Army continued to view transformation as centered on improving the capability of the soldier. The posture statement also related four goals for transformation, which were restructure into brigade-sized forces, realign soldier skills in order to meet the new demand, stabilize soldiers in units in order to improve unit effectiveness and improve morale, and improve business functions. The posture statement endorsed experimentation by stating that the Army planned a "continuous cycle of experimentation and innovation, informed by experience."[26]

In order to cope with the increasing demands of the global terrorist threat, operations in Afghanistan, and the insurgency in Iraq, the Army formed an Asymmetric Warfare Group (AWG) with a purpose to develop methods to "defeat current and future asymmetric threats." Since no opponent could face the conventional U.S. military power, these opponents adopted asymmetric capabilities to attack the United States. One of the AWG's initial priorities was to seek ways to defeat the improvised explosive device (IED) threat faced by U.S. and coalition forces in Iraq.[27]

The development of new concepts continued within the Army's TRADOC. In 2005, these efforts produced a capstone concept to guide Army operations within the framework of joint operations. TRADOC described the Army mission as providing "sustained land combat power." The document listed "seven key operational ideas." Shaping and entry operations are necessary to set the conditions for decisive maneuver. Operational maneuver from strategic distances sets the condition for the force to occupy a position of advantage. Intratheater operational maneuver extends the ability of the joint commander to use Army forces. Decisive maneuver achieves campaign objectives. Army forces will conduct concurrent and subsequent stability operations. Freedom of action will rely on distributed support and logistics. Situational understanding will result from network-enabled battle command.[28]

The terrorist attacks of September 11, 2001, affected Army transformation by focusing the energy and resources of the Army more on current operations than on preparing for a future war that might fit a wide range of types of operations. While the Future Combat System program continued, the Comanche and Crusader programs ended. The emphasis on mobility shifted from seeking a system that could deploy quickly to forming smaller modular brigades, which would be more deployable. Instead of seeking joint interoperability, the Army chose to seek joint interdependence as an essential capability in order to win on the battlefield. These changes reduced the emphasis on revolutionary change in order to allow the Army to engage in current operations. Nonetheless, change continued in multiple areas.

OTHER MILITARY SERVICE TRANSFORMATION INITIATIVES

Transformation was, of course, not the sole purview of the Army. The joint staff, joint commands, and the other services were pursuing their own transformation efforts during this time as well. A few examples follow in order to present an overview of transformation in the other services.

In its *Joint Vision 2020*, the U.S. Department of Defense Joint Chiefs of Staff stated that the primary focus of future joint operations was to achieve "full spectrum dominance" by the "interdependent application of dominant maneuver, precision engagement, focused logistics, and full dimensional protection." The military services were to achieve this through the application of new technologies and modernized equipment in addition to new developments in doctrine, organizations, training, education, and personnel actions.[29] Guidelines like this served to focus all of the military services on a vision of using developing technologies to produce a set of capabilities for multi-service combat action.

The U.S. Joint Chiefs of Staff also stated that the core competencies of the individual military services provide the foundation on which to build the synergy that achieves full spectrum dominance. Information superiority is crucial as an enabler. The U.S. military services must make better decisions and make them faster than an enemy. Innovation will provide our military forces with new ways to use our strengths against an enemy. In order to have innovation, the joint force must also experience continuous learning with the necessary feedback mechanisms to facilitate such an approach. Experimentation must include room for errors in order to reinforce innovative approaches.[30]

The U. S. Department of Defense *Quadrennial Defense Review (QDR)* was under way when the terrorist attacks of September 11, 2001, occurred. The *QDR* noted that the United States was now fighting a war that it did not choose. The report also posited that in order to fight this war, the military services must adopt a capability-based approach for planning in order to deny an enemy an asymmetric advantage. Enhancements in technology would provide the opportunity to change the conduct of military operations.[31]

The challenge to change to a capability-based force instead of a threat-based force was not trivial. Any analysis or training program must contain some sort of threat to oppose the force in the experiment or training regimen. Nonetheless, a focus on capabilities would provide a more flexible force, meaning one not optimized to defeat a specific threat such that it cannot defeat other threats. In 2002, U.S. Joint Forces Command (JFCOM) reiterated that the U.S. military services were moving from a threat-based force structure approach to a capability-based one. U.S. JFCOM proposed the use of rapid decisive operations (RDO) to exploit capabilities to seize the initiative to defeat an enemy quickly. Maintaining a knowledge advantage relative to an opponent is a key enabler. Effect-based operations (EBO) were a supporting functional concept. The JFCOM stated that EBO depended on a complete understanding of the direct and indirect effects that are achievable by balancing the full range of our military power used against the enemy.[32]

With transformation well under way, the U.S. Department of Defense defined transformation as "a process that shapes the changing nature of military competition and cooperation through new combinations of concepts, capabilities, people and organizations that exploit our nation's advantages and protect against our asymmetric vulnerabilities to sustain our strategic position, which helps underpin peace and stability in the world" in 2003. Using present capabilities as a baseline, the military services would explore new concepts, organizational constructs, doctrine, and capabilities in order to define new standards supporting the ability to accomplish missions previously considered impossible. It was clear that the changes in the security environment demanded that the military services change in order to meet the new demands.[33]

More guidance continued to flow from the senior leadership of the Department of Defense. The joint staff stated that the characteristics of the conduct of military operations were changing throughout the military services of the United States. Operations were once sequential and segmented but would now be simultaneous, distributed, and parallel. Simultaneous referred to operations occurring concurrently with real-time planning and execution. Distributed operations are dispersed across time and space. Parallel operations occur simultaneously across strategic, operational, and tactical levels of war and require greater integration in the past.[34]

The joint staff also concluded that joint warfare in the future would no longer be either attrition-based or maneuver-based. Instead, attrition and maneuver will merge into a seamless attack throughout the depth of the battlefield while exploiting the strengths of the joint U.S. forces and the vulnerabilities of an opponent. The commander of future joint forces will control the tempo of operations and "shock, dislocate, disrupt, or paralyze, an adversary's political and military cohesion, will and capacity for continued resistance."[35]

U.S. JFCOM began development of a joint operating concept to address the changing environment and requirements. Concepts such as this go through many revisions and updates. A 2004 version stated that joint interdependence depends on the network of information technology now available and expected to be available in the future. However, breaking down the interservice cultural barriers and rivalries is even more important if we are to achieve true interdependence. The relationships among the services and other governmental agencies are dynamic today and will be that way in the future. Information technologies provide the opportunity to integrate these various agencies and forces more than ever before. Access to capabilities that would not be available without interdependence will help commanders cope with the uncertainties on the future battlefield.[36]

Battlefield effects can be lethal or nonlethal and should produce an "enemy's disintegration, disorientation, dislocation, or destruction." Using an effect-based approach directly links the desired end state to the tasks and methods of achieving the effects. This concept of effect-based operations relies on a complete understanding of the commander's intent, as it filters through the chain of command, so that subordinates act in compliance with the commander's plan. The effect is a behavioral or physical reaction to the actions of a friendly unit.[37]

This brief review of a small amount of the joint services literature on transformation over time shows a clear change from the past. Key ideas were a change from a threat-based approach to force development to one of capability-based force development. Joint operations would now be the norm, and such operations would require military service interdependence, not simply the ability to cooperate. Time and space conditions had now changed, so that operations that might have been sequential in the past would now occur simultaneously. The interaction of the effects of such actions must be understood. The purpose of operations would now be to produce a specific effect, physical or psychological, on an enemy and not simply to destroy the enemy forces or systems.

The other military services began transformation initiatives during this same period. Brief summaries of the other services' transformation programs as provided by their documentation follow. These programs all fall under the overall guidance from the Department of Defense. Each military service charted its transformation course based on its unique characteristics and requirements.

The U.S. Air Force produced a *Transformation Flight Plan* in 2003 that stated that it would strive to enhance future operations, pursue innovation, create flexible and agile units, develop capabilities and effect-based planning and programming, support the transformational goals of the QDR, and adopt modern business practices in its effort to transform to meet the requirements of the future security environment. Three core competencies would guide this effort. They are developing Air Force personnel, integrating operations, and bringing technology to operations.[38]

The U.S. Air Force planned to continue to develop its Air Expeditionary Force organization and develop a new Combat Wing Organization, as well as more fully integrating Air Force Reserve and active duty personnel. The Air Force questioned whether the changes in capabilities would actually result in a revolution in military affairs; however, the Air Force emphasized that profound change would occur. Transformation requires changes in capabilities, organization, doctrine, and concepts of operation.[39]

In 2004, the U.S. Marine Corps (USMC) reported that it would use its core competencies to face the challenges of a changing security environment. The USMC core competencies include being ready to fight and win, having an expeditionary culture, conducting forcible entry from the sea, using Marine Air-Ground Task Forces (MAGTF) to conduct combined arms operations, conducting joint and multinational operations, and integrating reserve components. Basing operations at sea becomes the foundation for conducting operations ashore and supports the Marine Corps concepts of "Operational Maneuver from the Sea" and "Ship to Objective Maneuver." A "Global Concept of Operations" seeks to better integrate naval forces in order to meet the challenges of the new security environment. New materiel will improve Marine Corps capabilities.[40]

The U.S. Navy wrote that naval forces provide unique capabilities to support the defense of the United States. Asymmetric capabilities include maritime dominance, mobility, decision superiority, stealth, precision, and persistence. The Navy-Marine Corps team will rely on several new concepts referred to as "Sea Strike," "Sea Shield," and "Sea Basing." The Navy's information network concept, "FORCEnet," will link the forces, executing these concepts into a cohesive element.[41]

The U.S. Navy described "Sea Strike" as projecting "decisive and persistent offensive power anywhere in the world" as well as being able to initiate operations from the sea. The Navy expects improvements in information systems to enable a major change in the ability to target hostile forces. Deployment of marines directly from ships to an objective will provide the Navy the ability to attack targets ashore without a costly logistic buildup on a beach.[42]

"Sea Shield" is the concept for protecting United States' and allies' territory, forces off shore, and forces ashore from missile and air threats as well as other enemy forces. "Sea Basing" includes the ability to avoid having to establish support facilities ashore in order to conduct operations. Retaining key naval assets at sea will add to their protective posture and ensure maximum flexibility in their use. The Navy planned for an integrated force of enhanced Navy and U.S. Marine Corps aircraft, manned and unmanned, as well as naval surface and submarine forces in order to implement this transformation. Compressing the time and increasing the lethality of naval strikes are goals.[43]

Table 9.1 summarizes the characteristics of the U.S. Air Force, the U.S. Marine Corps, and the U.S. Navy transformation programs reviewed in this research. The conclusions as to whether the changes described would

Table 9.1 Other Military Service Transformation Programs

Military service	Operational concept changes	Weapon system changes	Organization changes	Technological changes	Fundamental change in warfare
U.S. Air Force	Emphasis on joint operations and precision strike	Technology to enhance information network and precision strike	Integration of active and reserve forces; Combat Wing	Improvement in aircraft technology and information systems	No
U.S. Marine Corps	Maneuver directly from ships to an objective	Improved amphibious, land, and aviation systems	Continued use of the Marine Air-Ground Task Force	Information technology	No
U.S. Navy	Sea Strike, Sea Basing, Sea Shield	Air, surface, and submarine forces; more unmanned aerial vehicles	A more integrated Navy and Marine force	Enhanced information systems for command and control and intelligence operations	No

result in a fundamental change in warfare and be revolutionary in nature are based upon the criteria defining revolutionary change discussed earlier. This comparison is not a thorough review of the other military services' transformation programs. The discussion instead provides a brief review of other transformation efforts within the U.S. Department of Defense in order to provide an understanding of the efforts within all of the military services to effect change as part of the reaction to the new security environment.

TRANSFORMATION CONCLUSION

All military services regardless of national origin must be prepared to change in order to adapt to new circumstances. The security environment may change. Technology will change and enable weapons to change. Operational concepts will change because technology changes will inspire new ideas, or new operational concepts will influence research and result in new technologies being developed. New methods of organizing these forces will flow from attempts to maximize military utility.

This review of military transformation is not all-inclusive and was outdated the moment it was put on paper. All of the services change constantly. Some change efforts are larger than others. Change is not always progress. Whether because of resources or a lack of viable ideas or technological improvements, change may not be in the best interest of one service or all of them collectively. The leadership of the Department of Defense, the executive, and the Congress ultimately decide the level of change needed or possible through their decisions regarding programs and other issues affecting resources available.

The U.S. military forces are undergoing great change while simultaneously fighting a war conducted around the world against a nontraditional enemy motivated by hatred of the very culture of freedom and democracy that is the cornerstone of America's might. Maintaining a focus on programs of change in any circumstances faces many challenges. The U.S. Department of Defense faces the added challenge of war. Regardless, some effort must continue to strive to prepare for the future.

10

Ensuring Transformation

Ensuring that transformation actually occurs is not a simple task. Any major program that changes a large segment of such a large organization as the Army will consume a great deal of resources whether time, money, people, or materiel. Several actions or considerations are critical in maintaining progress toward a transformed organization or Army.

Maintaining a vision for the change is important. Leadership will determine if the program succeeds or fails in the eyes of members of the organization. Pilot groups support instituting change. A learning driven organization is more apt to succeed in making a major change occur. A systems approach to organizing the effort will help ensure that all aspects or impacts of the program are clear. Maintaining relevance with the environment, coping with problems, and a system of assessment and measurement are essential. The Army leadership must be prepared to react to true believers and detractors to the ideas included in transformation. The Army structure may change in important or subtle ways. Finally the leadership must decide if revolutionary or evolutionary change is in the best interests of the force.

MAINTAINING THE VISION OF TRANSFORMATION

John Kotter posited that implementing a major change is not easy. A sense of urgency and guiding coalition are important. Vision and strategy are necessary, along with communicating them to the organization. Enabling action throughout the organization and producing short-term successes help solidify support. Continuing the process through new ideas and projects maintains the momentum for change. Change becomes permanent when the organization's culture institutionalizes the change.[1]

The Army has produced a number of documents that discuss the vision and strategy for completing the transformation initiative. Such references provide the general guidance for the Army major command organizations to follow in order to achieve success in transforming. However, the production of reference materials alone does not ensure that someone will read them or accept them as valid.

Changes in the security environment have affected Army transformation. The terrorist attacks on September 11, 2001, ushered in a new challenge to the security of the United States. The decisions to attack Afghanistan and Iraq resulted in a major expenditure of funds, which might have otherwise been spent on future programs. This new security environment also generally coincided with a change in the senior leadership of the Army. General Peter Schoomaker replaced General Eric Shinseki as the chief of staff of the Army during the transformation program. Shortly after these changes occurred, the Army cancelled the Comanche and Crusader programs, which had been components of transformation. The Army also began a major shift in organizational design by restructuring current brigades into smaller, more easily deployed brigades. This decision produced more brigades that also relied more on joint capabilities for combat power than their predecessor designs.

Maintaining the original vision of a major change effort is difficult. As shown by this discussion, a change in the external environment can have a major impact. Prior to the September 11, 2001, terror attacks, the Army was accepting risk with modernization by seeking a revolutionary change through the Future Combat System program. The Army expected the new weapon systems and technological change accompanied by new operational and organizational concepts to exploit these materiel systems would dramatically change the battlefield and the Army's ability to deploy to that battlefield. Such change would ensure that the Army maintained an advantage over any future opponent. However, the terrorist attacks forced the Army to adapt to a real threat that had attacked the United States. The requirements of a shooting war diverted resources from the major program of change.

Such a change in the external environment can also affect industry. Any major program of change will begin within a given environmental setting. Competitor actions can change a window of opportunity for making change, so that the window closes. Governmental action could change a regulatory requirement, which demands attention and shifts focus. Natural phenomenon may cause damage to facilities and divert resources.

Any organization contemplating a major change program must provide for flexibility in the program to cope with external environmental changes. A failure to do so will place the program of change at risk should the environment change. Flexible plans can help an organization confront an external environmental change and decrease its negative impact.

The senior leadership is especially important in maintaining a program of change over an extended period of time. The length of time required to implement all aspects of Army transformation make it clear that more than one chief of staff of the Army will participate in decisions supporting the program. The change in senior leadership at the same time as the external environment change of the terrorist attacks affected transformation. General Schoomaker had no choice but to respond to the new security environment. He could not help but place his own emphasis on transformation based on his experience and his judgment in order to balance the requirement to defend the nation and continue preparations to meet future perceived threats and use potential new capabilities.

Any change in senior leadership for an organization puts all ongoing programs at risk because the new leadership may choose to alter priorities and the allocation of resources. For a program of change such as Army transformation to succeed, a series of successive senior leaders must share the vision of revolutionary change. If they do not, transformation will become evolutionary change and hence simply a modernization program rather than an opportunity to fundamentally change the nature of warfare.

Any organization carrying out a revolutionary change program faces the same dilemma. The best catalyst for revolutionary change is to maintain consistency of the senior leadership. That may be simpler in industry than the military because senior leader rotation is not a requirement in industry as it is in the military services. Regardless of the setting, it is important that the senior leadership maintain the vision of a major change program if it is to occur. The senior civilian level leadership in the Department of Defense can assist in this by selecting subsequent senior leaders who share in the vision of transformation.

Short-term successes are important for maintaining momentum and encouraging an organization's members to support the change program. The loss of Crusader and Comanche are examples of the failure to gain short-term successes. The Army must strive to ensure that such major component programs within transformation do not fail again.

Organizations facing a major change should continue to reward individuals and component elements, recommending additions to the transformation program. Additions to major programs of change ensure that momentum continues to drive change forward. Rewarding people who support change programs helps inculcate the change in the organization culture. Personnel who view support to the program as a path to success in the organization will support the effort to change. An organization with a formal structure such as the Army will reorient as the senior leaders dictate. However, simply following an order does not guarantee immediate agreement or complete acceptance that a new policy is correct.

THE IMPORTANCE OF LEADERSHIP

John Kotter has discussed the need for organizations to retain and motivate lower level leaders. Recruiting the right people is extremely important as is providing adequate compensation and training. Clearly it is important for successful organizations to expend resources on growing future leaders.[2] Military organizations must do this just as civilian industries must.

Kotter also noted that driving people out of their comfort zone in order to change an organization is difficult. The lack of a crisis can inhibit change as can low standards of performance and internal settings that indicate success. Changing these factors can set the foundation for beginning a program of change.[3] The military services were already preparing for major changes prior to the terrorist attacks on September 11, 2001. However, it is also apparent that these attacks spurred the services to alter the planned change. Transformation shifted emphasis to address more near term requirements.

Educating an organization's membership is crucial for the purpose of a major change to be understood. This education must include middle managers as well as lower level employees. However, scheduling briefings and publishing pamphlets is not enough. Relying on public announcements will also not suffice to ensure that the organization's membership understand the change program. Organizations must provide a means of assessing the understanding and acceptance of the characteristics of the change program. Providing a means for middle managers to partcipate in pilot projects or to provide input for decisions on implementation of programs within a major program of change are ways to encourage support from middle managers and to assess their understanding of the components of a major program. Announcing successful participation in a pilot project and giving credit to managers who propose worthwhile additions to a program of change would further encourage middle managers to support the effort to change.

Middle management acceptance is crucial for change to be implemented. Organizations must develop a means to explain the purpose of a program of change. Organizations should also develop a means to monitor understanding and acceptance of the vision and the details of any program of change. Ensuring that middle mangers as well as first-line supervisors and all employees understand the vision and requirements of a major change program will reduce anxiety in the workforce and facilitate successful implementation.

Military chains of command provide units with leaders who have the authority, responsibility, and accountability to ensure that actions occur. Staffs provide a network of leaders to enforce and supervise actions. Senior leaders, civilians, and general officers, provide the executive level leadership to create the environment that will allow change to occur.

Military leaders must work together to ensure that the Army has an environment that allows innovation to occur and then reinforces the spread of innovative ideas to the rest of the force. Leaders must be mentors and coaches and inculcate a "learning organization"[4] culture in the Army. The Army must continuously learn from its environment and adapt to a changing world. Episodic training will not suffice. Learning must be continuous. Otherwise the rapidity with which the security environment changes or a specific enemy reacts and adapts to us will result in our inability to respond effectively to a threat.

A key role of leadership is to guard against a focus on the innovative act or idea rather than the impact on the culture and capabilities of the Army as a whole. This may result in such "pushback" that the Army's efforts to change could fail.[5] Time and materiel resources will always be short. Some soldiers will not understand the relevance of the change. Certain leaders may not support the change. Much anxiety will ensue. Leaders must work hard to overcome these challenges.

Several tactics can reinforce the transition to a new system. Leaders must be consistent in the message about the purpose and focus of transformation. People who are engaged in the change experience must enjoy personal success in order to maintain enthusiasm. Symbolizing the new identity is important to reinforce the new organizations being formed. It is also important to celebrate the successes of transformation.[6]

Time

There never seems to be enough time to accomplish all of the tasks that leaders plan to accomplish. Crises arise at inconvenient times and derail long laid plans and divert attention. Leaders say that a project is important, but they then rarely attend meetings themselves. A subordinate often replaces them. Teams form, but then members change, as important missions outside the task at hand arise and demand attention. However, the true problem is not a lack of time. The real problems are prioritizing time and time flexibility.[7]

It is important to help soldiers have flexibility in scheduling their time, so that they can then prioritize their efforts in support of transformation while maintaining the ability to conduct operations today. There are several techniques to consider in helping soldiers manage time more effectively. Integrating new concepts and functions may save resources and help focus effort. Setting aside time to accomplish specific tasks and refusing to interrupt the effort focused on certain tasks can help soldiers maintain their focus. A third method is to trust soldiers to control their time. Allow them the freedom to manage their time within the constraints of mission accomplishment and maintaining discipline. Protecting time that soldiers can spend with their families is very important since the repetitive deployments to fight terrorism and support nation-building put a great strain on soldiers and their families.[8]

Leaders need unstructured time to think about their profession. They need the opportunity to read and ponder the lessons of the past and the opportunities of the future. It is not possible to mandate new ideas and creative thinking, but it is possible to provide the time for them to occur. Leaders need time away from the daily pressures, so they can think.[9]

Coaches and Mentors

Senior leaders must help junior leaders transform the Army. Junior leaders must help soldiers do the same. This is important with the new modular brigades and will be important in the first Future Combat System brigades that function as pilot groups. Assistance and guidance from the chain of command will reduce frustration and the potential for rejection of new concepts and initiatives. It is important in units not modernizing, so that they continue their focus on current operations and do not lose sight of their missions. It is also important in the institutional Army, so that tomorrow's leaders adopt a learning organization culture with innovation as a constant. The Army cannot allow junior leaders and soldiers to think that there is no help available for them as we transform. Military schools and centers must include transformation and the change process in their programs of instruction.[10]

"Great coaching is artful, compassionate, and incisive."[11] This is true whether referring to industry or the Army. Coaches must encourage interaction. They cannot dictate actions but must help their partners learn how to succeed. Good coaches must enjoy their profession. They must focus on the end state. The interaction between coaches and their partners must be based on honesty. Good coaches feel accountable for the outcome of their efforts.[12]

As mentors, senior leaders must guide a subordinate in preparing for the future. Good relationships in mentoring are reciprocal. Both parties commit to the relationship and support each other. Mentors facilitate learning rather than simply providing solutions. Without integrity in an organization, mentoring relationships cannot develop. Mentoring relationships do not have a specific time associated with them. They are not permanent. Mentoring junior leaders and soldiers who have shown great potential will help the Army benefit from their talents at an earlier date than that which might otherwise occur. Mentoring can help the Army by identifying the talented soldiers needed for the future.[13]

As soldiers grapple with the changes that are part of transformation, leaders must be prepared to help them cope with the emotional responses that may occur. This transition can result in soldiers going through the grieving process. Emotions may range from anger to sadness to disorientation.[14] Leaders must guide their subordinates through this process and ensure that our soldiers understand why transformation is necessary. Communication is vital. It must be two-way. Leaders must ensure that soldiers understand the purpose of transformation, and leaders must be open to feedback from soldiers regarding transformation's successes and shortcomings.

Walking the Talk

Leaders set the example. They will be on center stage throughout the transformation process. This is true in industry just as it is in the Army. Leaders are accountable for their actions. Their conduct sets the tone for the Army. When there is a mismatch between a leader's values and those associated with the changes being implemented, the leader must change or move on. If the Army's leaders do not accept transformation as necessary, it will breed distrust in the Army. Distrust will tear apart the cohesion that we must have to face the challenges today and in the future. Leaders must display the attitude and cultural change demanded by transformation. Failure to do so will be a failure of "walking the talk."[15]

Transformation involves making change throughout the Army, including the adoption of new concepts, the integration of new organization designs, fielding new equipment, and changing the structure of the institutional Army. This massive degree of change demands commitment from all soldiers. The Army leadership cannot simply dictate that the change will occur. Soldiers must adopt the new methods and opportunities and work to succeed. This also places a great demand of trust on the leadership. There will be successes and failures. Soldiers will learn through both. Leaders must underwrite their actions and avoid a "zero defect" mentality. Soldiers must know that they can trust their leaders to help. Otherwise a "trust gap" will develop and cripple the Army's efforts to transform. Goals and values must be credible and clear.[16]

Leaders set the climate that allows honest discussion and reflection. This will help ensure that soldiers align their personal goals and ambitions with those of the Army. Success in transforming the Army is predicated on support from its soldiers. Leaders must ensure the credibility of transformation initiatives through demonstrating their worth, not simply talking about them.[17]

Leaders need trusted agents who can provide advice and honest criticism. Command sergeants major, chaplains, and inspectors general are advisors who leaders can go to for honest answers. Leaders must also work hard to be patient with subordinates and superiors when under great pressure. This will help junior leaders and soldiers do the same. Being calm under the pressure of change should not be more difficult than being calm when under fire in combat. Leaders must not be remote. Leaders must be seen and be ready to talk about the Army's values and how important they are to soldiers.[18] Leaders must also be careful of relying too much on data analysis. The Army is a human organization. Numbers are useful, but they can hide the human element. Leaders must observe soldiers at work and not simply rely on numbers and their interpretation. Leaders must engage one another in the process of change.[19]

PILOT GROUPS

An idea used in civilian industry with positive effect is that of a pilot group. They can be of varying size and functional characterization. An organization may use one or several in order to implement change. Regardless of characteristics, the idea is that all new ideas must begin small and then grow in order to last.[20]

The Army is already using pilot groups and must seek ways to use them effectively. The process to change the 3rd Infantry Division from a division with three maneuver brigades to a more deployable headquarters with four modular brigades was an example of a pilot group. This has led the Army toward a brigade-based Army providing commanders with enhanced flexibility and joint interoperability.

AUTHORITY VS. LEARNING-DRIVEN CHANGE

The basic command structure of the Army makes a reliance on authority-driven change a process that is easy to slip into. Such change can be very efficient and also effective in the near term. However, a learning-driven culture of change is more apt to last for a long time.[21]

It may be necessary initially to rely on change that is driven by the chain of command. This certainly is a way to overcome the reluctance of others to adopt new ideas. However, the Army must also change its education system to ensure young soldiers and leaders grow up in a culture of perpetual learning and innovation.

In order to ensure transformation becomes a permanent element in Army culture, the Army should reflect on several initiatives that are common in major change programs. First, changes should be associated with actual work objectives and processes. The changes should involve an improvement in performance. People involved in the change must have the power to take action. The changes should seek a balance between action and reflection. People involved in the change must have time to think about the change. Overall the change should be intended to improve people's individual and collective capability to perform. Finally, change should focus on learning.[22]

Transformation certainly fits this description. The Army is transforming in order to better serve the nation. By using new technologies, reorganizing brigades, and becoming joint interdependent, the Army intends to improve unit and soldier lethality, survivability, and relevance in operations worldwide. The Army leadership must empower soldiers and lower level leaders to implement transformation. A challenge is to provide the time to reflect on the initiatives being implemented. The pace of change is so rapid and the needs of the Army so sufficiently profound as the United States conducts a war and prepares for the future that it is easy to ignore this need for time to think. Nonetheless, providing such time for leaders, soldiers, and institutions is important.[23]

For any organization to make a major change in how it operates, it is essential for that organization to inspire its members to commit their imagination and energy to make the change occur. It is also important for the organization to take care of its members' needs, personal and family. Without caring for the people who must implement the change, the innovation will not be sustained.[24]

Instilling the proper mindset in soldiers is a key aspect of transformation. However, transformation requires much more than a commitment from our soldiers to be expeditionary and joint in their thinking. Stabilizing soldier assignments is important for unit cohesion and in taking care of soldier families. Individual training must prepare all soldiers to fight and win. Soldiers must know how to think instead of what to think. This is important for them to be able to adapt to the unexpected, which will be with us as long as we face an adaptive enemy. Equipping soldiers must remain our top priority. All soldiers must have the tools they require for their mission and the equipment necessary for their survival on the battlefield.[25]

SYSTEMS APPROACH TO CHANGE

The Army is composed of many systems. Systems synchronize combat power on the battlefield. Systems manage personnel and budgets. The interaction among all of these systems provides the Army the means of conducting operations around the world constantly. Changing an organization also requires a complex system to lead that change.[26]

The Army is a human system, since soldiers compose it. The Army is a living organism, an open system. It is more than the simple sum of its parts. An open system changes the inputs to the system and the organization to which it belongs.[27] Likewise, the Army changes the inputs to itself. The Army transforms civilians into soldiers. The Army transforms technologies into functioning combat systems. The merging of soldiers and weapons systems into cohesive units completes the transformation of the civilian into the Army.

The Army's dependence on people clearly makes it a social system. Three areas proposed by Charlotte Roberts and Art Kleiner are worth review in order to ascertain the interplay of social systems with transformation initiatives.[28] The Army should review the interaction of the various internal organizations or agencies. Schools and centers, major command staffs, and the acquisition community must cooperate for transformation to succeed. The second social system effect worthy of monitoring is the perceptions of soldiers and civilians regarding the impact of transformation. Lastly the Army's leaders must determine whether soldiers and civilians understand the goals assigned. Process systems follow the flow of information.[29] Changes in this flow will occur as we change the Army. By mapping current processes, the Army can ascertain whether they best meet the needs of current and future operations. Formal and informal information flows are important. Current reporting systems may not serve the Army in the future as well as in the past. As it transforms, the Army must examine these processes and institute changes as needed.

The Army is also a living system.[30] Change is not new in the Army. There has always been a need to conduct current operations of some type while also looking to the future for new requirements. Change has occurred in order for the Army to grow new capabilities to respond to a changing domestic and international environment. Change will always be with the military services. Integrating change within the Army without inhibiting the ability to conduct current operations is essential.

Transforming the Army "is a process that shapes the changing nature of military competition and cooperation through new combinations of concepts, capabilities, people, and organizations." Transformation will change Army processes by simultaneously developing future capabilities and accelerating the fielding of selected capabilities into the current force. This interaction between the present force and future force will include leveraging insights and lessons learned from operations, concept development, and experimentation to enhance joint interdependence. Future force attributes that will guide this transformation include the Army being fully integrated with joint forces, expeditionary, networked, decentralized, adaptable, decision superior, and lethal. Experimentation, analyses, and capability assessments will ensure that new warfare concepts are ready for employment by Army and joint forces.[31]

MAINTAINING RELEVANCE

It is important for change to be relevant to the organization involved. Sometimes organization leaders fail to explain the need for change, which then dampens enthusiasm for the change initiatives. Relevance is important. If the change does not appear relevant to the organization, then the expenditure of resources and effort to make the change appears pointless. Simply stating that the change is important is not enough. The members of the organization must perceive that the change is relevant to the organization's purpose. People must consider any project to be important if their best effort is to be sustained over an extended period of time.[32]

There are several methods that may be used to avoid the stigma of being termed irrelevant. Key leaders must have strategic awareness of the change under way. Leaders should discuss relevance as an issue with members of the pilot group. They must keep communications open with the pilot group and provide more information to them. Leaders must ensure that training remains linked to the organization's purpose or output. If information indicates that someone support the change initiatives out of the norm, then the organization should investigate to determine if time is being diverted from more important tasks. Finally, leaders should periodically revisit the idea of relevance in order to ensure that concerns do not arise and interfere with the change.[33]

Transformation is relevant for the Army. The changes in the international security environment mandate change in order to meet those challenges. The worldwide threat of terrorism is very different from the old state-based opponents such as the Soviet Union or North Korea. Deployment challenges must be overcome, so the Army can more rapidly put soldiers on the ground. Technological change provides new capabilities that enable a change in warfare methods. The Army must transform in order to ensure our continued relevance. Senior leaders must use the techniques discussed earlier in order to ensure that soldiers and civilians understand the relevance as change.

Senior Department of Defense leaders must also address this relevance with the nation's political leadership in order to ensure that they understand the relevance of transformation to maintaining a safe America. The political leadership must understand the need for continued excellence in ground combat capability, so they will provide the funding to procure the technologies needed to support the Army's continued relevance.

Maintaining a history of successes and failures in transformation is important. As Richard Ross and Art Kleiner pointed out, every "change initiative has a history."[34] Recognizing this history will help others learn about the actions taken and reasons for change. Interviewing a range of people is important because no one person will have a complete understanding of everything that has happened. Understanding the history of transformation initiatives will help us ensure the Army maintains its relevance in today's world. A historical record would ensure that we remember the lessons of the past that we are learning today.

BUMPS IN THE TANK TRAIL

Transforming the Army into a learning organization with campaign quality and a joint and expeditionary mindset will not simply happen. However, developing this learning capability is essential for profound change. Leadership will help the Army sustain this program of change. If the Army fails to sustain transformation, future soldiers will not be ready for the challenges of tomorrow. Several bumps in the tank trail could arise and interfere with these efforts. Potential challenges include resistance due to fear and anxiety, assessment and measurement, and the conflict between believers and nonbelievers. Army leaders must try to smooth these bumps in order to continue our efforts to transform.

Fear and Anxiety

In the military services' authoritarian-based culture, it is very easy for leaders to fail to understand the fear and anxiety that a major change, such as transformation, might cause. The Army tends to adopt a can-do attitude. No challenge is too great. Failure is not an option. Anyone who has spent any time in the Army knows that soldiers pride themselves on being able to accomplish the impossible with limited resources and regardless of the obstacles in our path. Soldiers often ignore the obstacles or refuse to accept that they exist.

In a learning-based organization, the obstacles become apparent. Fear and anxiety are not viewed as problems but are instead seen as natural responses to new conditions. Open communication channels throughout the chain of command are necessary for this learning attitude to exist. Soldiers must feel that they can discuss concerns without fear of reprisal, and they must know that their opinions are important. They must feel ownership of transformation for it to succeed.[35]

Some leaders may flinch at this idea of openness, but they should not. The Army has been conducting After Action Reviews (AAR) at training centers and in unit training for years. Soldiers have provided a free exchange of ideas and professional discussion in training environments throughout this process in units large and small. This willingness to provide constructive criticism and have open discussion must permeate the Army and not stop with training events. In this manner the Army can grow as a learning organization. The enemies who we face in the world will adapt to our actions. If the Army is a learning organization, it will enhance our ability to maintain the initiative in operations and evolve operations faster than our enemies can adapt.

Open discussion supports integrity. It is normal for people to be concerned about making a mistake and for others to know that they have. People fear exposing their errors and hurting themselves and other people. As change to a learning capability progresses, some people begin to experience fear and anxiety because of the openness that follows. Leaders must show them that such emotional responses are natural and that they will not suffer punishment for being open.[36]

Fear and anxiety becomes a problem for change if an "openness gap" develops. This occurs when learning capabilities of the group grow more quickly than the learning capabilities of the individuals. A lack of confidence in their ability to cope with open, candid discussion can result in this gap. This conflict can force the change to a halt because people's emotional responses cripple their ability to continue. It becomes important then for leaders to have the skills to encourage discussion and candor without automatically evoking a defensive reaction. The overall environment for safe comment is crucial for people to overcome their concerns.[37]

William Bridges warned that as concern rises, productivity can fall dramatically because people focus on their fears and not on the task at hand. Absenteeism is typically higher. Old weaknesses that may have been hidden could once again become apparent. People feel overloaded and polarize into opposing groups.[38]

Soldiers are people, too. They will react in a similar fashion. With the Army's performance reporting procedures, it would be very easy for officers and noncommissioned officers to be concerned about a completely open learning environment. The Army's senior leadership must dispel such concerns through selection and assignment decisions. The reactions of senior leaders will set the tone in the Army. Junior leaders will be watching closely. If open discussion results in promotions, it will continue. If the reverse is apparent, open discussion will end. This open discussion must include criticisms of transformation.

Enthusiasm for the chief of staff's program must not be allowed inadvertently to squelch honest criticism and questions. The Army will learn through an open debate. There will be good ideas and bad ones that develop during the course of the Army's evolution into the future Army. All of the military services must have a spirited, professional debate, so that they can learn from one another. The Army cannot afford for debate to be smothered as it was before World War II with regard to tank employment, where the careers of Dwight Eisenhower and George Patton were almost ruined due to their authoring controversial periodical articles.[39] A learning organization welcomes such discussion. True transformation must have it.

There are several strategies that can be used to confront difficult issues. Start small and build momentum for change before confronting major issues that are sure to evoke a negative emotional response. Avoid a direct attack on an issue that is sure to raise concerns. Set an example for allowing candor and open discussion. Accept diversity as an asset and not a hindrance. Use the different skills and experiences of subordinates to enhance the group's capabilities to handle a range of actions. Use a failure as an opportunity to learn and not criticize. Whenever possible, make participation in pilot groups a volunteer act and not a forced one. Help people learn to accept this openness by being a good coach, so they learn to be aware of the impact of their actions on others. Work to develop a common framework around the vision for the future and the reality of today. Be careful of demanding openness in such a way that it actually results in people hiding their views. Finally, remind people that their fear and anxiety are natural.[40]

These strategies are related to command climate. Commanders set the environment within their units. If the leadership is open to professional candor, then the soldiers will provide honest input regarding their concerns and their views of the true status of the unit and the transformation process. Leaders must determine the attitudes and abilities of their subordinates and then develop an appropriate strategy to enhance change and innovation for their soldiers. The abilities of soldiers will vary greatly. Harnessing these differences is part of the challenge of leadership. The evolution of the Army today into the future design is a constant process. Transformation involves the current force and the future Army. Units from both will share the battle-field as we field new equipment and operational capabilities and concepts. A shared framework that includes the realities of today with the vision for the future is essential to ensure that our units regardless of their state of change can operate effectively together. The United States cannot afford to have disjointed operations.

Roberts warned of the concept of unilateral control.[41] Leaders must guard against grabbing unilateral control when they feel fear and anxiety. This would stifle the change into a learning organization because it will end open discussion. Leaders must accept an open environment. This is a special concern in the Army because the hierarchical structure with its emphasis on a commander being responsible for all that a unit accomplishes or fails to accomplish makes it very easy for leaders to be fearful and anxious regarding openness. The senior leadership must guard against subordinate leaders adopting unilateral control as a defense mechanism. It will backfire on the Army.

Assessment and Measurement

Any change will call into question how success is measured. Some people will argue for changes in the assessment process, while others will argue that traditional techniques are fine. Leaders and organization members may resent any claims that long-standing measures are no longer adequate. This disagreement can inhibit change.[42]

Quantitative measures are a common form of assessing performance in industry today and carry more weight than more subjective forms of measurement. However, relying solely on quantitative measurements does not tell the entire story. Focusing only on numbers can hide the interactions in the real world.[43]

The Army is certainly familiar with quantitative measures. Whether talking about equipment readiness, reenlistment rates, or training tasks, we very quickly begin to use charts and graphs to track and display current status and trends. Clearly such quantitative techniques are useful. However, leaders must be prepared to see the entire picture and to extrapolate beyond the numbers in order to understand the real status of the Army. War is part art and part science. Quantitative measures whether tracking ammunition on hand or soldiers reporting for duty are necessary in order to provide a clear understanding of the baseline capability of our forces. This is the science element of warfare. However, war is also partially art. The human element is not based on a number approach. A learning organization harnesses this human component. Morale is a key element of this human dimension. The Army must pay close attention to this human dynamic in order to address the qualitative aspects of Army operations.

Transformation may require new measures of performance in order to monitor progress as discussed previously. But leaders must also be patient while awaiting improvements, whether defined by new measures or old ones. A way to view this is as a "result gap." There may be a time delay in improvements expected from a change. A profound change can also produce results that appear negative when compared to old standards. Leaders must be careful when comparing pilot group results to existing organizations. Time must be provided for the change to produce results, and leaders must be aware that new measures may be needed.[44]

In order to be prepared to deal with these issues of changes to assessment, leaders should consider several strategies. Leaders must be prepared to accept that being able to measure improvements may be delayed by unforeseen factors or challenges. Partner with other leaders in assessing transformation and the processes used to measure success. Learn to recognize progress when it occurs through setting interim goals, watching for unanticipated improvements, and keeping a record of the changes in people's views. Make the assessment process a priority for change. Discuss assessment early. Look for new measures. Do not blame the bearer of bad news for the occurrence of bad news.[45]

Rather than looking at data, leaders need to look at processes. The interactions inherent in the flow of work are often neglected, but they are also often the source of performance improvement. Be sensitive to this process flow. The interplay among processes produces the output often measured in traditional quantitative accounting systems.[46]

The Army is a very complex system of systems. The interaction among these systems ultimately determines our success or failure. The Army leadership must examine these interactions in its experiments in order to understand the interplay among them. The Army must also develop ways to assess this interaction in order to develop methods of measurement and assessment for the transformed force. Personal interaction with soldiers will help in maintaining awareness of the attitudes of soldiers and their understanding of the changes underway. Leaders should use discussion groups in officer and noncommissioned officer leader development training sessions in a rock drill or map exercise format to investigate transformation processes and concepts.

The Army should not eliminate measurement. Quantitative data provides useful information. But leaders must understand the processes that produced the data. George Roth recommended a new definition for assessment. He recommended that it include gathering the information, comparison of current and past results, an open discussion of the meaning of the data gathered, the means used to obtain the data, and the implications for the future.[47]

Open discussion requires loyalty and trust throughout the chain of command. Whether leader or subordinate, candid conversations entail a degree of personal risk. Success and failure must be shared for an open exchange to occur.[48] The Army's After Action Review process sets the example for this type of communication. Soldiers who are free to discuss success and failure with subordinates and superiors without fear of reprisal can learn from their experience and the experiences of others.

True Believers and Nonbelievers

Major change programs can produce individuals who are too committed to change and are then known as "true believers." They can actually inhibit change because their belief in the processes of change can border on fanaticism. Should this occur, expect a negative response from people who are not that committed to change. Isolation of the group fostering change may occur. This division of the organization into camps of believers and nonbelievers can fragment effort and tear apart the cohesion of the organization. Walls go up, and people take sides. This can drive change into conflict.[49]

Another danger associated with this is that success can result in pilot groups becoming arrogant and intolerant.[50] Conduct such as this further separates them from others in the group. The Army cannot afford for this to happen with its current modular brigade. The Army must have interaction among its soldiers and leaders in the new modular brigades as well as its regular brigades in order for a free exchange of lessons learned to take place. This becomes even more important as we move toward the future Army. The Army will eventually be composed of present-day brigades, modular brigades, and Stryker-equipped brigades as well as future brigades equipped with the Future Combat System.[51]

Communities in the Army are not new. Branch parochialism has always been with us. We have also always had divisions among the combat and noncombat arms as well as the airborne, air assault, and armor communities. This competition has generally been friendly; however, the Army cannot afford to have competition to the point of arrogance, where units cannot work together. Soldiers must be able to work with one another, or we will never be able to establish a good working relationship with the other military services and achieve joint interdependence.

The Army must cultivate the ability to be multicultural.[52] Soldiers must be able to function whether assigned to a Stryker brigade or a 3rd Infantry Division modular brigade. Schools and centers can help this through educating our soldiers on how to think and making training courses available to help soldiers operate the wide variety of equipment that will be in the force for many years. Soldiers, regardless of rank, must be open to new warfare concepts and to learning how to operate new equipment. The Army must have the flexibility to assign soldiers to the unit where they are needed and not to be forced to develop several different armies due to the transition period while changing from the Army today to the future Army.

Leaders can also help prevent this division into true believers and non-believers by mentoring younger leaders and soldiers on this need to operate as one Army and not several. Leaders can help their subordinates bridge gaps and resolve misunderstandings. They can also help members of pilot groups build functional relationships with the larger Army. Leaders also must remember that many people fear change. They need reassurance that the change is for the best.[53]

The Army must rely on its values as a foundation of its character. They transcend all change and are indicative of our cultural heritage. Transcendent values lay a foundation for change that provides a sense of identity.[54] The values of leadership, duty, respect, selfless service, honor, integrity, and personal courage remain important regardless of whether a soldier is in a transforming unit or in one that has not yet changed.[55]

Transformation requires a cultural change in the Army to adopt a joint and expeditionary mindset. Becoming a learning organization also requires a cultural change to progress beyond relying on commanders dictating action and reaction. Edgar Schein recommended several steps to follow in inculcating a cultural change. First clarify the purpose in changing culture. Next assemble a group of people to lead the change. Observe the organization in its work setting, and note the visible cultural signs. Using the small group, identify the organizational culture and look for inconsistencies. Then discuss the inconsistencies and ways to make a cultural change within the group.[56]

The Army leadership must continue to explain why it is transforming. The security environment provides the requirement. Technology provides the capability. Current force brigades and the futures groups at Training and Doctrine Command headquarters and its schools and centers will provide the people to manage change. These futures groups must look for ways to study the Army and the new brigade structures in particular in order to monitor the cultural change under way. School assistance visits will provide an opportunity to stay up to date with lessons from the field.

ARMY STRUCTURE

Transformation must include a continuing review of the structure of the Army to ensure that it supports preparation for the future. The military hierarchical structure came into being long before the technological changes being experienced today and expected in the future. This calls into question the best method of governance for the Army. The changing environment that we face also means diffusion of information and effort is even more critical today than in the past. Strategy and purpose must evolve to address the changing threat environment.

Governance

Transformation will not change the basic governance of the Army. The structure of the president as commander in chief followed by the secretary of defense and then the Army will remain in place. Nothing in Army transformation proposes a change to the policies of civilian control or this chain of command that then flows through the Army and its major commands. However, major change efforts in the corporate world are affecting how businesses view governance. The interdependence in industry requires the rethinking of hierarchical structures[57] just as the required interdependence of the Army on joint forces means that we must rethink the Army's structure.

Industry is discovering that hierarchical structures are not meeting organizational governance needs in the information-dominated world today. The rapidly changing geopolitical and technological environment is calling into question previous views of efficient and effective governance structures. Decisions must be made faster, which argues for more local autonomy rather than facing the time delays inherent in a typical hierarchical structure. Traditional decision-making at the top of an organization with obedience by the majority of employees fostered a level of dependence that no longer seems best for the world of today.[58]

Pilot groups encounter the issues of power and autonomy in the course of their development. Any change process necessitates decisions in an organization. Some of these decisions will be outside the authority of a pilot group. This can result in conflict between a pilot group and another element of the larger organization, as both components seek an answer to a question.[59]

The Army is a hierarchical structure. Nonetheless, the operation tempo on today's and tomorrow's battlefields will not allow for decision-making to be concentrated in the hands of senior leaders alone. The technological change affecting society at large is affecting all military services as well. We must take advantage of the opportunities provided by information technology or, we run the risk of an enemy doing so and being able to make decisions faster than we can. That would result in a loss of initiative and put our forces at risk. The leaders and soldiers on the ground must be empowered to make decisions. Speed and survival demand it.

Hierarchies will not disappear whether in industry or the Army. But the basic reason for the existence of the hierarchical structure of an organization should be reviewed based on the changing environment. Elliott Jaques stated that the reason management hierarchies exist is to differentiate accountability over time.[60] The Army must differentiate operational responsibility over time and space. The present hierarchical structure has served well for many years. But certain relationships require a change. The Army must exploit information technology and assets in space in order to provide the basic structure for network-centric battle command to function.[61]

Operations in the future will be "simultaneous, distributed, noncontiguous, and nonlinear." The Army will participate in joint service interdependent, network-centric, and effect-based campaigns. The seamless interaction among the components of the joint force is crucial to success. The Army will provide the land component of this force.[62]

The current plan to develop modular force designs is the correct path. Brigade-sized units will form the basic building block for Army forces. All higher level division and corps headquarters will be modular. Both should be capable of functioning as joint task force headquarters.[63]

In order to execute leadership on the battlefield, the Army must prepare its leaders for battle command, which is "the art and science of applying leadership and decision making to achieve mission success." Battle command occurs within a joint framework and relies on modern information technology to support communications, decision-making, and intelligence operations. These systems must provide a commander the capability to understand the situation faster and more accurately than an enemy. Battle command must also provide the capability to synchronize the operations of the current Army and the units in the future Army in addition to those from other services and allies. The focus must be on assisting the commander's role and not on maintaining statistics demanded by the staff. Distributed, continuous, and high tempo operations will characterize the future battlefield. The systems supporting battle command must enable and not hinder a commander's actions in such a fluid environment.[64]

A network collaborative information environment (NCIE) will support battle command in the future. The purpose is to enable simultaneous collaborative planning and operation execution among multiple command levels and adjacent units. A collaborative decision-making environment is a revolutionary change in how we operate. This requires an open architecture of systems, so that other services and functional units can interact seamlessly. Allies must also be able to enter this environment in order for the Army to conduct effective operations around the world.[65]

For the Army to execute such a command paradigm shift, we must be knowledge-based and function as a learning organization. Open communications are essential. Collaborative planning requires real-time interaction between superiors and subordinates, commanders and staffs. This will dramatically reduce the time required to gather information, plan, make a decision, and disseminate that decision. It also requires superiors and subordinates to be free to air opinions and ask questions without fear of ridicule. The open channels inherent in a learning organization facilitate this approach. Our traditional authoritative approach to decision-making and information sharing will not work. Information sharing and open discussion will preclude us from making mistakes such as the inability to synchronize Army and Navy plans before World War II that then doomed the Philippines garrison to death and capture. No one dared to point out the fallacy of holding the islands while waiting for relief from the sea when this relief attempt had no realistic chance of success.[66]

Unit wiring diagrams should flatten with the ability to reduce the levels of command between physical action on the battlefield and higher levels of decision-making. With modular brigades that possess joint interdependence and connectivity to a global information network, there seems little reason to demand the number of intervening headquarters that characterize our organizations today. Reducing the layers of command speeds the time between decision and action, which will help maintain the initiative and stay ahead of an opponent. Reducing these layers will also save personnel and reduce equipment requirements. This can provide more soldiers and equipment at the cutting edge of the force. That means more combat power where it is needed.

The basic hierarchical structure of the Army will remain in place. Commanders will still command. Leaders will be responsible for their actions. But information technology and our new organizations will allow more shared planning and decision-making, which will speed the battle command process and ensure that we set the pace of operations rather than our enemies doing so.

Diffusion

Diffusing or sharing innovative ideas is a problem for most organizations. Many companies have teams that develop new and innovative methods but then have difficulty sharing these ideas with the remainder of the company. Industry has invested a great deal of resources in information management systems to aid in sharing new ideas, but many continue to fail. Evidence of the failure of innovative ideas to be shared includes the discovery that another team has already developed the same idea and resistance to a new idea because another element of the organization invented it. The complexity may result in other people not understanding the new idea. One team may jump on the program but execute the idea poorly because it does not really understand it. People may be sufficiently arrogant to indicate that there is nothing new for them to learn. A lack of curiosity in an organization regarding new ideas can also inhibit the transfer of information.[67]

For the diffusion of new ideas to occur in an organization, innovators need someone who can coach them regarding how the organization functions. Organizational boundaries must be sufficiently permeable that new ideas can be considered. Communication channels must support the transfer of information. The organization must also have a learning culture that fosters collaboration and the sharing of new ideas and concepts.[68]

Since diffusion depends on the transfer of information, it is important to identify network leaders and to facilitate their actions as agents of change by passing information and by helping people respond to new requirements. Leaders must exploit formal and informal communication links, make information available, and not hide the work or new ideas being proposed. Leaders must also hold meetings with the people affected by new ideas and provide information directly to them. Army leadership should seek better means to disseminate information than those that currently exist, use the advances in information technology to disseminate information, and encourage people to think outside of the box. It is also important not to ridicule ideas even if they initially seem outside typical behavioral norms. Leaders should hold their subordinate leaders accountable for staying abreast of new ideas while also helping them learn how to maintain awareness of the latest conceptual issues and combat development programs.[69]

Making a profound change in an organization requires a long-term commitment. Change does not come overnight. People who are experts in the processes being changed must be available to one another in order to share experiences. Everyone in the organization must be prepared to learn. The organization must demonstrate the key elements of the program of change.[70] Army transformation is no different.

Changing the culture of the Army will take years. The materiel fielding of the equipment in the Future Combat System program will continue beyond 2020.[71] The company commanders of today will be the battalion commanders and brigade commanders using the equipment fielded as a result of transformation. The Army must begin to prepare them now, so that they are ready to lead our fighting units when the time comes. Combat developers and the soldiers in the present-day Army brigades must exchange ideas and experiences. The Army as an institution must adopt the culture and concepts that flow from this change process. Candor will reinforce integrity. The Army will learn from open discussion of our successes and our failures.

STRATEGY AND PURPOSE

Profound change requires consideration of the strategy and purpose of such action because change will leave a legacy—whether good or bad. Leaders must be aware of the impact of their actions and the actions of others. Negative feelings can last a long time and penalize future actions. Senior leader reactions are especially important because they can so quickly reinforce or terminate open discussion.[72]

New ideas about strategy and purpose can bump into obstacles that will not easily move. Discussing these issues opens decisions normally relegated to senior leaders to comment from junior members of an organization. If senior leaders discourage such open discussion, people with innovative ideas will be discouraged and seek fulfillment elsewhere.[73]

John Gordon and Jerry Solinger proposed a change in how the Army portrays itself to the civilian leadership. They believe that the Army should be more flexible in its view of its role on the battlefield. Gordon and Solinger believe the Army should focus on the lower end of the spectrum of conflict more because operations like Desert Storm and Iraqi Freedom occur much less frequently than support and stability operations in the Balkans or elsewhere. Army forces are clearly the dominant service in such environments. The emphasis on rapid deployment is too high. The Army must be able to deploy rapidly, but the present requirements under transformation are too restrictive. They also feel the Army must realize that in certain environments, the Army's campaign concepts may not prevail any longer. The improvements in precision weaponry and all-weather strike by aircraft dominate their reasoning for the Army rethinking its force structure and the use of land forces.[74]

The discussion of rethinking Army warfare roles is encouraging whether any of these ideas are adopted or not. The Army should reexamine what it does and how it functions in light of the changing environment. Sister services' capabilities have changed as well. Growing interdependence among all of the services may provide the opportunity to change how we use military power against an opponent. This rethinking must be critical and thorough. The Army cannot afford to sacrifice a needed capability solely in the interest of appearing politically correct or more joint than another service, but it also must be open to the discussion. Good ideas may result.

MAKING REVOLUTIONARY OR EVOLUTIONARY CHANGE

Maintaining the focus on revolutionary change is difficult for any organization. The time required to develop new materiel for the Army complicates this process because support for the change must continue for many years and through several changes of senior level leaders. Nonetheless, implementing revolutionary change promises the opportunity to inject surprise onto the battlefield. Surprise provides an opportunity to maintain the initiative in setting the conditions of interaction between combatants.

Revolutionary change can provide any organization an opportunity to surprise a competitor. A fundamental change in the manner of conducting operations can provide an advantage to the organization best able to make such change in comparison to other organizations with similar goals. Therefore, any organization may benefit from making a revolutionary change in comparison to a competitor. Revolutionary change may not be possible due to the inability to provide a basis for it; however, revolutionary change should be an organization's goal as long as it is in a competitive environment.

The external situation cannot be controlled; however, an organization's reaction to it can be. When envisioning a major change in operations, an organization's leadership should prepare the implementation plans while analyzing the impact against foreseeable changes in the external environment. Such analysis can provide for flexibility in plans, so that the likelihood of a major disruption due to external factors is reduced.

Revolutionary change can afford an organization the opportunity to set the terms for competition instead of being reactionary with regard to the environment. Evolutionary change allows an organization to maintain capability in relation to changes in technology or other external factors; however, this only promises to maintain the status quo or produce greater efficiencies in operations. Revolutionary change provides an opportunity to use the external environment as an advantage and not as a constraint. Revolutionary change also provides the opportunity to achieve an advantage over a competitor rather than simply compete. Therefore, if achievable within resource constraints, revolutionary change promises success. Implementation of such a level of change requires flexible planning, maintaining a clear vision, and ensuring understanding at all levels within an organization.

11

Future War

Violence will certainly continue as a means to settle disputes among nations for many years. There is nothing evident in human nature that implies that violence will end as a means to resolve conflicts. The collapse of the Soviet Union has made a major land war in Europe unlikely. This is good for Europeans and Americans because a major war would destroy virtually everything worth having and make large segments of land uninhabitable for years. However, exploring the future provides the opportunity to avoid a catastrophe resulting from a future surprise. Without a crystal ball, no prediction can hope to be precise. A useful goal is to minimize the error in the prediction through flexible preparation.[1]

CONTINUING COMPETITION

The changes in the European political environment in the last years of the twentieth century have brought more stability in Europe even if tensions remain in certain areas. Communism was a failure as implemented as a political and economic philosophy in Europe. The eastern European nations that formed the Warsaw Pact buffer zone for the Soviet Union have turned their backs on the Soviet system. The Soviet Union has collapsed into a group of independent nations with only a loose confederation remaining from a once seemingly monolithic empire. While this reduced tension regarding war in Europe is real, the stability that accompanied the previous bipolar world has not extended universally into the present and expected future.

For 45 years, western Europe was polarized into two camps, one prodemocracy and pro-United States, the other pro-Soviet Union. The threat of war revolved around the tension between the two superpowers, the United States and the Soviet Union. Western Europe (and some might say the world) was bipolar. These two powers, whether directly or indirectly, held others at bay. The conflict solidified the diverse cultures and nationalistic feelings against common enemies. Whether this solidification was voluntary or forced was immaterial. The important factor was that two relatively predictable groups existed. Foreign affairs in Europe focused on keeping the peace between two parties. That has now changed.

The democratic revolution in eastern Europe has reawakened nationalistic sentiments. The enforced alliance necessary to hold together the Soviet satellite nations has died. The final outcome of this process is unclear. Freedom-loving, tolerant, democratic governments may last. If so, peace in Europe may continue for a long time. However, if the old rivalries that tore at Europe for years reawaken, war may actually be more likely to occur. Fortunately, since the fall of the Soviet Union, only the Balkans and now the pervasive existence of terrorism have threatened an otherwise peaceful region.

Competition and the need to constrain the actions of other nations will continue. Power will continue to come from several sources. Military strength will be one source of power to achieve political objectives. Any event or need that interferes with peaceful interaction among nations will foster conflict. Nations, just like people, will continue to desire other nations' possessions, if those possessions will fulfill a real or perceived need. There is no reason to believe all nations are ready to forgo using their power to affect other nation's actions. A quick look around the world shows that many nations remain more than willing to exploit their power, including military power, to constrain and restrain other nations or to remove such limitations upon themselves.

The future will most likely continue the trend of less use of large military units fighting large military units than that normally envisioned when discussing land warfare. This does not mean another Desert Storm or Operation Iraqi Freedom will not occur. The United States must be ready to deploy heavy and light forces to protect its interests anywhere in the world. Other nations must be prepared to protect their interests as well. Certain nations will muster all of their military resources to fight other nations. Stress points still exist where major combat operations could occur. The Korean Peninsula is one such area. Iran remains a concern to its neighbors and much of the world due to its strategic location concerning the world's oil supply and its support of terrorist organizations. Tension between India and Pakistan could as yet explode into a major regional conflict that today might even include nuclear weapons. The world certainly is not going to be peaceful.

This belief that there is less likelihood of major combat operations than in the past in no way rules out the use of military forces. Conventional land, sea, and air forces will remain tools available to nations to protect themselves or destroy an enemy. Special operations will continue to be necessary in order to combat terrorism, rescue hostages, protect citizens in foreign nations, conduct peacekeeping operations, or perform other special missions as a government may require.

Larger states may also arm or otherwise support less powerful nations in exchange for their willingness to use military power to enforce the will of the major power. Such third-party help can be particularly useful if coercive violence of this kind cannot be traced to the major power but still serves the major power's needs. The Soviet Union used Cuba for years in this role.

Smaller nations will continue to fight each other. Some will have help from a major power or another nation. Others will have no help. As long as reasons exist for conflict, nations will use military power as a means to resolve the conflict. Some governments will also use their military forces, or police forces armed in a similar manner as military forces, to enforce unpopular policies on unwilling citizens.

Armed conflict will continue as long as national suicide is a necessary outcome of the conflict. Nations facing an opponent armed with nuclear weapons will take care not to excite a punitive response resulting in national suicide through a nuclear exchange. However, nuclear weapons are a threat only if their use is perceived to be likely. If the potential belligerent is convinced that nuclear weapons will not be used against it, then the nuclear weapons serve only to absorb resources and provide no benefit. Western nations will continue to face threats to their citizens and way of life due to small groups like terrorists and drug traffickers.

Security assistance through grants and loans of money or weapons and equipment will continue to be a way to assist an ally without becoming directly involved in a violent confrontation. Allies will remain important in order to protect economic ties, maintain peace in a geographical region, preserve an ideal such as freedom or democracy, and share the sacrifices required for a military response.

Coalition warfare has become increasingly important for the United States. The "peace dividend" that many called for when the Soviet Union no longer appeared to pose a major threat to American vital interests encouraged many to call for a reduction in the size of the U.S. military forces. The current war against insurgents in Iraq, nation-building in Afghanistan, and operations against terrorists around the world have made this dividend elusive indeed. The U.S. military is smaller today than it was at the height of the Cold War, when the Soviet Union was the perceived major threat. The coalition assembled by the United States to fight Iraq during Operation Desert Storm was necessary in order to ensure positive world opinion and the isolation of Iraq. This large team of nations was then able to generate sufficient combat power to overwhelm the Iraqi military quickly. By the time of Operation Iraqi Freedom, it was clear that the strength of the Iraqi military was an illusion.

The concept of a peace dividend was very popular in America. However, the reality has proved deceptive. It seemed logical that a reduced foreign threat should have meant a reduced military force requirement. However, the loss of the Soviet Union as a direct threat to Europe (and often by proxy to the rest of the world) has not eliminated all enemies of democracy and a freedom-loving way of life. The rise of radical anti-Western Islamic hatred has spawned the widespread instances of terrorism as a threat. Terrorism is not new, of course. However, this shift to nonstate and religious-based terrorism has made Islamic terrorism a difficult threat to counter.

The U.S. military will remain a mixture of forward deployed (i.e., overseas) and continental U.S.– or CONUS–based forces. However, the size of the force maintained overseas in permanent duty stations will reduce. CONUS forces are less expensive because their support costs such as transportation to move everything from people to rations to repair parts are smaller. Maintaining bases in this country also helps local economies. Basing in the United States makes support to families easier because their families are nearer and the culture is familiar. CONUS basing also provides more flexibility in the use of military forces because they are not already committed to a specific type of operational environment as can happen if stationed permanently overseas.

Actual military intervention will always be a possibility, since American citizens live and work outside national boundaries and America's economic well-being depends in part on international trade. Military action will occur if their lives or livelihood are endangered and if the government feels violent action is necessary to save them and is within the nation's best interests. Such action may be worth the cost in military lives and equipment in order to protect valuable national resources or to uphold the moral obligation a nation has to protect its citizens.

FORCE STRUCTURE

These changes in the threat should affect the military force structure. If the U.S. military fails to adjust its force structure, budget, materiel, and doctrine to meet any new threat, it would betray the trust the nation shows in it. Certainly, adjustments will occur. Argument among various elements of the government will occur as well as opinions provided by all the self-proclaimed or universally accepted experts. Congress will eventually reach some type of budgetary consensus. Money will decide the changes that result.

The United States and other nations will need naval forces to ensure free trade on the sea, show a presence in foreign lands, and deploy land forces overseas. If an army is to be a strategic force, it must be able to reach the point of conflict. Sea transport will remain a viable means of transporting merchandise. Water covers three-fourths of the globe. Ships will remain a relatively secure and inexpensive way to carry large amounts of raw materials or finished goods.

The extensive U.S. coastline and the expanse of water covering the globe will ensure the continued need for naval forces. There is no reason to believe oceangoing craft will be obsolete in the future. As long as ships remain an important means of economic interaction between nations, we will need a navy to protect America's economic interaction with other nations. Unless aircraft somehow exceed the cargo capacity or loiter time of ships, we also will need naval warships to project combat power worldwide. This will continue to include firepower and the transportation of forces capable of operating over land.

A navy will remain an easy way to display a national presence or threat of violence around the world. Surface ships are a visible symbol of national power, and many possess awesome firepower. When combined with naval-based land power forces such as the U.S. Marine Corps, a warship task force can provide air, naval, and land fires as well as naval and land maneuver forces. Functionally joint by nature, such a task force would provide a nation with a very flexible response to a threat.

Nations will need air forces to quickly reach foreign lands in order to deploy soldiers, support soldiers once deployed, and counter foreign air threats. Aircraft will continue to provide rapid transport, but the size of the cargo will limit the utility of aircraft for mechanized or armored forces. This is not meant to imply that aircraft will be less important than today. On the contrary, inland support of large land forces will require aircraft just as now. Given the need to rapidly deploy armored forces for contingency missions, armored vehicles must decrease in size and weight. This will then allow aircraft to more easily deploy and support armored forces. Light infantry forces must have some form of armored tank-killing system. Even third-rate powers have tanks.

Countering a sophisticated air threat will continue to demand a sophisticated air force. This is in addition to naval aircraft from aircraft carriers. Reaching a great distance inland will demand air forces supported by an established airbase on land. Any major war on land will require air forces to defeat the air threat and provide resupply by air and aerial fires against ground targets.

Armies will remain oriented toward conducting land operations. To do this, the U.S. Army will consist of forward-based and continental-based forces. As Edward Dewey has suggested, the active Army must be able to sustain itself for at least sixty days due to the War Powers Act requirement for Congressional approval and until reserve component units can mobilize and deploy.[2]

SPACE

Space system support for terrestrial forces is critical today with the increased reliance on information technologies that use platforms based in space for communication relay. Preventing a similarly equipped opponent from using such space support indicates the need to be able to attack another nation's space systems while defending friendly space systems. The farther we look into the future, the more extensive facilities in space and reliance on such support becomes.

Armies have always sought to seize terrain affording unrestricted observation of other terrain such as a battlefield. Outer space provides a dramatic leap in observation potential. The U.S. Army and the other U.S. military services must be interested in space. Observing the Earth or another celestial object from space is a vital concern of any military force. Whether viewed from that of exploitation or protection from observation from that medium, current and future military forces must consider their ability to operate in space or use assets positioned in space or the same abilities in the hands of a potential opponent.

The continued need for communication and navigation support from satellites is obvious. No reason exists to throw away this present capability. However, any type of combat action in space is more open to debate. The move to develop antisatellite missiles, lasers, satellites, or other weapons is not new. But the final outcome on the type of the weapon deployed will depend as much on arms control agreements as on technological feasibility. Whether through arms control, a weapon to destroy hostile systems, or a means to protect our own, the military leadership must determine how to employ and defeat space systems.

The more complicated issue, but rarely discussed in forums other than those associated with science fiction, is the question of combat involving manned systems. If war occurs between nations having astronauts in space, they could provide an observation or antisatellite platform. What do the nations do? Are astronauts worthy targets? Is there a way for them to defend themselves?

Obviously, any threat whether manned or unmanned is a valid target. Counteraction is permissible. If a nation has the ability to remove the threat, it should do so. Any other action would be irrational. Therefore, space systems are vulnerable because they cannot hide behind a physical object and still perform their function. They are valid targets.

Given that space systems are potential targets, who should defend them? Should each military service protect its own systems? Who should defend systems used by multiple services? Who should defend nonmilitary systems? Should we defend any of them?

Whether to defend space systems will be decided by the political leadership through the allocation of money. However, the military leadership must advise the political leaders as to appropriate options. The military leadership must plan to defend all national assets within the limits of available resources. Where resources do not allow successful defense, military leaders must point out the risk associated with this lack of resources. Government leaders then must decide if the risk is acceptable.

As with any question involving multiservice operations, decisions should rest on the capabilities or potential capabilities while considering the various services' traditional roles and strengths. However, space operations complicate this process, since all services have performed many of the same types of functions in space, including launching rockets, supplying astronauts, and using communication and navigation satellites. Just as with today's combatant commands in the U.S. Department of Defense, military operations in space must be the business of joint task forces, and as the name indicates, all services must participate.

LAND OPERATIONS

Military forces will continue to have utility in nontraditional roles. The military services are today and will remain in the future a source of organized and disciplined manpower and skilled workmen for combat and noncombat missions. Domestic threats will continue to plague nations. Armies will still represent a reserve manpower pool that can be used to fight forest fires, clean up after floods or hurricanes, or provide any other types of disaster relief. To expect otherwise would be foolish because a nation's political leadership must be able to use all resources at its disposal to overcome the difficulties it faces. Of course, such missions detract from attempts to train for combat—the present and future purpose of all military forces.

The military services must retain training for combat as a major focus. Training provides a national government a force that is capable of performing its missions. If the military services fail to train for war, they will not be able to fight when called upon. A failure to train in the future will result in needless deaths and the inability to win in battle.

Operations will be joint and often combined. Land operations will continue to require support in the air to attack deep targets and for protection from hostile aircraft. Land and air will remain inseparable, as both intend to control the ground and the population that resides there.

Land operations in the future will be nonlinear—or noncontiguous. Weapon lethality and range will continue to encourage organized bodies of combatants to disperse on the battlefield as far as is practical. Improvements in communications and sensors will enable military organizations to function while not in physical or even visual contact. A nonlinear battlefield has large spaces between units. Commanders must mass forces dispersed spatially in order to focus combat power on the destruction of an enemy force.

Smaller conventional forces with greater capabilities have the ability to disperse farther apart and dominate the same amount of land as much larger forces did many years ago. Improvements in sensor technology and long-range attack will enable this domination. Desert Storm was an indicator of the characteristics of this environment. The units on the western flank conducted operations with open flanks and great distances between adjacent units. They massed maneuver and fire support assets from multiple directions onto groups of Iraqi units. The combined effects of surprise, speed, and concentrated firepower unhinged the Iraqi defense.

In this case, the western flank coalition forces overwhelmed the linear Iraqi defensive plan with a nonlinear approach to fighting. Whether such a nonlinear operation was intended or not is immaterial. The effect on the ground was nonlinear. The physical and mental agility, technological superiority, training readiness, and leadership ensured that the risks inherently part of nonlinear operations such as dispersed forces with unprotected flanks did not become a problem. The coalition forces overwhelmed the Iraqis before they could stabilize the battlefield in order to exploit the advantages of the defense.

TECHNOLOGY

Technological advances will also continue to change the face of warfare. Anyone who dares to gaze too deeply into a crystal ball risks looking very foolish. Concepts that appear to have promise today may turn out to be only figments of an overactive imagination tomorrow. Resources may be insufficient to support the concept. Priorities for resource allocation may change. The basic infantryman will undergo radical change. Body armor has already improved dramatically and saved soldiers' lives in Iraq and Afghanistan. The use of improvised explosive devices has resulted in a large number of limb amputations, while current helmet and body armor advances have saved vital organs. Until a complete armored suit can be fielded, ballistic protection will not be all inclusive. However, soldier protection has certainly improved a great deal in recent years.

The U.S. Army's Land Warrior and Future Force Warrior programs may radically change how infantrymen and other soldiers fight. If the programs succeed, the individual soldier will have the level of decision support and situational awareness that is today only available to soldiers physically inside a vehicle or platform of some sort. This will provide the opportunity for radical change in how small units operate on the battlefield.

If soldiers and small units know where they and the enemy are located with the precision to mass effects from a range that provide the inherent protection of distance, then these small elements can maintain a freedom of maneuver that is well beyond that of today. Small units would have the ability to prosecute attacks against multiple hostile targets in quick succession while maintaining a protective posture. Spatial separation of small units and possibly soldiers themselves would rely on the range of weapons rather than including the added necessity of a leader personally and physically indicating a point of attack. Fire and maneuver will remain essential elements of small unit tactics; however, the distances separating small units and soldiers could increase. It remains to be seen how far apart soldiers can be and still function coherently over time. The physical presence of another person will always be important for psychological and emotional reinforcement, but physical presence of several soldiers will not be required for navigation and communication.

Someday an armored suit may be possible once power and exoskeletal mechanical systems mature; however, even this will not make the infantryman impervious to attack. No body armor or fully armored suit will be able to withstand the impact of a cannon-launched projectile. Any improvement in armor may be followed by a corresponding improvement in antiarmor weaponry. However, an armored infantryman could withstand attack by today's riflemen. Such an infantryman would have great utility as long as the opposing infantry were not armored. In an age of declining numbers of uniformed personnel as well as the shrinkage in the pool of young people available for recruitment, anything that enhances the combat capability of the individual soldier is worth consideration.

Improved situation awareness and protection would be particularly useful in certain special operations. An armored infantry could assault a terrorist/hostage situation without having to worry about being injured by the terrorists. The armored infantry personnel could concentrate on shooting terrorists or any enemy not similarly equipped without fear of injury to themselves.

Using some sort of exoskeletal suit would also allow the infantry personnel to carry additional weaponry. The structure of the suit should support carrying multiple systems such as an automatic weapon system and possibly an antitank or antiaircraft missile system. Accuracy of the weapon system would depend on the sighting system built into the suit helmet.

Armored vehicles will provide a protected weapon system and a means of transporting personnel and materiel. Advances in armor technology should enhance the protection they provide. Composite armor will reduce the weight of armored vehicles and allow the hardening of logistical vehicles. Common chasses for multiple vehicle types will ease repair parts resupply and reduce the training necessary for mechanics and operators. Commonality among system operation and maintenance requirements will provide a redundancy of functional capability in both areas.

Directed energy weapons will change the manner in which targets are attacked and the requirements for physical protection. It has been clear for years that laser rangefinders pose an eye hazard. Even if the United States does not allow the use of lasers to intentionally blind people, the step to a system designed to inflict eye or other injury to soldiers is not an insurmountable one. Laser weapons also have the potential to damage hostile optical systems. As technology reduces the size of laser weapons they will become more and more useful.

The age of the handheld ray gun so popular in science fiction may not yet be here, but it seems reasonable to estimate that such weapons are not an impossible technical challenge. The U.S. Air Force has developed a rifle-sized eyesight dazzler laser weapon. Lasers are undergoing testing to destroy vehicles from the air if mounted on airborne platforms, as well as mines and explosives from ground systems. Lasers have also shown that they can destroy indirect fire munitions while the munitions are in flight.[3] Lasers will alter the types of defensive systems necessary for protection as well as the medical skills required to care for the wounded. As with any new device, new logistical requirements and training programs will follow.

Lasers are not the only types of directed energy weapon systems that may operate on the future battlefield. Experimentation is aimed at using high-powered microwaves to disable vehicles. Millimeter wave technology can be used to repel humans by agitating the water molecules under a person's skin to make the person feel extreme heat when hit with the beam. This can be a deterrent to actions or movement in a certain direction.[4]

Directed energy will have an impact on much more than ground operations and the soldiers located there. Given the power and fire control system required, directed energy could be used for lethal and nonlethal attacks in air, naval, and space operations. Atmospheric conditions will continue to be a consideration when planning to use directed energy weapons. Nonetheless, such weapons will be factors on the future battlefield.

New propellants will provide increased range for indirect fire systems. Liquid propellants could provide the capability to precisely measure the propellant required to fire a projectile to a specific range. This would enhance the precision of indirect fire systems by only providing the propellant to launch a projectile a specific distance. Using liquid propellants would also change the storage requirements for ammunition. The precise metering of charges would decrease the amount of excess propellant that is today associated with bags of artillery powder. Instead of boxes or tubes of powder, propellant could be stored in drums or barrels.

Electromagnetic propulsion is another possible weapon improvement, using electrical energy to accelerate a projectile through a gun tube at extremely high speeds. This would provide greater range possibilities as well as a reduced logistical burden. Storing and transporting powder would cease to be a burden. However, the power system to support such a system is not yet practical for land warfare platforms.

New fuels should reduce the logistical structure necessary to support the heavy, or armored, force. More efficient engines coupled with more powerful fuels will reduce the fuel usage rates and the amount of fuel required to support a given force size. This will allow forces to move greater distances more quickly by using vehicles that move faster and having a smaller logistical train to project forward.

The need to deploy ground forces rapidly to a distant shore will force an improvement in sealift and airlift capability for the United States. Whether through new and larger aircraft or faster shipping, the United States and any other nation relying on deployment from a sanctuary home to an area of operations some distance away must produce the sealift and airlift to support the requirement.

Robotic system developments will reduce the crews of many systems. This could eventually eliminate the crews for certain weapon systems. Robotics may allow tank crew reduction to two, possibly one soldier. If a sophisticated fighter aircraft with a one-man crew is possible, a one-man tank platform with a weapon system ought to be feasible. Performing routine maintenance might exceed the capability of one person; nonetheless placing fewer crew members at risk in combat ought to be possible.

Remotely piloted vehicles, or unmanned aerial vehicles or unmanned aerial systems, have already shown the possibility of separating a vehicle from its crew. The U.S. Army's Future Combat System program includes a number of robotic or unmanned systems for reconnaissance and attack. Separating the crew and the vehicle complicates the target attack process but also increases crew protection through separation. As long as technological advances continue to improve the artificial intelligence capability that can be integrated with a remotely controlled or even semiautonomous vehicle, the ability to maneuver combat and surveillance platforms without a dedicated onboard crew will grow. Employment of robotic vehicles will grow as a means of protecting that most precious resource of people.

Computer advances will speed information transfer and processing. This will allow the immediate collection, sorting, and prioritization of massive amounts of information. Computers will provide more accurate fire control to allow precise target engagement over greater distances than today. Commanders will rely more on computers for information and analysis of that information. Information exchange and processing will form the basis for all technological advances included in future forces.

There is a danger in this reliance on computers. Reliance on computers could rob us of our ability to use our minds. If we rely on a black box for every answer and assume the black box is always right, we run a terrible risk. A computer will only provide a correct answer if the parameters of the problem match its program. Failure may result if the unexpected, meaning not programmed, occurs. Military leaders must always remember that decisions must rest in the hands of people, not machines. When a machine makes a decision, it is simply running a program.

Intelligence collection and target acquisition capabilities will increase, so that deception and operation security will become more important than ever. Deception will be more difficult and will rely on electronic signals in order to mislead sensors. Sensor improvements will challenge the ability to process the raw information into usable intelligence.

Units will need to remain dispersed as much as possible but be capable of massing their fires, direct and indirect, on enemy targets. The threat of weapons of mass destruction whether nuclear, chemical, or biological will demand that units remain physically separated in order to avoid presenting a lucrative target. Physical separation will also make deceiving an opponent as to objectives and the correlation of forces on the battlefield more difficult. Massing the effects of the available fires will be the method of destroying an enemy. Indirect fires and long-range direct fires will be the primary means of killing.

WEAPONS OF MASS DESTRUCTION

Weapons of mass destruction will remain a threat. The risk of their use between major powers has diminished. It is highly unlikely that Russia or any member of the North Atlantic Treaty Organization (NATO) will launch a nuclear attack. However, the likelihood of their use in other conflicts including terrorist attacks will increase. More nations will seek nuclear capability as proof of their technological and military might. Chemical weapons will remain a threat as long as nations can produce the compounds. Biological weapons such as anthrax are difficult to harness but are threats that nations must be prepared to face. Industrial chemicals and homemade bombs made from items such as fertilizer will continue to be threats as well. For standard military forces, dispersion combined with the capability to mass the effects of fires over great distances will minimize the target array presented for destruction.

As less powerful nations enhance their weapon production capabilities through the spread of technology, they will rely less on foreign-supplied arms whether conventional or the basis of weapons of mass destruction. This will reduce the U.S. and other Western nations' ability to deter war in the world by pressuring other more highly developed nations to limit arms sales to potential areas of conflict. Once nations or groups hostile to a nation or group of nations develop the ability to produce threats without having to rely on more developed countries' technological base, the ability to deter their use becomes problematic.

The rise of Islamic fundamentalist terrorism that is hostile to Western democratic civilization is a special concern. Religious fervor tends toward the extreme. One need only consider the events of September 11, 2001, where three aircraft rammed buildings and a fourth would have done so if it were not for the courageous resistance by the passengers and crew in order to understand the danger of religious extremism. When someone believes God tells them to act, there is no limit to the believer's willingness to do so. Such misguided people are a very dangerous threat to society at large and civilization in general. An attack by a religiously motivated terrorist using a weapon of mass destruction promises to impose extreme horror on his victims. In this case, religion will encourage a terrorist to inflict the maximum amount of pain on innocent people—people who are generally considered innocent in Western culture's eyes but not in the eyes of the terrorist. Instead the victims are guilty by association with Western society or simply the cost of imposing God's will. This runs in stark contrast to the general Christian belief that such intent to hurt the innocent is morally wrong.

A NEW FORM OF WAR?

Thomas Hammes has proposed that a new form of warfare has developed, Fourth Generation Warfare or 4GW. Mao Tse-tung began this form of warfare when confronted with a conventional opponent that he cold not defeat through conventional means. Changes in society have continued to affect the concepts of insurgent actions in order to confront an adversary with a large degree of military power. The process has been painful for the people who have exercised this style of warfare with losses in combat often being the principal means of learning.[5]

Hammes posits that the U.S. military and industrial leadership focuses too much on technology as a solution to future warfare concerns; however, the United States has erred because technology is not the sole answer and technology applied to old methods of fighting actually sets the United States behind present and future opponents. The U.S. Department of Defense continues to use technology to centralize decision-making, when much of the world is using technology to support decentralization of decision-making.[6]

Fourth Generation Warfare focuses political, economic, social, and military networks on defeating an enemy's political leadership. Hammes contends that warfare evolves; there are no revolutions in warfare. Fourth Generation Warfare is an evolution of insurgency as a means of defeating an opponent's political will while avoiding direct military confrontation where possible.[7]

Mao Tse-tung stated that guerilla warfare is not new and that such warfare is characteristic of the struggle against an invader. He also pointed out that every guerilla war has its own special characteristics. He emphasized the importance of ensuring that soldiers waging a guerilla war and the people who reside in the area of operations understand the political aspects of such a struggle.[8]

Whether this is a new form of warfare or simply a case of smart people adapting to the situations that they face, it is clear that the rise of nonstate groups opposing nations on the level seen today requires study and a broad approach to combat. Military action alone is not the answer. The underlying reasons for the violence are important, not simply opposing every act of violence with military action. Targeting action whether political, economic, or military is difficult when faced with an opponent lacking an obvious base or open leadership for negotiation or destruction. The disparate groups who seem to join forces to combat nations complicate identifying a decisive point or center of gravity upon which to focus action. Nonetheless this complexity then demands thorough analysis and a multifaceted approach for the application of power against such an opponent. The difficulty in achieving peace and security in Afghanistan and Iraq are examples of the challenges that political and military leaders face in devising an appropriate strategy and the operations and tactics to implement that strategy.

Witnessing Israel's 2006 invasion of Lebanon in order to destroy Hezbollah terrorist forces that have attacked Israel for years and kidnapped two Israeli soldiers is an example of the difficulty of defeating a nonstate group that hides in the population of a third party, Lebanon, and then projects a sympathetic image to segments of the world. Israel has a great deal of experience fighting terrorists and surrounding hostile Arab states. However, the difficulty in selective targeting to avoid "innocent" civilian deaths while still killing sufficient enemy fighters causes another question to come to mind. Instead of trying to fight insurgents or 4GW practitioners in this complex environment without causing harm to the surrounding population, does the only way to win and end the conflict require resorting to the Third Generation Warfare approach of the World War II generation? Is it possible to win in today's environment without resorting to extreme violence and the virtual annihilation of an opponent?

By these questions, I am not advocating such an approach. However, the frustration of trying to achieve security in such a violent world as exists in certain regions brings to mind this issue. Maybe my concern evolves from my bias as having been raised in a world that looked to the conventional military actions of World War II as the only satisfactory way to fight a war: commit to the destruction of an opponent—inflict sufficient pain, so that everyone in the target country knows that they lost.

Certainly the best means to achieve victory or security today requires study and consideration. Devising means to combat these nonstate actors and religion-based groups and even nations merits attention, or someone may be faced with surrender or all-out military action to annihilate an opponent regardless of the collateral damage (dead and injured noncombatants). Finding a means of dealing a shock to the opponents so that they understand that they have lost the war is becoming more difficult in this age of international media exposure and a general reluctance to impose violence on noncombatants. If the liberal democracies fail to devise a means of changing the conditions that give birth to radical religious or other ideologies, then the demands and fears associated with war will encourage either surrender or the use of more massive levels of violence to avoid destruction.

PRIMARY CONSTANT

In many ways, the face of war will change, but in many other ways it will remain the same. Technology will produce new weapons and equipment. The competition for resources and power over one's environment will continue to result in conflict among nations. Regardless of the changes in technology or the environment, people will remain the one indispensable resource necessary for waging war or conducting other military operations. That will never change.

People will always be the linchpin of all military actions. They will fire the weapons, make decisions, and repair equipment just as now. No leader, military or civilian, who attempts to use military force can succeed if he or she neglects people, the essence of war's moral nature. To do so would be to invite disaster. Such catastrophes will occur, of course. History is full of such failures, and there is no reason to believe humankind is smart enough not to make such mistakes in the future. However, those who want to avoid mistakes will do well to remember this warning: War's moral nature is inescapable. Ignore it or abuse it at great risk.

12

The Constants

War is a human drama with many faces. It is a tool of national power. It is a means for one nation to force another to do its bidding. It is a way to constrain and restrain the actions of another or to eliminate the same imposed by another. War enslaves and it frees. War protects and it destroys. War can bring glory and fame to a victor while inflicting great pain on a loser.

A nation derives power from the use of this tool. A successful outcome in war provides a nation the freedom to act in its best interests. It also provides a nation the ability to force other nations or opponents to act in its best interest.

War is also too restrictive a term when discussing the breadth of feasible military actions. An army can do much more than fight. Military personnel are principally trained and organized to use violence or the threat of violence to enforce a nation's will. However, they also remain a disciplined, organized body of people who can maintain themselves in difficult circumstances. This makes them useful in nation support tasks such as disaster relief. They are also available to train an ally's military forces, which can support national goals by precluding commitment of a nation's military to support an ally. Strong allies can protect themselves.

To ensure a nation's military is prepared to perform nonviolent missions these tasks must be seen as valuable and appreciated. Soldiers, as do all people, find fulfillment when they see a positive gain from an action. The goal must be one they can achieve. The rewards must equal those provided to soldiers who perform other missions.

A great danger in using soldiers to perform missions other than war is that it diverts their time and attention from their primary mission. Associated with this is the problem of the soldiers' inclination to fully apply the violence possible from their weapons if also required to show restraint in the use of such force. Soldiers may show insufficient or too much restraint at the wrong time.

Defining a spectrum of conflict or range of possible options of the use of military power is not simple. Lists exist. However, there are no universal criteria for categorizing military actions that seem able to survive the periodic reviews of doctrine. Any system is prone to leave out or not fully explain a critical element.

Categorizing military operations in the various ways to portray a spectrum of conflict hides the interaction of the different types of operations. Special operations can support conventional armored formations. Nation-building can occur at the same time as armies grapple for supremacy in a major battle. Clear divisions do not exist. Trying to force operational descriptions into distinct groups that do not overlap is unwise. One type of operation may dominate the others; however, today's military forces must be prepared for multiple types of missions occurring simultaneously in close proximity to one another.

Levels of war also lack clear divisions. The central issue of constraint and restraint binds together actions along the continuum of levels of war. However, even though the divisions are not clear, differences exist among the levels when examining the issues of time, space, and objective.

Rather than focusing on levels of war and the force sizes associated with them, the cognitive activities associated with these descriptions is important. Strategy establishes the ultimate goal. Tactics is the employment of forces on the battlefield. The operational level links a series of tactical outcomes to accomplish the strategic end state.

Operational art really describes a style of warfare that came into being as the size of armies and technology expanded the battlefield in the late nineteenth century. This expansion resulted in a single battle not deciding the outcome of a war. Instead, a series of operations distributed in time and space became necessary to ensure victory.

Another way to view war is through its three natures—physical, cognitive, and moral. The physical nature includes those observable, measurable, and quantifiable factors that compose the environment in which war takes place. War occurs within a physical environment that must be overcome or exploited. Technology cannot be ignored in any study of war. It provides the weapons and equipment that armies use. It imposes limitations on actions and may provide one belligerent an advantage over another.

The cognitive nature of war encompasses the decision-making process that governs military actions. Leaders establish the focus or vision that guides all action. The command and control process ensures that subordinates attain the goal set.

The moral nature of war addresses the human factor. Wars cannot be fought without people. War affects people, and people affect war. War's moral nature is the crucial element that must not be forgotten. War evolves from human conflict.

Regardless of the elements of power used to resolve the conflict, a battlefield will exist. The term signifies the arena for conflict resolution. In war a physical space serves as the battlefield, but the minds of the opponents are critical when employing a national will or political power. Financial institutions and markets serve as the focus when economic power is at work.

Today all elements of power interact in varying degrees in all conflicts. Recognition of this complexity is critical if an appropriate plan of action is to be found.

The future will bring many changes, but many things will also remain unchanged. Technology will provide new weapons and equipment. Allies may change, but military forces will remain a tool of power.

War remains a human activity. People operate the weapons and equipment used to prosecute any effort. People also establish the end state desired and design the plan to achieve it. The moral domain, then, permeates every aspect of war. Those contemplating the use of military force must always remember this principal characteristic of war.

As long as people exist, war will continue in one form or another. The desire for power over others and our communal instinct will ensure that groups, such as nations, exist and compete with one another. Some might consider it a curse. It is a fact.

Attempts to eliminate conflict are commendable because war is so terrible; however, short of the end of times predicted by numerous religions, true peace among all peoples is unlikely. Conflict, even if only in an economic vein, will continue.

That is no reason to stop trying to bring peace or to swamp the world with our military arsenal. That is also no reason to commit suicide because there is no end in sight to the violent strife that composes war. Unless you are prepared to withdraw from the human race, you must reconcile yourself to our competitive nature and deal with it as best you can. In other words, people and nations must confront the issue of war and deal with it, not ignore it. They must also be prepared to accept the consequences of the decisions, good or bad. Anything else is folly. Military force is one way to deal with conflict.

Nations must assemble the military force they need to accomplish their objectives in the manner in which they want to accomplish them within the resources available. Leaders with the responsibility to protect the nation must then use the tools available to do so. Military force will not always be the preferred alternative, but it will always be one option. Force is sometimes the only answer.

Notes

CHAPTER 1

1. Carl von Clausewitz, *On War*, ed. and trans. by Michael Howard and Peter Paret (Princeton: Princeton University Press, 1976), 88.

2. Thomas Hobbes, *Leviathan*, ed. by Richard Tuck (Cambridge: Cambridge University Press, 1991), 70–71.

3. Carl von Clausewitz, *On War*, 69, and 87–88.

4. Ibid., 75.

5. William C. Johnson, *Public Policy: Policy, Politics, and Practice*, 2nd ed. (Madison, WI: Brown and Benchmark Publishers, 1996), 2. Portions of this chapter are extracts from an unpublished paper from my doctoral studies; see John M. House, "What is Public Administration?" (student paper, Northcentral University, January 4, 2004).

6. Ibid., 6–8.

7. Ibid., 15–17

8. David M. Walker, "9/11: The Implications for Public-sector Management," *Public Administration Review*, 62, special Issue (September 2002): 94–95.

9. William C. Johnson, *Public Policy*, 18.

10. Woodrow Wilson, "The Study of Administration," in Richard J. Stillman, *Public Administration: Concepts and Cases*, 6th ed. (Boston: Houghton Mifflin Company, 1996), 6.

11. Richard J. Stillman, *Public Administration: Concepts and Cases*, 6th ed. (Boston: Houghton Mifflin Company, 1996), 54—56 and 63–64.

12. Ibid., 86–87.

13. Ibid., 104–106.

14. H. Kaufman, "Major players: Bureaucrats in American Government," *Public Administration Review* 61, no.1 (January–February 2001): 18–42.

15. These elements of power are a compilation of concepts from my notes after attending the command and general staff officers course and the school of advanced military studies at Fort Leavenworth's Command and General Staff College and the Naval War College.

16. U.S. Department of State, Papers Relating to the Foreign Relations of the United States, 1917, Supplement 2, The World War, Vol. 1, message from acting secretary of the treasury to the secretary of state, 6 July 1917, 536; U.S. Congress, Senate, "Loans to Foreign Governments," S. Doc. 86, 67th Cong., 2nd sess., 1921, 89; Richard Goldhurst, *The Midnight War* (New York: McGraw-Hill, 1978), 27.

17. National Archives, M917, Reel 10, Graves, "Operations to 30 June 1919," 13–14.

18. John Spanier, *Games Nations Play*, 5th ed. (New York: CBS College-Holt, Rinehart and Winston, 1984), 80–81.

19. Geoffrey Blainey, *The Causes of War* (New York: The Free Press, 1973), 111–112.

20. Carl von Clausewitz, *On War*, 75–76, 96–97, and 149.

21. Kim R. Holmes, "Defining National Security and American Interests," in *A Safe and Prosperous America: A U.S. Foreign and Defense Policy Blueprint* (Washington, DC: The Heritage Foundation, 1994), 8, 13, and 16.

22. Barry R. Posen and Andrew L. Ross, "Competing U.S. Grand Strategies," in *Strategy and Force Planning* (Newport, RI: U.S. Naval War College, 1995), 117–118.

23. Ibid., 125–126, and 129–130.

24. Ibid., 122–123.

25. Ibid., 119–120.

26. Richard K. Betts, "Systems for Peace or Causes of War? Collective Security, Arms Control, and the New Europe," *International Security* 17, no. 1 (Summer 1992): 6 and 9.

27. Richard N. Haass, "Paradigm Cost," *Foreign Affairs* 72, no. 1 (January–February 1995): 51.

28. Charles A. Kupchan and Clifford A. Kupchan, "The Promise of Collective Security," *International Security* 20, no. 1 (Summer 1995): 58.

29. Richard K. Betts, "Systems for Peace or Causes of War?" 17–19.

30. Ashton B. Carter, William J. Perry, and John D. Steinbruner, *A New Concept of Cooperative Security* (Washington, DC: The Brookings Institution Press, 1992), 7.

31. Edward C. Luck, "Making Peace," *Foreign Policy*, no. 89 (Winter 1992–1993): 149.

32. James E. Nolan, "The Concept of Cooperative Security," in Global Engagement and Security in the 21st Century, ed. James E. Nolan (Washington, DC: The Brookings Institution Press, 1994), 5.

33. Michael Howard, *The Causes of War*, 2nd ed., (Cambridge, MA: Harvard University Press, 1983), 15 and 131.

34. Carl von Clausewitz, *On War*, 75–76, 96–97, and 149.

35. Samuel P. Huntington, *The Clash of Civilizations and the Remaking of World Order* (New York: Simon & Schuster, 1996), 97, 128–130, 215, and 310–311.

CHAPTER 2

1. U.S. Army, *FM 100-20: Low-Intensity Conflict* (Washington, DC: U.S. Government Printing Office, 1981), 14.

2. Barry Crane, Joel Lesan, Robert Plebanek, Paul Shemella, Ronald Smith, and Richard Williams, "Between Peace and War: Comprehending Low-Intensity Conflict," *Special Warfare* 2 (Summer 1989): 7.

3. Ibid.

4. Ibid., 8.

5. Ibid.

6. Ibid.

7. Carl von Clausewitz, *On War*, ed. and trans. by Michael Howard and Peter Paret (Princeton: Princeton University Press, 1976), 77.

8. U.S. Department of Defense, *The National Defense Strategy of the United States of America* (Washington, DC: U.S. Government Printing Office, March 2005), 2–3.

9. U.S. Army, *FM 1: The Army* (Washington, DC: U.S. Government Printing Office, June 2005), 3–4.

10. Ibid., 3–7.

11. Ibid., 3–5.

CHAPTER 3

1. U.S. Army, *Oaths of Enlistment and Oaths of Office*, http://www.army.mil/cmh-pg/faq/oaths.htm (accessed July 31, 2006).

2. Alexander Hamilton, James Madison, and John Jay, "Paper No. 8: The Federalist," in *"American State Papers; the Federalist, on Liberty; Representative Government; Utilitarianism—Great Books of the Western World Series, No. 43* (Chicago: Encyclopedia Britannica, Inc., 1952), 44.

3. Alexander Hamilton, James Madison, and John Jay, "Paper No. 28," in *"American State Papers; the Federalist, on Liberty; Representative Government; Utilitarianism—Great Books of the Western World Series, No. 43* (Chicago: Encyclopedia Britannica, Inc., 1952), 96.

4. John M. Gates, *Schoolbooks and Krags: The United States Army in the Philippines, 1898–1902* (Westport, CT: Greenwood, 1973), 277–281.

5. Robert E. Quirk, *An Affair of Honor: Woodrow Wilson and the Occupation of Veracruz* (New York: W.W. Norton and Company, 1967), 129–153.

6. Craig T. Trebilock, "The Myth of Posse Comitatus," *Journal of Homeland Security* (October 2000), http://www.homelandsecurity.org/journal/articles/Trebilcock.htm (accessed December 8, 2005).

7. John R. Brinkerhoff, "The Posse Comitatus Act and Homeland Security," *Journal of Homeland Security* (February 2002), http://www.homelandsecurity.org/journal/Articles/brinkerhoffpossecomitatus.htm (accessed December 8, 2005).

8. David Isenburg, "Posse Comitatus: Caution is Necessary," *CDI Terrorism Project*, August 6 2002, http://www.cdi.org/terrorism/pcomitatus-pr.cfm (accessed December 8, 2005).

9. Bonnie Baker, "The Origins of Posse Comitatus," *Air & Space Chronicles* (November 1, 1999), http://www.airpower.maxwell.af.mil/airchronicles/cc/baker1.html (accessed December 8, 2005).

10. John R. Brinkerhoff, "The Posse Comitatus Act and Homeland Security."

CHAPTER 4

1. U.S. Department of Defense. *Joint Publication 3-0: Doctrine for Joint Operations* (Washington, DC: U.S. Government Printing Office, September 10, 2001), II-2. Portions of Chapter 4 are extracts from a major paper written for one of my master's degrees; see John M. House, "Do Doctrinal Buzzwords Obscure the Meaning of Operational Art?" (master's major paper, U.S. Army Command and General Staff College, SAMS, Fort Leavenworth, KS, April 1989).

2. Carl von Clausewitz, *On War*, ed. and trans. by Michael Howard and Peter Paret (Princeton: Princeton University Press, 1976), 128.

3. Antoine H. Jomini, *The Art of War*, trans. by G.H. Mendell and W.P. Craighill, reprint ed. (Westport, CT: Greenwood, 1977), 69.

4. Baron von der Goltz, *The Conduct of War: A Brief Study of Its Most Important Principles and Forms*, trans. by Joseph T. Dickman (Kansas City, MO: Franklin Hudson Co., 1896), 30.

5. John G. Burr, *The Framework of Battle* (Philadelphia: J.B. Lippincott Co., 1943), 17–20.

6. Quincy Wright, *A Study of War* (Chicago: The University of Chicago Press, 1971), 291–292.

7. Michael Howard, *Studies in War and Peace* (New York: The Viking Press, 1971), 170–175.

8. Trevor N. Dupuy, *Understanding War: History and Theory of Combat* (New York: Paragon House, 1987), 68 and 70.

9. Edward N. Luttwak, *Strategy: The Logic of War and Peace* (Cambridge, MA: The Belknap Press, 1987), 4.

10. David M. Glantz, "The Nature of Soviet Operational Art," *Parameters* 15, no. 1 (Spring 1985): 2–3; V.D. Sokolovskiy, *Soviet Military Strategy*, ed. and trans. by Harriett Fast Scott (New York: Crane, Russak, and Company, Inc., 1985), 239–240.

11. U.S. Army, *FM 100-2-1: The Soviet Army: Operations and Tactics* (Washington, DC: U.S. Government Printing Office, July 16, 1984), 2–1.

12. Aleksandr A. Svechin, *Strategy* (Minneapolis: East View, 1992) 69.

13. William K. Naylor, *The Principles of Strategy* (Fort Leavenworth, KS: General Services Schools Press, 1920), 13, 14 and 206; U.S. Army, *The Principles of Strategy for an Independent Corps or Army in a Theater of Operations* (Fort Leavenworth, KS: The Command and General Staff School Press, 1936), 7.

14. U.S. Army, *FM 100-5: Field Service Regulations—Operations* (Washington, DC: U.S. Government Printing Office, 1962), 4.

15. U.S. Army, *FM 100-5: Operations* (Washington, DC: U.S. Government Printing Office, 1982), 2–3.

16. U.S. Army, *FM 100-5: Operations* (Washington, DC: U.S. Government Printing Office, 1986), 9.

17. U.S. Army, *FM 100-1: The Army* (Washington, DC: U.S. Government Printing Office, 1986), 13; U.S. Army, *FM 100-6: Large Unit Operations*, coordinating draft (Fort Leavenworth, KS: U.S. Army Command and General Staff College, September 30, 1987), 1–1.

18. Joint Chiefs of Staff, *JCS Pub 1: Dictionary of Military and Associated Terms* (Washington, DC: U.S. Government Printing Office, June 1, 1987), 232, 244, and 350.

19. U.S. Army, *FM 3-0: Operations* (Washington, DC: U.S. Government Printing Office, June 2001), 2–2; U.S. Army, *FM 3-0: Operations* (Washington, DC: U.S. Government Printing Office, February 2008), 6–2.

20. Joint Chiefs of Staff, *Joint Publication 3-0: Doctrine for Joint Operations* (Washington, DC: Joint Chiefs of Staff, 2001), GL-16.

21. Joint Chiefs of Staff, *Joint Publication 3-0: Joint Operations* (Washington, DC: Joint Chiefs of Staff, September 17, 2006); Joint Chiefs of Staff, *Joint Publication 3-0: Joint Operations*, incorporating Change 1, (Washington, DC: Joint Chiefs of Staff, February 13, 2008), GL-26. See also Joint Chiefs of Staff, *Joint Publication (JP) 1-02: Department of Defense Dictionary of Military and Associated Terms* (Washington, DC: Joint Chiefs of Staff, April 12, 2001); Joint Chiefs of Staff, *Joint Publication 1-02: Department of Defense Dictionary of Military and Associated Terms*, amended version, (Washington, DC: Joint Chiefs of Staff, August 2005), 509 for a similar definition.

22. *Merriam-Webster's Collegiate Dictionary*, 9th edition (Springfield, IL: Merriam-Webster, Inc., 1987), 1165.

23. Carl von Clausewitz, *On War*, 128.

24. Antoine H.Jomini, *The Art of War*, 322.

25. John G. Burr, *The Framework of Battle*, 18.

26. Quincy Wright, *A Study of War*, 291.

27. Trevor N. Dupuy, *Understanding War*, 71.

28. B.H. Liddell Hart, *Strategy*, 2nd revised edition (New York: Frederick A. Praeger, 1967), 335.

29. U.S. Army, *FM 100-2-1*, 2–1.

30. U.S. Army, *The Principles of Strategy for an Independent Corps or Army*, 8.

31. U.S. Army, *FM 100-5* (1982), 2–3.

32. U.S. Army, *FM 100-5* (1986), 10.

33. Joint Chiefs of Staff, *JCS Pub 1*, 363.

34. *Merriam-Webster's*, 1201.

35. U.S. Army, *FM 3-0* (2001), 2-5; U.S. Army, *FM 3–0* (2008), 6–3.

36. Joint Chiefs of Staff, *JP 1-02* (2001), 526.

37. David M. Glantz, "The Nature of Soviet Operational Art," 3.

38. James J. Schneider, "The Theory of Operational Art" (theoretical paper no. 3, draft, SAMS, Fort Leavenworth, KS, March 1, 1988), 9–11.

39. Chris Bellamy, *The Future of Land Warfare* (New York: St. Martin's Press, 1987), 105.

40. Ibid., 105; David M. Glantz, "The Nature of Soviet Operational Art," 4–5; Jacob Kipp, *Mass, Mobility, and the Red Army's Road to Operational Art, 1918–1936* (Fort Leavenworth, KS: Soviet Army Studies Office, U.S. Army Combined Arms

Center, n.d.), 5 and 8; David M. Glantz, "Soviet Operational Art in Perspective," in *The Art of War Quarterly, Volume III, pages 1-37* (Carlisle Barracks, PA: U.S. Army War College, February 1, 1984), 13.

41. Richard E. Simpkin, *Race to the Swift* (New York: Brassey's Defense, 1985), 14. For a discussion of the history of operational theory, see Shimon Naveh, *In Pursuit of Military Excellence: The Evolution of Operational Theory* (London: Frank Cass, 1997).

42. Clayton R. Newell, "Exploring the Operational Perspective," *Parameters* 16, no. 3 (Autumn 1986): 19, 36.

43. U.S. Army, *FM 100-5* (1986), 10.

44. Joint Chiefs of Staff, *JCS Pub 1*, 34, 370.

45. Dwight L. Adams and Clayton R. Newell, "Operational Art in the Joint and Combined Arenas," *Parameters* 18, no. 2 (June 1988): 36.

46. U.S. Army, *FM 100-5* (1986), 10.

47. Joint Chiefs of Staff, *JCS Pub 1*, 34, 370.

48. U.S. Army, *FM 100-6*, 2–3, 2–5, and 2–6.

49. John F. Meehan, III, "The Operational Trilogy," *Parameters* 16, no. 3 (Autumn 1986): 14.

50. U.S. Army, *FM 100-5* (1986), 10; U.S. Army, *FM 100-1*, 13.

51. William K. Naylor, *The Principles of Strategy*, 150.

52. U.S. Army, *FM 100-5* (1982), 2–3.

53. *Merriam-Webster's*, 199.

54. William H. Janes, "Operational Art in NATO" (Student monograph, SAMS, Fort Leavenworth, KS, January 10, 1988), 10.

55. Joint Chiefs of Staff, *JCS Pub 1*, 60.

56. U.S. Army, *FM 100-6*, 4-2, and 4-2.

57. William W. Mendel and Floyd T. Banks, "Campaign Planning: Getting It Straight," Parameters 18, no. 3 (September 1988): 45; William A. Williamson, "Campaign Planning," *Parameters* 14, no. 4 (Winter 1984): 25.

58. U.S. Army, *FM 100-5* (1986), 10.

59. William M. Naylor, *The Principles of Strategy*, 19.

60. Baron von der Goltz, *The Conduct of War*, 66.

61. Trevor N. Dupuy, *Understanding War*, 70.

62. Wayne M. Hall, "A Theoretical Perspective of AirLand Battle Doctrine," *Military Review* 66, no. 3 (March 1986): 39.

63. Dwight L. Adams and Clayton R. Newell, "Operational Art in the Joint and Combined Arenas," 36.

64. U.S. Army, *FM 100-2-1*, 2-1.

65. Christopher Donnelly, *Red Banner* (Alexandria, VA: Jane's, 1988), 213–214.

66. David M. Glantz, "Soviet Operational Art," 29.

67. James J. Schneider, "The Theory of Operational Art," 18 and 31.

68. Stephen E. Runals, "A Different Approach," *Military Review* 67, no. 10 (October 1987): 46.

69. Richard E. Simpkin, *Race to the Swift*, 24.

70. U.S. Army, *FM 3-0* (2001), 2-2 to 2-3; U.S. Army, *FM 3-0* (2008), 6-3.

71. Joint Chiefs of Staff, *JP 1-02* (2001), 391.

72. Joint Chiefs of Staff, *JP 3-0* (2001), GL-14; Joint Chiefs of Staff, *JP 3-2*, 2006 with change 1 2008, p. GL-21.

73. Thomas C. Schelling, *The Strategy of Conflict* (Cambridge, MA: Harvard University, 1976), 5, 9, and 13.

74. James J. Schneider, "Vulcan's Anvil: The American Civil War and the Emergence of Operational Art" (theoretical paper no. 4, SAMS, Fort Leavenworth, KS, June 16, 1991), 1, 23, 30–31, and 40–44. Dr. Schneider was instrumental in my continuing research and in the theoretical discussions throughout the program at the School of Advanced Military Studies.

75. Ibid., 23–32.

76. Ibid., 11, 23, and 31.

77. Leonard D. Holder "A New Day for Operational Art," *Army* 45, no. 3 (March 1985): 27.

78. Shimon Naveh, *In Pursuit of Military Excellence*, 306–307.

CHAPTER 5

1. James J. Schneider, "Foundations of Military Theory," Advanced Military Studies Program Course 1: Syllabus AY 88/89 (SAMS, Fort Leavenworth, KS, June 28, 1988), 1-15-1; during my attendance of SAMS, Dr. Schneider discussed three domains of war—physical, cybernetic, and moral. J.F.C. Fuller, *The Foundations of the Science of War* (London: Hutchinson & Co, 1925), 63 (page reference from original), reprinted by the Army War College in 1983; he writes of military power expressing itself as a function of mass, or body, and energy, or activity, within three spheres—mental, moral, and physical. I prefer to categorize these concepts as natures of war rather than domains or spheres, and I prefer cognitive to describe this nature of war that focuses on command and control and the mental processes associated with war.

2. Joint Chiefs of Staff, *Joint Publication 1-02: Department of Defense Dictionary of Military and Associated Terms*, amended version, (Washington, DC: Joint Chiefs of Staff, August 2005), 538; Joint Chiefs of Staff, *Pub 3-0* with Change 1 (Washington, DC: Joint Chiefs of Staff, February 13, 2008), GL-28. Much of this description of the battlefield is based on my personal notes from the Advanced Military Studies Course 1: Lesson 9. I modified an explanation provided by Professor James J. Schneider in which he was outlining a linkage between the classical levels of war (grand strategy, strategy, grand tactics, tactics, and minor tactics), space, time, and policy execution. The base diagram follows:

Level	Space	Time	Policy Execution
Grand strategy	Theater of war	War	Policy decision; plans for war
Strategy	Theater of operations	Campaign	Executing war plans; planning campaigns
Grand tactics	Position	Battle	Executing campaign plans; battles
Tactics	Field	Engagement	Executing battle plans; planning engagements
Minor tactics	Point	Combat	Executing engagements; plan executed

My summary note under the diagram would read, "Basically how Clausewitz looks at war in Jomini's terms."

3. Joint Chiefs of Staff, *Pub 3-0* (2008), GL-28; see also Joint Chiefs of Staff, *JP 1-02*, 539.

4. Ibid.

5. U.S. Army, *FM 100-5: Operations* (Washington, DC: U.S. Government Printing Office, 1986), 19–21; U.S. Army, *FM 100-5: Operations*, preliminary draft (Washington, DC: Department of the Army, August 21, 1992), 7–15.

6. U.S. Army, *FM 100-5* (1986), 19.

7. U.S. Army, *FM 3-0: Operations* (Washington, DC: U.S. Government Printing Office, June 2001), 4–25; U.S. Army, *FM 3-0: Operations* (Washington, DC: U.S. Government Printing Office, February 2008), D-4.

8. U.S. Army, *FM 3-0* (2001), 4–25.

9. Ibid., 4–26.

10. Ibid., p. 4–27.

11. U.S. Army TRADOC, *TP 525-3-0: The Army in Joint Operations; The Army's Future Force Capstone Concept 2015-2024*, version 2.0 (Fort Monroe, VA: TRADOC, April 7, 2005), 14, 19, and 64; *TP 525-3-2: The United States Army Concept for Tactical Maneuver, 2015-2024*, version 1.0 (Fort Monroe, VA: TRADOC, October 2, 2006), 5, 13, and 50.

12. Antoine H. Jomini, *The Art of War*, trans. by G.H. Mendell and W.P. Craighill, reprint ed. (Westport, CT: Greenwood, 1977), 70 and 186.

13. Joint Chiefs of Staff, *JP 3-0* (2008), GL-12; see also Joint Chiefs of Staff, *JP 3-0* (2001), GL-8.

14. Joint Chiefs of Staff, *JP 3-0* (2001), GL-5; Joint Chiefs of Staff, *JP 3-0* (2008), GL-7.

15. Carl von Clausewitz, *On War*, ed. and trans. by Michael Howard and Peter Paret (Princeton: Princeton University Press, 1976), 248, 260, and 485–486.

16. Ibid., 595–596.

17. John L. Romjue, "AirLand Battle: The Historical Perspective," *Military Review*, 66, no. 3 (March 1986): 55.

18. Chris Bellamy, *The Future of Land Warfare* (New York: St. Martin's Press, 1987), 142.

19. Ferdinand O. Miksche, *Attack: A Study of Blitzkrieg Tactics*, reprint ed., Art of War Colloquium publication, Carlisle, PA: U.S. Army War College, December 1, 1983), 2.

20. James Kievit, "Operational Art in the 1944 Ardennes Campaign" (Student monograph, SAMS, Fort Leavenworth, KS, May 10, 1987), 31.

21. John F.Meehan III, "The Operational Trilogy," *Parameters* 16, no. 3 (Autumn 1986): 14.

22. Antoine H. Jomini, *The Art of War*, 86–88.

23. Joint Chiefs of Staff, *Pub 3-0* (2008,) GL-11; Joint Chiefs of Staff, *JP 3-0* (2001), GL-8.

24. Carl von Clausewitz, *On War*, 567–569.

25. Charles D. Franklin, "Time, Space, and Mass at the Operational Level of War: The Dynamics of the Culminating Point" (Student monograph, SAMS, Fort Leavenworth, KS, April 28, 1986), 9–12.

26. Carl von Clausewitz, *On War*, 566.

27. Ibid., 528.

28. James D. Coomler, "The Operational Culminating Point: Can You See It Coming?" (Student monograph, SAMS, Fort Leavenworth, KS, May 16, 1986), 30.

29. Carl von Clausewitz, *On War*, 572.

30. Ibid., 370 and 383

31. U.S. Army, *FM 100-5* (1986), 77.

32. Antoine H. Jomini, *The Art of War*, 71.

33. Ibid., 69.

34. Martin Van Creveld, *Supplying War* (New York: Cambridge University Press, 1980), 175, 199–200.

35. Van Creveld says no. Ibid., 235.

36. Shimon Naveh, *In Pursuit of Military Excellence: The Evolution of Operational Theory* (London: Frank Cass, 1997), 324.

CHAPTER 6

1. Lord Moran, *The Anatomy of Courage* (Garden City Park, NY: Avery, 1987), 180, 183, and 199–200.

2. Ibid., 198 and 202.

3. Aleksandr A. Svechin, *Strategy* (Minneapolis: East View, 1992), 328.

4. Eliot A. Cohen and John Gooch, *Military Misfortunes: The Anatomy of Failure in War* (New York: The Free Press, 1990), 21–22.

5. Carl von Clausewitz, *On War*, ed. and trans. by Michael Howard and Peter Paret (Princeton: Princeton University Press, 1976), 117–120 and 140.

6. Ibid., 140.

7. Ibid., 119.

CHAPTER 7

1. James J. Schneider, "Foundations of Military Theory," Advanced Military Studies Program, Course l: Syllabus AY 88/89(U.S. Army Command and General Staff College, SAMS, Fort Leavenworth, KS, 1988), 1-21-1. Portions of Chapter 7 are extracts from a major paper written for one of my Master's degrees; see John M. House, "The Moral Domain of Low-Intensity Conflict" (master's major paper, U.S. Army Command and General Staff College, SAMS, Fort Leavenworth, KS, December 1988).

2. Carl von Clausewitz, *On War*, ed. and trans. by Michael Howard and Peter Paret (Princeton: Princeton University Press, 1976), 184 and 186.

3. Anthony Kellett, *Combat Motivation: The Behavior of Soldiers in Battle* (Boston: Kluwer Boston, Inc., 1982), 231–269.

4. Samuel A. Stouffer, Arthur A. Lumsdaine, Marion H. Lumsdaine, Robin M. Williams, Jr., M. Brewster Smith, Irving L. Janis, Shirley A. Star, and Leonard S. Cottrell, *Studies in Social Psychology in World War II, Vol. II; The American Soldier: Combat and Its Aftermath* (Princeton: Princeton University Press, 1949–50), 77; Anthony Kellett, *Combat Motivation*, 272.

5. U.S. Army, *FM 26-2: Management of Stress in Army Operations* (Washington, DC: U.S. Government Printing Office, 1986), 12–16.

6. Richard Holmes, *Acts of War: The Behavior of Men in Battle* (New York: The Free Press, 1985), 177.

7. Ibid., 179.

8. Herbert Hendin, *Wounds of War: The Psychological Aftermath of Combat in Vietnam* (New York: Basic Books, 1984), 4.

9. Americas Watch Committee, *Land Mines in El Salvador and Nicaragua: The Civilian Victims* (New York: Americas Watch Committee, 1976), 2 and 12.

10. Bernard E. Trainor, "US Sides with Captain of Vincennes," *Kansas City Times*, August 20, 1988, A-15; "Report Exonerates Crew of Vincennes," *Kansas City Times*, August 20, 1988, A-1 and A-14.

11. Herbert Hendin, *Wounds of War*, 48 and 233–234.

12. Lord Moran, *The Anatomy of Courage* (Garden City Park, NY: Avery, 1987), 16.

13. Charles J.J.J. Ardant du Picq, *Battle Studies*, trans. by John N. Greely and Robert C. Cotton (Harrisburg, PA: The Military Service Publishing Company, 1958), 48.

14. Ibid., 141.

15. Lord Moran, *The Anatomy of Courage*, 26 and 61.

16. Ibid.,113.

17. Anthony Kellett, *Combat Motivation*, 232.

18. Lord Moran, *The Anatomy of Courage*, 81.

19. Roger A. Beaumont and William A. Snyder, "Combat Effectiveness: Paradigms and Paradoxes," in *Combat Effectiveness: Cohesion, Stress, and the Volunteer Military*, edited by Sam C. Sarkesian, Sage Research Progress Series on War, Revolution and Peacekeeping (Beverly Hills, CA: Sage, 1980), 49.

20. S.L.A. Marshall, *Men Against Fire*, reprint ed. (Gloucester, MA: Peter Smith, 1978), 44.

21. James J. Schneider, "The Theory of the Empty Battlefield," *Journal of the Royal United Services Institute for Defense Studies* 132, no. 3 (September 1987): 42–44.

22. Lord Moran, *The Anatomy of Courage*, 19.

23. U.S. Army and U.S. Air Force, *FM 100-20/AFP 3-20: Military Operations in Low Intensity Conflict* (Washington, DC: U.S. Government Printing Office, 1990), 4-1 to 4-7.

24. Ramesh Thakur, *Peacekeeping in Vietnam: Canada, India, Poland and the International Commission* (Edmonton, AB, Canada: The University of Alberta Press, 1984), 7.

25. U.S. Army and U.S. Air Force, *FM 100-20/AFP 3-20*, 5-8.

26. Ben Shalit, *The Psychology of Conflict and Combat* (New York: Praeger, 1988) 183; Ruth Lunn, "Conscientious Objection in Israel During the War in Lebanon," *Armed Forces and Society* 12, no. 4 (Summer 1986): 490 and 500.

27. Edgar O'Ballance, *Terror in Ireland: The Heritage of Hate* (Novato, CA: Presidio Press, 1981) 259.

28. Steven E. Hodgkins, "The Reporting of Terrorism by the Media" (M.S. thesis, California State University, 1987), 17, 22, and 29.

29. Lord Moran, *The Anatomy of Courage*, 69.

30. U.S. Army and U.S. Air Force, *FM 100-20/AFP 3-20:*, 3-1 and 3-7.

31. Ibid., 3-5.

32. Arthur Campbell, *Guerrillas: A History and Analysis from Napoleon's Time to the 1960s* (New York: The John Day Co., 1968), 88 and 93–5.

33. Steven Metz, "The Ideology of Terrorist Foreign Policies in Libya and South Africa," *Conflict* 7, no. 4 (1987): 387.

34. S.L.A. Marshall, *Men Against Fire*, 78.

35. William V. O'Brien, *The Conduct of Just and Limited War* (New York: Praeger, 1981), 185–186.

36. Robert M. Pockrass, "The Police Response to Terrorism: The Royal Ulster Constabulary," *Conflict* 6, no. 4 (1986): 289–290.

37. Neil C. Livingstone, "States in Opposition: The War Against Terrorism," *Conflict* 3, no. 2–3 (1981): 116–120.

38. Lord Moran, *The Anatomy of Courage*, 145.

39. Dale B. Flora, "Battlefield Stress: Causes, Cures, and Countermeasures" (MMAS thesis, U.S. Army Command and General Staff College, Fort Leavenworth, KS, 1985), 235–243.

40. Lord Moran, *The Anatomy of Courage*, 101–102.

41. Ibid., 101.

42. Alistair Horne, *A Savage War of Peace: Algeria 1954–1962*, revised ed. (Hong Kong: Elisabeth Sifton Books–Penguin Books, 1987), 25–27.

43. Edgar O'Ballance, *Terror in Ireland*, 154.

44. Desmond Hamill, *Pig in the Middle: The Army in Northern Ireland 1969–1984* (London: Methuen, 1985), 247.

45. Rick Maze, "Panama Harassment Down, U.S. Officials Say, Despite Reports," *Army Times*, October 24, 1988, 8.

46. Alexandre Bennigsen, "The Soviet Union and Muslim Guerrilla Wars, 1920–1981: Lessons for Afghanistan," *Conflict* 4, no. 2–3–4 (1983): 310.

47. Anthony Kellett, *Combat Motivation*, 222.

48. Alistair Horne, *A Savage War of Peace*, 100 and 112.

49. "IRA Shootings Are Deemed Lawful," *Kansas City Times*, October 1, 1988, A-18.

50. Edward B. Glick, *Peaceful Conflict: The Non-Military Use of the Military* (Harrisburg, PA: Stackpole Books, 1967), 36 and 41.

51. Lieutenant General (Retired) Don Holder stated that the scale of operations in low-intensity conflict affects the concerns over death and injury. The medical system may have the time and resources in low-intensity conflict to focus on the casualties that occur. "Death and wounds are rare in Ireland. Hence, they are particularly shocking. On the other hand, medical care is focused on a few cases and evacuation is normally easy."

52. S.L.A. Marshall, *Men Against Fire*, 50.

53. Desmond Hamill, *Pig in the Middle*, 283.

54. Charlie Schill, "Treating Delayed Trauma," *Army Times*, October 24, 1988, 22.

55. For an example of security action force organization, see William P. Johnson and Eugene N. Russell, "An Army Strategy and Structure," *Military Review* 66, no. 8 (August 1986): 69–77.

CHAPTER 8

1. Keith Davis, *Human Behavior at Work: Human Relations and Organizational Behavior* (New York: McGraw-Hill, 1972), 160–163, and 166–167. Portions of Chapter 8 including the tables are extracted from my Ph.D. dissertation; See John M. House, "A Study of Army Operational Transformation Strategy: Evolutionary Vs. Revolutionary Change" (Ph.D. dissertation, Northcentral University, 2005).

2. John P. Kotter, "Problems of Human Resource Management in Rapidly Growing Companies," *California Management Review* 21, no. 2 (Winter 1978): 29–36.

3. John P. Kotter, "How Leaders Grow Leaders," *Across the Board* 25, no. 3 (March 1988): 38–40.

4. John P. Kotter, *Leading Change* (Boston: Harvard Business School Press, 1996), 10–14, 25, and 47.

5. John P. Kotter, "Kill Complacency," *Fortune* 134, no. 3 (August 5, 1996): 168–170.

6. John P. Kotter, "Transforming Organizations," *Executive Excellence* 13, no. 9 (September 1996): 13.

7. David A. Nadler and Michael L. Tushman, "Beyond the Magic Leader: Leadership and Organizational Change," in *The Management of Organizations: Strategies, Tactics, Analyses*, edited by M. L. Tushman, C. O'Reilly, and D. A. Nadler (New York: Harper & Row, 1989), 533–537.

8. Yvan Allaire and Mihaela Firsirotu, "How to Implement Radical Strategies in Large Organizations," in *The Management of Organizations: Strategies, Tactics, Analyses*, edited by M. L. Tushman, C. O'Reilly, and D. A. Nadler (New York: Harper & Row, 1989), 508–515.

9. Peter Senge, "The Leadership of Profound Change," in *The Dance of Change: The Challenges to Sustaining Momentum in Learning Organizations*, by Peter Senge, Art Kleiner, Charlotte Roberts, Richard Ross, George Roth, and Bryan Smith (New York: Currency/Doubleday, 1999), 15 and 18.

10. Roger T. Burlton, *Business Process Management: Profiting from Progress* (Indianapolis, IN: Sams, 2001), 9, 11, and 14.

11. David S. Alberts and Richard E. Hayes, *Campaigns of Experimentation* (Washington, DC: Department of Defense Command and Control Research Program, 2005), 43 and 46.

12. Samuel P. Huntington *The Soldier and the State: The Theory and Politics of Civil–Military Relations* (Cambridge, MA: Belknap Press, 1957), 229–230, 364, and 366.

13. Harold R. Winton, *To Change an Army: General Sir John Burnett-Stuart and British Armored Doctrine, 1927–1938* (Lawrence, KS: University Press of Kansas, 1988), 202, 203, 227, and 229–230.

14. Stephen Rosen, *Winning the Next War: Innovation and the Modern Military* (Ithaca, NY: Cornell University Press, 1991), 2, 9, 21–22, and 52–53.

15. Alvin Toffler and Heidi Toffler, *War and Anti-War* (New York: Warner Books, 1993), 20, 32–34, 36, 47, 51–63, and 66–72.

16. Andrew F. Krepinevich, "Cavalry to Computer," *The National Interest*, no. 37 (Fall 1994): 30–31 and 36–40.

17. Larry H. Addington, *The Patterns of War Since the Eighteenth Century*, 2nd ed. (Bloomington, IN: Indiana University Press, 1994), 325.

18. Carl H. Builder, "Looking in All the Wrong Places?" *Armed Forces Journal International* 132, no. 10 (May 1995): 38–39.

19. Robert H. Scales, "Cycles of War: Speed of Maneuver Will Be the Essential Ingredient of an Information Age Army," *Armed Forces Journal International* 134, no. 12 (July 1997): 38–42.

20. Williamson Murray and Thomas O'Leary, "Military Transformation and Legacy Forces," *Joint Force Quarterly*, no. 30 (Spring 2002): 21.

21. William A. Owens, "The Once and Future Revolution in Military Affairs," *Joint Force Quarterly*, no. 31(Summer 2002) 56–68.

22. Robert B. Killebrew, "Winning Wars," *Army* 55, no. 4 (April 2005): 28.

23. David A. Nadler and Michael L. Tushman, "A Diagnostic Model for Organizational Behavior" (Research Paper No. 4, Graduate School of Business, Columbia University, New York, November 1975), 8–9, 11, 15–17, and 21.

24. David A. Nadler and Michael L. Tushman, *Strategic Organization Design: Concepts, Tools, & Processes* (New York: HarperCollins, 1988), 24–25, 29, and 42–44.

25. Ibid., 165–166 and 172–173.

26. David A. Nadler and Michael L. Tushman, *Competing by Design: The Power of Organizational Architecture* (New York: Oxford University Press, 1997), 26–28 and 187–189.

27. David E. Johnson, *Fast Tanks and Heavy Bombers: Innovation in the U.S. Army, 1917–1945* (Ithaca, NY: Cornell University Press, 1998), 220–223 and 229.

28. Robert A. Doughty, *The Evolution of U.S. Army Tactical Doctrine, 1946–76* (Leavenworth Paper No. 1, Combat Studies Institute, U.S. Army Command and General Staff College, Fort Leavenworth, KS, 1979), 1, 16, 19, and 46.

29. Ibid., 29 and 48–49.

30. John L. Romjue, *The Army of Excellence: The Development of the 1980s Army* (Fort Monroe, VA: Office of the Command Historian, U.S. Army Training and Doctrine Command, 1993), 125–127.

31. John L. Romjue, *American Army Doctrine for the Post–Cold War* (Fort Monroe, VA: U.S. Military History Office, Army Training and Doctrine Command, 1996), 5, 100, 117, 119, 121, and 123–125.

32. Combat Studies Institute (CSI), "History of Transformation," *Military Review* 80, no. 3 (May–June 2000): 17.

33. Ibid., 17–18.

34. Ibid., 19–20; Robert A. Doughty, *The Evolution of U.S. Army Tactical Doctrine, 1946–76*, 6.

35. CSI, "History of Transformation," 20.

36. Ibid., 20–21.

37. Ibid., 21; Robert A. Doughty, *The Evolution of U.S. Army Tactical Doctrine, 1946–76*, 40.

38. CSI, "History of Transformation," 22; Robert A. Doughty, *The Evolution of U.S. Army Tactical Doctrine, 1946–76*, 46.

39. CSI, "History of Transformation," 23.

40. Ibid., 24.

41. Ibid., 25.

42. John L. Romjue, *From Active Defense to AirLand Battle: The Development of Army Doctrine, 1973–1982* (Fort Monroe, VA: Historical Office, U.S. Army Training and Doctrine Command, June 1984), 19, 69, and 72–73.

43. CSI, "History of Transformation," 26.

44. Ibid., 26.

45. Peter Senge, "Toward an Atlas of Organizational Change," in *The Dance of Change: The Challenges to Sustaining Momentum in Learning Organizations*, by Peter Senge, Art Kleiner, Charlotte Roberts, Richard Ross, George Roth, and Bryan Smith (New York: Currency/Doubleday, 1999), 5.

46. George W. Bush, *2002 State of the Union Address* (Washington, DC: The White House, January 29, 2002), http://www.whitehouse.gov/news/releases/2002/01/20020129-11.html (accessed March 16, 2004).

47. Eliot A. Cohen and John Gooch, *Military Misfortunes: The Anatomy of Failure in War* (New York: Anchor Books, 2003), 235–239.

48. General (Retired) Montgomery Meigs, "Unorthodox Thoughts about Asymmetric Warfare," *Parameters* 33, no. 2 (2003): 4, 7, 9, and 16.

49. Peter F. Drucker, *Managing in a Time of Great Change* (New York: Truman Talley Books, 1995), 79.

50. David. A. Nadler and Michael L. Tushman, *Strategic Organization Design*, 25–29 and 42–44.

CHAPTER 9

1. U.S. Department of Defense, *Joint Vision 2010* (Washington, DC: Joint Chiefs of Staff, Pentagon, 1996), 1–2 and 13. Portions of Chapter 9 including the tables are extracted from my Ph.D. dissertation; see John M. House, "A Study of Army Operational Transformation Strategy: Evolutionary vs. Revolutionary Change" (Ph.D. dissertation, Northcentral University, 2005).

2. U.S. Army, *The Annual Report on the Army After Next Project to the Chief of Staff of the Army* (Fort Monroe, VA: U.S. Army Training and Doctrine Command, Deputy Chief of Staff for Doctrine, July 1997), 2–5.

3. Robert H. Scales, *AAN Roundtable: Summary of Comments* (Fort Monroe, VA: U.S. Army Training and Doctrine Command, Office of the Deputy Chief of Staff for Doctrine, July 7, 1997), 1–3.

4. "Army Announces Vision for the Future," Army News Service, October 12, 1999, http://www4.army.mil/ocpa/print.php?story_id_key=2703 (accessed July 6, 2005).

5. Gerry J. Gilmore, "Army to Develop Future Force Now, Says Shinseki," Army News Service, October 13, 1999, http://www4.army.mil/ocpa/print.php?story_id_key=2703 (accessed July 6, 2005).

6. Louis Caldera and Eric K. Shinseki, "Army Vision: Soldiers on Point for the Nation . . . Persuasive in Peace, Invincible in War," *Military Review* 80, no. 5 (September–October 2000): 3–5.

7. U.S. Army, *The United States Army White Paper: Concepts for the Objective Force* (Washington, DC: U.S. Army, n.d.), 6, http://www.monroe.army.mil/futurescenter /oftf/Key%20Docs/white_paper.htm (accessed March 13, 2004).

8. Jack Siemieniec, "Chief of Staff Expands on Army Vision," Army News Service, January 31, 2000, http://www4.army.mil/ocpa/print.php?story_id_key=4162 (accessed July 6, 2005).

9. U.S. Army, *The United States Army Posture Statement, Fiscal Year 2001* (Washington, DC: U.S. Army, 2001), iii and 2, http://www.army.mil/aps/aps_pdf. htm (accessed June 17, 2005).

10. Ibid., 3–4, 16–18, and 21.

11. Ibid., 23–24, 26, and 30.

12. Joe Burlas, "Crusader Howitzer Gets the Axe," Army News Service, May 8, 2002, http://www4.army.mil/ocpa/print.php?story_id_key=905 (accessed June 18, 2005).

13. Marcia Triggs, "New Vision: More Brigades—Smaller but Lethal," Army News Service, October 8, 2003, http://ww4.army.mil/ocpa/read.php?story_id_key= 5300 (accessed March 16, 2004).

14. Tonya K. Townsell, "Enhancements in Store for Future Stryker Brigades," Army News Service, December 23, 2003, http://www4.army.mil/ocpa/read. php?story_id_key=5536 (accessed March 16, 2004).

15. Gary Sheftick, "Army to Reset into Modular Brigade-Centric Force," Army News Service, n.d., http://www4.army.mil/ocpa/read.php?story_id_key=5703 (accessed March 13, 2004).

16. "Army's Future Combat System Passes Major Milestone," Army News Service, May 19, 2003, http://www4.army.mil/ocpa/print.php?story_id_key=178 (accessed July 6, 2005).

17. Douglas A. Macgregor, *Transformation under Fire: Revolutionizing How America Fights* (Westport, CT: Praeger, 2003), 16, 54, 59, and 86.

18. Steven Metz and Raymond A. Millen, *Future War/Future Battlespace: The Strategic Role of American Landpower* (Carlisle Barracks, PA: U.S. Strategic Studies Institute, Army War College, March 2003), 1–3, http://www.carlisle.army.mil/ssi/ (accessed August 24, 2003).

19. U.S. Army, *United States Army Transformation Roadmap 2003* (Washington, DC: U.S. Army, November 1, 2003), ix, xii–xiii, and xv, http://www.army.mil/ 2003Transformation Roadmap/RoadmapFull.pdf (accessed April 14, 2004).

20. Joe Burlas, "Army Requests Comanche Termination," Army News Service, February 23, 2004, http://www4.army.mil/ocpa/print.php?story_id_key=5697 (accessed June 18, 2005).

21. Les Brownlee and Peter J. Schoomaker, "Serving a Nation at War: A Campaign Quality Army with Joint and Expeditionary Capabilities," *Parameters* 34, no. 2 (Summer 2004): 7–10 and 13–16.

22. U.S. Army, *The United States Army 2004 Army Transformation Roadmap* (Washington, DC: U.S. Army, July 2004), viii–xi, http://call.army.mil/products/ACP/ acprefs.html (accessed January 9, 2005).

23. Huba Wass de Czege, *Task Force Modularity White Paper Part III: Brigade Units of Action* (unpublished manuscript prepared for the chief of staff of the Army, May 24, 2004), 3 and 13–14.

24. U.S. Army, *Providing the Best Quality Force to Our Nation: A Commitment to Excellence* (Washington, DC: U.S. Army, March 31, 2004), 2 and 6–7, http:// call.army.mil/products/ACP/acprefs.html (accessed January 9, 2005).

25. U.S. Army, *Unit of Employment (UE) Operations*, white paper version 3.1 (Fort Leavenworth, KS: Combined Arms Doctrine Directorate, Combined Arms Center, April 20, 2004), 9–10, 16, and 22.

26. U.S. Army, *The United States Army 2005 Posture Statement* (Washington, DC: U.S. Army, February 6, 2005), ii and 3, http://www.army.mil/aps /aps_pdf.htm (accessed June 17, 2005).

27. James J. Lovelace and Joseph L. Votel, "The Asymmetric Warfare Group: Closing the Capability Gaps," *Army 55*, no. 3 (March 2005): 29–31.

28. U.S. Army Training and Doctrine Command (TRADOC), *The Army in Joint Operations: The Army's Future Force Capstone Concept 2015-2024*, version 2.0 (Fort Monroe, VA: TRADOC, April 7, 2005), i, 18, 21, 23, 27, and 33.

29. Joint Chiefs of Staff, U.S. Department of Defense, *Joint Vision 2020* (Washington, DC: U.S. Government Printing Office, 2000), 3.

30. Ibid., 34–35.

31. U.S. Department of Defense, *Quadrennial Defense Review Report* (Washington, DC: U.S. Department of Defense, September 30, 2001), iii–iv, 2, and 6, http://call.army.mil/products/ACP/acprefs.html (accessed January 9, 2005).

32. Joint Warfighting Center, U.S. Joint Forces Command, *Pamphlet for Future Joint Operations* (Suffolk, VA: Joint Warfighting Center, March 1, 2002) 2, 7–8, 9, 11, and B-2.

33. U.S. Department of Defense, *Transformation Planning Guidance* (Washington, DC: U.S. Department of Defense, April 2003), 3, http://www.oft.osd.mil/library/ library_files/document_129_Transformation_Planning_Guidance_April_2003_1.pdf (accessed January 9, 2005).

34. The Joint Staff, U.S. Department of Defense, *An Evolving Joint Perspective: U.S. Joint Warfare and Crisis Resolution in the 21st Century* (Washington DC: The Joint Staff, J7, January 24, 2003), 1, 6, 18, and 37.

35. Ibid., 9.

36. U.S. Joint Forces Command, *Major Combat Operations Joint Operating Concept*, version 1.1, draft working paper (Suffolk, VA: U.S. Joint Forces Command, J-9, June 8, 2004), 15.

37. Ibid., 27.

38. U.S. Air Force, *The U.S. Air Force Transformation Flight Plan* (Washington, DC: U.S. Air Force, November 2003), ii and 1–3, http://www.af.mil/library/ posture/ AF_TRANS_FLIGHT_PLAN-2003.pdf (accessed May 11, 2004).

39. Ibid., iv and 9–10.

40. U.S. Marine Corps, *Concepts and Programs 2004* (Washington, DC: U.S. Marine Corps, 2004), 4–6 and 8–9, http://hqinet001.hqmc.usmc.mil/p&r/concepts/ 2004/toc1.htm(accessed May 11, 2004).

41. U.S. Navy, *Naval Transformation Roadmap: Power and Access . . . from the Sea* (Washington, D.C.: U.S. Navy, n.d.), 1–2, http://www.onr.navy.mil/ctto/docs/ naval_transform_roadmap.pdf (accessed May 23, 2004).

42. Ibid., 2–3.

43. Ibid., 3–4 and 9–11.

CHAPTER 10

1. John P. Kotter, "Transforming Organizations," *Executive Excellence* 13, no. 9 (September 1996): 13. Portions of Chapter 10 are extracted from one of my Ph.D. coursework papers and dissertation; see John M. House, "Enhancing

Transformation—Challenges to Sustaining Change" (unpublished paper, Northcentral University, July 2004) and John M. House, "A Study of Army Operational Transformation Strategy: Evolutionary Vs. Revolutionary Change" (Ph.D. dissertation, Northcentral University, 2005).

2. John P. Kotter, "How Leaders Grow Leaders," *Across the Board* 25, no. 3 (March 1988): 38 and 40.

3. John P. Kotter, "Kill Complacency," *Fortune* 134, no. 3 (August 5, 1996): 168–170.

4. Art Kleiner, Charlotte Roberts, Richard Ross, George Roth, Peter Senge, and Bryan Smith, "The Challenges of Profound Change," in *The Dance of Change: The Challenges to Sustaining Momentum in Learning Organizations*, by Peter Senge, Art Kleiner, Charlotte Roberts, Richard Ross, George Roth, and Bryan Smith (New York: Currency/Doubleday, 1999), 22.

5. Ibid., 26.

6. William Bridges, *Managing Transitions: Making the Most of Change*, 2nd ed. (Cambridge, MA: Perseus, 2003), 69–72.

7. Peter Senge, Art Kleiner, Charlotte Roberts, Richard Ross, George Roth, and Bryan Smith, *The Dance of Change: The Challenges to Sustaining Momentum in Learning Organizations* (New York: Currency/Doubleday, 1999), 67–68.

8. Ibid., 70–71.

9. Ibid., 71.

10. Ibid., 103.

11. Ibid., p. 106.

12. Bryan Smith and Richard Ross, "From to Golf to Polo," in *The Dance of Change: The Challenges to Sustaining Momentum in Learning Organizations*, by Peter Senge, Art Kleiner, Charlotte Roberts, Richard Ross, George Roth, and Bryan Smith (New York: Currency/Doubleday, 1999), 108–109.

13. Bill O'Brien, Peter Collins, John Hogan, and Mike Rowe, "Precepts for Mentors," in *The Dance of Change: The Challenges to Sustaining Momentum in Learning Organizations*, by Peter Senge, Art Kleiner, Charlotte Roberts, Richard Ross, George Roth, and Bryan Smith, (New York: Currency/Doubleday, 1999), 129–132.

14. William Bridges, *Managing Transitions*, 29.

15. Peter Senge, Art Kleiner, Charlotte Roberts, Richard Ross, George Roth, and Brian Smith, *The Dance of Change*, 194–195.

16. Ibid., 196–197.

17. Ibid., 198–199.

18. Ibid., 200–203.

19. David Marsing, "How to Walk the Talk without Falling Off a Cliff," in *The Dance of Change: The Challenges to Sustaining Momentum in Learning Organizations*, by Peter Senge, Art Kleiner, Charlotte Roberts, Richard Ross, George Roth, and Bryan Smith (New York: Currency/Doubleday, 1999), 215

20. Peter Senge, "Establishing a Pilot Group," in *The Dance of Change: The Challenges to Sustaining Momentum in Learning Organizations*, by Peter Senge, Art Kleiner, Charlotte Roberts, Richard Ross, George Roth, and Bryan Smith (New York: Currency/Doubleday, 1999), 39–40.

21. Ibid., 41.

22. Peter Senge, Art Kleiner, Charlotte Roberts, Richard Ross, George Roth, and Bryan Smith, *The Dance of Change*, 43.

23. Les Brownlee and Peter Schoomaker, "Serving a Nation at War: A Campaign Quality Army with Joint and Expeditionary Capabilities," *Parameters* 34, no. 2 (Summer 2004): 10–14.

24. Peter Senge, Art Kleiner, Charlotte Roberts, Richard Ross, George Roth, and Bryan Smith, *The Dance of Change*, 47.

25. Les Brownlee and Peter Schoomaker, "Serving a Nation at War," 15–17 and 21.

26. Charlotte Roberts and Art Kleiner, "Five Kinds of Systems Thinking," in *The Dance of Change: The Challenges to Sustaining Momentum in Learning Organizations*, by Peter Senge, Art Kleiner, Charlotte Roberts, Richard Ross, George Roth, and Bryan Smith (New York: Currency/Doubleday, 1999), 137.

27. Ibid., 138

28. Ibid., 140.

29. Ibid., 142.

30. Ibid., 144.

31. U.S. Army, *United States Army Transformation Roadmap 2003* (Washington, DC: Government Printing Office, November 1, 2003), ix and 1-5-1-8, http://www.army.mil/2003Transformation Roadmap/RoadmapFull.pdf (accessed April 14, 2004).

32. Peter Senge, Art Kleiner, Charlotte Roberts, Richard Ross, George Roth, and Bryan Smith, *The Dance of Change*, 159–160.

33. Ibid., 161–164.

34. Richard Ross and Art Kleiner, "The History Map," in *The Dance of Change: The Challenges to Sustaining Momentum in Learning Organizations*, by Peter Senge, Art Kleiner, Charlotte Roberts, Richard Ross, George Roth, and Bryan Smith (New York: Currency/Doubleday, 1999), 186.

35. Peter Senge, Art Kleiner, Charlotte Roberts, Richard Ross, George Roth, and Bryan Smith, *The Dance of Change*, 242.

36. Ibid., 242–243.

37. Ibid., 245–246.

38. William Bridges, *Managing Transitions*, 40–41.

39. David E. Johnson, *Fast Tanks and Heavy Bombers: Innovation in the U.S. Army, 1917–1945* (Ithaca, NY: Cornell University Press, 1998), 74–75.

40. Peter Senge, Art Kleiner, Charlotte Roberts, Richard Ross, George Roth, and Bryan Smith, *The Dance of Change*, 247–250.

41. Charlotte Roberts, "Unilateral Control," in *The Dance of Change: The Challenges to Sustaining Momentum in Learning Organizations*, by Peter Senge, Art Kleiner, Charlotte Roberts, Richard Ross, George Roth, and Bryan Smith (New York: Currency/Doubleday, 1999), 252–254.

42. Peter Senge, Art Kleiner, Charlotte Roberts, Richard Ross, George Roth, and Bryan Smith, *The Dance of Change*, 281–282.

43. Ibid., 284.

44. Ibid., 285–287.

45. Ibid., 288–290.

46. David E. Johnson, *Fast Tanks and Heavy Bombers*, 291–295.

47. George Roth, "Cracking the "Black Box" of a Learning Initiative Assessment," in *The Dance of Change: The Challenges to Sustaining Momentum in Learning Organizations*, by Peter Senge, Art Kleiner, Charlotte Roberts, Richard Ross, George Roth, and Bryan Smith (New York: Currency/Doubleday, 1999), 305.

48. Ibid., 310.

49. Peter Senge, Art Kleiner, Charlotte Roberts, Richard Ross, George Roth, and Bryan Smith, *The Dance of Change*, 319–321.

50. Ibid., 321.

51. U.S. Army, *United States Army Transformation Roadmap 2003*, 8-12–8-14.

52. Peter Senge, Art Kleiner, Charlotte Roberts, Richard Ross, George Roth, and Bryan Smith, *The Dance of Change*, 328.

53. Ibid., 328–333.

54. Ibid., 333.

55. U.S. Army, *Army Values* (n.d.), http://www.army.mil/ArmyBTKC/gov/values.htm (accessed July 23, 2006).

56. Edgar Schein, "How to Set the Stage for a Change in Organizational Culture," in *The Dance of Change: The Challenges to Sustaining Momentum in Learning Organizations*, by Peter Senge, Art Kleiner, Charlotte Roberts, Richard Ross, George Roth, and Bryan Smith (New York: Currency/Doubleday, 1999), 335–341.

57. Peter Senge, Art Kleiner, Charlotte Roberts, Richard Ross, George Roth, and Bryan Smith, *The Dance of Change*, 365.

58. Ibid., 362.

59. Ibid., 363.

60. Elliott Jaques, cited in Peter Senge, Art Kleiner, Charlotte Roberts, Richard Ross, George Roth, and Bryan Smith, *The Dance of Change*, 365.

61. U.S. Army, *United States Army Transformation Roadmap 2003*, xi.

62. U.S. Army, *United States Army Transformation Roadmap 2003*, 1-9.

63. U.S. Army, *United States Army Transformation Roadmap 2003*, 1-11.

64. U.S. Army, *United States Army Transformation Roadmap 2003*, 2-1–2-4.

65. U.S. Army, *United States Army Transformation Roadmap 2003*, 3-8.

66. Ronald H. Spector, *Eagle Against the Sun: The American War with Japan* (New York: Vintage Books, 1985), 56–57.

67. Petr Senge, Art Kleiner, Charlotte Roberts, Richard Ross, George Roth, and Bryan Smith, *The Dance of Change*, 418–419.

68. Ibid., 425–426.

69. Ibid., 425–433.

70. Peter Block, "The School for Managing," in *The Dance of Change: The Challenges to Sustaining Momentum in Learning Organizations*, by Peter Senge, Art Kleiner, Charlotte Roberts, Richard Ross, George Roth, and Bryan Smith (New York: Currency/Doubleday, 1999), 451–452.

71. Paul L. Francis, *Defense Acquisitions: The Army's Future Combat Systems' Features Risks, and Alternatives*, GAO Report GAO-04-635T, (Washington, DC: Government Accounting Office, April 1, 2004), 1.

72. Peter Senge, Art Kleiner, Charlotte Roberts, Richard Ross, George Roth, and Bryan Smith, *The Dance of Change*, 488–90.

73. Ibid., 493–495.

74. John Gordon and Jerry Sollinger, "The Army's Dilemma," *Parameters* 34, no. 2 (Summer 2004): 42.

CHAPTER 11

1. I am not so bold as to assert I can predict with assurance the course of future events. However, the failure of the world's military to recognize the lethality of modern weaponry before World War I is a well-known catastrophe costing millions of casualties. Debate over the future may disclose opportunities to exploit and dangers to avoid. If interested in a notable prediction of World War I that did come true, see Jean De Bloch, *The Future of War in Its Technical, Economic and Political Relations*, trans. by R.C. Long (New York: Garland, 1972).

2. Edward J. Dewey, "A Blueprint for a Lean, Mean Army 21," *Army* 40, no. 6 (June 1990): 33.

3. Elihu Zimet, "High Energy Lasers: Technical, Operational, and Policy Issues," *Defense Horizons* (October 2002): 1–9, http://www.ndu.edu/inss/press/nduhp.html (accessed April 14, 2006); U.S. Air Force, Air Force Research Laboratory (AFRL), "Air Force Builds Portable Laser Weapon," fact sheet (Wright Patterson Air Force Base: AFRL, n.d.), 1–2, http://www.afrl.af.mil/successstories/2005/ emerging_tech/DE-S-06-01_Final.pdf (accessed April 14, 2006); Association of the United States Army (AUSA), AUSA News, "Zeus: A Very Big Deal," February 1, 2003, http://www.ausa.org/webpub/DeptAUSANews.nsf/byid/CCRN-6CGM64 (accessed April 14, 2006); Northrop Grumman, "Northrop Grumman Chosen to Proceed with Developing Solid-State Laser Technology for Military Applications," news release, January 5, 2006, http://biz.yahoo.com/pz/060105/91947.html (accessed April 14, 2006).

4. U.S. Air Force, Air Force Research Laboratory (AFRL), "High Powered Microwaves," fact sheet (Kirtland Air Force Base, NM: AFRL, September 2002), 2, http://www.de.afrl.af.mil/pa/factsheets/ (accessed April 14, 2006); U.S. Air Force, AFRL, "Active Denial System," fact sheet (Kirtland Air Force Base, NM: AFRL, September 2005), 1, http://www.de.afrl.af.mil/ (accessed April 14, 2006).

5. Thomas Hammes, *The Sling and the Stone* (St. Paul, MN: Zenith Press, 2004), 5–6 and 52–55.

6. Ibid., 204–206.

7. Ibid., 207–208.

8. Mao Tse-tung, *On Guerilla Warfare*, trans. and ed. by Brigadier General (ret.) Samuel B. Griffiths (New York: Praeger, 1961), 58 and 88–89.

Bibliography

Adams, Dwight L. and Clayton R. Newell. "Operational Art in the Joint and Combined Arenas." *Parameters* 18, no. 2 (June 1988): 33–39.

Addington, Larry. *The Patterns of War since the Eighteenth Century*. 2nd edition. Bloomington, IN: Indiana University Press, 1994.

Alberts, David S. and Richard E. Hayes. *Campaigns of Experimentation*. Washington, DC: Department of Defense Command and Control Research Program, 2005.

Allaire, Yvan and Mihaela Firsirotu. "How to Implement Radical Strategies in Large Organizations." In *The Management of Organizations: Strategies, Tactics, Analyses*, edited by Michael L. Tushman, C. O'Reilly, and David A. Nadler. New York: Harper & Row, 1989.

Americas Watch Committee. *Land Mines in El Salvador and Nicaragua: The Civilian Victims*. New York: Americas Watch Committee, 1976.

Ardant du Picq, Charles J.J.J. *Battle Studies*. Translated by John N. Greely and Robert C. Cotton. Harrisburg, PA: The Military Service Publishing Company, 1958.

"Army Announces Vision for the Future." Army News Service, October 12, 1999, http://www4.army.mil/ocpa/print.php?story_id_key=2703 (accessed July 6, 2005).

"Army's Future Combat System Passes Major Milestone." Army News Service, May 19, 2003, http://www4.army.mil/ocpa/print.php?story_id_key=178 (accessed July 6, 2005).

Association of the United States Army (AUSA) News. "Zeus: A Very Big Deal." February 1, 2003, http://www.ausa.org/webpub/DeptAUSANews.nsf/byid/CCRN-6CGM64 (accessed April 14, 2006).

Baker, Bonnie. "The Origins of Posse Comitatus." *Air & Space Chronicles* (November 1, 1999). http://www.airpower.maxwell.af.mil/airchronicles/cc/baker1.html (accessed December 8, 2005).

Bellamy, Chris. *The Future of Land Warfare*. New York: St. Martin's Press, 1987.

Bennigsen, Alexandre. "The Soviet Union and Muslim Guerrilla Wars, 1920–1981: Lessons for Afghanistan." *Conflict* 4, nos. 2,3, and 4 (1983): 301–324.

Betts, Richard K. "Systems for Peace or Causes of War? Collective Security, Arms Control, and the New Europe." *International Security* 17, no. 1 (Summer 1992): 5–43.

Blainey, Geoffrey. *The Causes of War*. New York: The Free Press, 1973.

Bridges, William. *Managing Transitions: Making the Most of Change*. 2nd edition. Cambridge, MA: Perseus, 2003.

Brinkerhoff, John R. "The Posse Comitatus Act and Homeland Security." *Journal of Homeland Security* (February 2002). http://www.homelandsecurity.org/journal/Articles/brinkerhoffpossecomitatus.htm (accessed December 8, 2005).

Brownlee, Les and Peter J. Schoomaker. "Serving a Nation at War: A Campaign Quality Army with Joint and Expeditionary Capabilities." *Parameters* 34, no. 2 (Summer 2004): 5–23.

Builder, Carl H. "Looking in All the Wrong Places?" *Armed Forces Journal International* 132, no. 10 (May 1995): 38–39.

Burlas, Joe. "Army Requests Comanche Termination." Army News Service, February 23, 2004, http://www4.army.mil/ocpa/print.php?story_id_key=5697 (accessed June 18, 2005).

———. "Crusader Howitzer Gets the Axe." Army News Service, May 8, 2002, http://www4.army.mil/ocpa/print.php?story_id_key=905 (accessed June 18, 2005).

Burlton, Roger T. *Business Process Management: Profiting from Progress*. Indianapolis, IN: Sams, 2001.

Burr, John G. *The Framework of Battle*. Philadelphia: J.B. Lippincott Co., 1943.

Bush, George W. "2002 State of the Union Address." The White House, Washington, DC, January 29, 2002, http://www.whitehouse.gov/news/releases/2002/01/20020129-11.html (accessed March 16, 2004).

Caldera, Louis and Eric K. Shinseki. "Army Vision: Soldiers on Point for the Nation . . . Persuasive in Peace, Invincible in War." *Military Review* 80, no. 5 (September–October 2000): 3–5.

Campbell, Arthur. *Guerrillas: A History and Analysis from Napoleon's Time to the 1960s*. New York: The John Day Co., 1968.

Carter, Ashton B., William J. Perry, and John D. Steinbruner. *A New Concept of Cooperative Security*. Washington, DC: The Brookings Institution Press, 1992.

Clausewitz, Carl von. *On War*. Edited and translated by Michael Howard and Peter Paret. Princeton: Princeton University Press, 1976.

Cohen, Eliot A. and John Gooch. *Military Misfortunes: The Anatomy of Failure in War*. New York: The Free Press, 1990.

Combat Studies Institute (CSI). "History of Transformation." *Military Review* 80, no. 3 (May–June 2000): 17–29.

Coomler, James D. "The Operational Culminating Point: Can You See It Coming?" Student monograph, School of Advanced Military Studies (SAMS), Fort Leavenworth, KS, May 16, 1986.

Crane, Barry, Joel Lesan, Robert Plebanek, Paul Shemella, Ronald Smith, and Richard Williams. "Between Peace and War: Comprehending Low-Intensity Conflict." *Special Warfare* 2 (Summer 1989): 7.

Creveld, Martin Van. *Supplying War*. New York: Cambridge University Press, 1980.

Davis, Keith. *Human Behavior at Work: Human Relations and Organizational Behavior*. New York: McGraw-Hill, 1972.

De Bloch, Jean. *The Future of War in Its Technical, Economic and Political Relations*. Translated by R.C. Long. New York: Garland, 1972.

Dewey, Edward J. "A Blueprint for a Lean, Mean Army 21." *Army* 40, no. 6 (June 1990): 31–38.

Donnelly, Christopher. *Red Banner*. Alexandria, VA: Jane's, 1988.

Doughty, Robert A. "The Evolution of U.S. Army Tactical Doctrine, 1946–76." Leavenworth Paper No. 1, Combat Studies Institute, U.S. Army Command and General Staff College, Fort Leavenworth, KS, 1979.

Drucker, Peter F. *Managing in a Time of Great Change*. New York: Truman Talley Books, 1995.

Dupuy, Trevor N. *Understanding War: History and Theory of Combat*. New York: Paragon House, 1987.

Flora, Dale B. "Battlefield Stress: Causes, Cures, and Countermeasures." MMAS Thesis, U.S. Army Command and General Staff College, Fort Leavenworth, KS, 1985.

Francis, Paul L. *Defense Acquisitions: The Army's Future Combat Systems' Features Risks, and Alternatives*. GAO Report GAO-04-635T. Washington, DC: Government Accounting Office, April 1, 2004.

Franklin, Charles D. "Time, Space, and Mass at the Operational Level of War: The Dynamics of the Culminating Point." Student monograph, SAMS, Fort Leavenworth, KS, April 28, 1986).

Fuller, J.F.C. *The Foundations of the Science of War*. London: Hutchinson & Co, 1925, reprinted by the Army War College. Carlisle Barracks, PA: Army War College, 1983.

Gates, John M. *Schoolbooks and Krags: The United States Army in the Philippines, 1898–1902*. Westport, CT: Greenwood, 1973.

Gilmore, Gerry J. "Army to Develop Future Force Now, Says Shinseki." Army News Service, October 13, 1999, http://www4.army.mil/ocpa/print.php?story_id_key=2703 (accessed July 6, 2005).

Glantz, David M. "The Nature of Soviet Operational Art." *Parameters* 15, no. 1 (Spring 1985): 2–12.

———. "Soviet Operational Art in Perspective." In *The Art of War Quarterly*, volume III, 1–37. Carlisle Barracks, PA: U.S. Army War College, February 1, 1984.

Glick, Edward B. *Peaceful Conflict: The Non-Military Use of the Military*. Harrisburg, PA: Stackpole Books, 1967.

Goldhurst, Richard. *The Midnight War*. New York: McGraw-Hill, 1978.

Goltz, Baron von der. *The Conduct of War: A Brief Study of Its Most Important Principles and Forms*. Translated by Joseph T. Dickman. Kansas City, MO: Franklin Hudson Co., 1896.

Gordon, John and Jerry Sollinger. "The Army's Dilemma." *Parameters* 34, no. 2 (Summer 2004): 33–45.

Haass, Richard N. "Paradigm Cost." *Foreign Affairs* 72, no. 1 (January–February 1995): 43–58.

Hall, Wayne M. "A Theoretical Perspective of AirLand Battle Doctrine." *Military Review* 66, no. 3 (March 1986): 32–43.

Hamill, Desmond. *Pig in the Middle: The Army in Northern Ireland 1969–1984.* London: Methuen, 1985.

Hamilton, Alexander, James Madison, and John Jay. "Paper No. 8: The Federalist." In *American State Papers; the Federalist; on Liberty; Representative Government; Utilitarianism—Great Books of the Western World Series No. 43.* Chicago: Encyclopedia Britannica, Inc., 1952.

Hammes, Thomas. *The Sling and the Stone.* St. Paul, MN: Zenith Press, 2004.

Hart, B. H. Liddell. *Strategy.* 2nd revised edition. New York: Frederick A. Praeger, 1967.

Hendin, Herbert. *Wounds of War: The Psychological Aftermath of Combat in Vietnam.* New York: Basic Books, 1984.

Hobbes, Thomas. *Leviathan.* Edited by Richard Tuck. Cambridge: Cambridge University Press, 1991.

Hodgkins, Steven E. "The Reporting of Terrorism by the Media." MS Thesis, California State University, 1987.

Holder, Leonard D. "A New Day for Operational Art." *Army* 45, no. 3 (March 1985): 22–32.

Holmes, Kim R. "Defining National Security and American Interests." In *A Safe and Prosperous America: A U.S. Foreign and Defense Policy Blueprint.* Washington, DC: The Heritage Foundation, 1994.

Holmes, Richard. *Acts of War: The Behavior of Men in Battle.* New York: The Free Press, 1985.

Horne, Alistair. *A Savage War of Peace: Algeria 1954–1962.* Revised edition. Hong Kong: Elisabeth Sifton Books/Penguin Books, 1987.

House, John M. "Do Doctrinal Buzzwords Obscure the Meaning of Operational Art?" Master's major paper, U.S. Army Command and General Staff College, School of Advanced Military Studies, April 1989.

———. "Enhancing Transformation—Challenges to Sustaining Change." Unpublished paper, Northcentral University, July 2004.

———. "The Moral Domain of Low-Intensity Conflict." Master's major paper, U.S. Army Command and General Staff College, School of Advanced Military Studies, December 1988.

———. "A Study of Army Operational Transformation Strategy: Evolutionary Vs. Revolutionary Change." Ph.D. dissertation, Northcentral University, 2005.

———. "What is Pubic Administration?" Unpublished paper, Northcentral University, January 2004.

Howard, Michael. *The Causes of War.* 2nd edition. Cambridge, MA: Harvard University Press, 1983.

———. *Studies in War and Peace.* New York: The Viking Press, 1971.

Huntington, Samuel P. *The Clash of Civilizations and the Remaking of World Order.* New York: Simon & Schuster, 1996.

———. *The Soldier and the State: The Theory and Politics of Civil–Military Relations.* Cambridge, MA: Belknap Press, 1957.

"IRA Shootings Are Deemed Lawful." *Kansas City Times*, October 1, 1988, p. A–18.

Isenburg, David. "Posse Comitatus: Caution is Necessary." CDI Terrorism Project, August 6, 2002, http://www.cdi.org/terrorism/pcomitatus-pr.cfm (accessed December 8, 2005).

Janes, William H. "Operational Art in NATO." Student monograph, SAMS, Fort Leavenworth, KS, January 10, 1988.

Johnson, David E. *Fast Tanks and Heavy Bombers: Innovation in the U.S. Army, 1917–1945.* Ithaca, NY: Cornell University Press, 1998.

Johnson, William C. *Public Policy: Policy, Politics, and Practice.* 2nd edition. Madison, WI: Brown and Benchmark, 1996.

Johnson, William P., and Eugene N. Russell. "An Army Strategy and Structure." *Military Review* 66, no. 8 (August 1986): 69–77.

Joint Chiefs of Staff. *JCS Pub 1: Dictionary of Military and Associated Terms.* Washington, DC: U.S. Government Printing Office, June 1, 1987.

———. *Joint Publication 1-02: Department of Defense Dictionary of Military and Associated Terms.* Washington, DC: Joint Chiefs of Staff, April 12, 2001 as amended August 2005.

———. *Joint Publication 3-0: Doctrine for Joint Operations.* Washington, DC: Joint Chiefs of Staff, 2001.

———. *Joint Publication 3-0: Joint Operations (Incorporating Change 1).* Washington, DC: Joint Chiefs of Staff, February 13, 2008.

———. *Joint Vision 2020.* Washington, DC: U.S. Government Printing Office, 2000.

The Joint Staff, U.S. Deparment of Defense. *An Evolving Joint Perspective: U.S. Joint Warfare and Crisis Resolution in the 21st Century.* Washington DC: The Joint Staff, J7, January 24, 2003.

Joint Warfighting Center, U.S. Joint Forces Command. *Pamphlet for Future Joint Operations.* Suffolk, VA: Joint Warfighting Center, March 1, 2002.

Jomini, Antoine H. *The Art of War.* Translated by G.H. Mendell and W.P. Craighill. Reprint edition. Westport, CT: Greenwood, 1977.

Kaufman, H. "Major players: Bureaucrats in American Government." *Public Administration Review* 61, no.1 (January–February 2001): 18–42.

Kellett, Anthony. *Combat Motivation: The Behavior of Soldiers in Battle.* Boston: Kluwer Boston, Inc., 1982).

Kievit, James. "Operational Art in the 1944 Ardennes Campaign." Student monograph, SAMS, Fort Leavenworth, KS, May 10, 1987.

Killebrew, Robert B. "Winning Wars." *Army* 55, no. 4 (April 2005): 25–32.

Kipp, Jacob. *Mass, Mobility, and the Red Army's Road to Operational Art, 1918–1936.* Fort Leavenworth, KS: Soviet Army Studies Office, U.S. Army Combined Arms Center, n.d.

Kotter, John P. "How Leaders Grow Leaders." *Across the Board* 25, no. 3 (March 1988): 38–42.

———. *Leading Change.* Boston: Harvard Business School Press, 1996.

———. "Kill Complacency." *Fortune* 134, no. 3 (August 5, 1996): 168–170.

———. "Problems of Human Resource Management in Rapidly Growing Companies." *California Management Review* 21, no. 2 (Winter 1978): 29–36.

———. "Transforming Organizations." *Executive Excellence* 13, no. 9 (September 1996): 13.

Krepinevich, Andrew F. "Cavalry to Computer." *The National Interest*, no. 37 (Fall 1994): 30–42.

Kupchan, Charles and Clifford A. Kupchan. "The Promise of Collective Security." *International Security* 20, no. 1 (Summer 1995): 52–61.

Livingstone, Neil C. "States in Opposition: The War Against Terrorism." *Conflict* 3, no. 2–3 (1981): 83–142.

Lovelace, James J. and Joseph L. Votel. "The Asymmetric Warfare Group: Closing the Capability Gaps." *Army* 55, no. 3 (March 2005): 29–34.

Luck, Edward C. "Making Peace." *Foreign Policy*, no. 89 (Winter 1992–1993): 137–155.

Lunn, Ruth. "Conscientious Objection in Israel During the War in Lebanon." *Armed Forces & Society* 12, no. 4 (Summer 1986): 489–511.

Luttwak, Edward N. *Strategy: The Logic of War and Peace*. Cambridge, MA: The Belknap Press, 1987.

Macgregor, Douglas A. *Transformation Under Fire: Revolutionizing How America Fights*. Westport, CT: Praeger, 2003.

Mao Tse-tung. *On Guerilla Warfare*. Translated and edited by Brigadier General (Ret.) Samuel B. Griffiths. New York: Praeger, 1961.

Marshall, S.L.A. *Men against Fire*. Reprint edition. Gloucester, MA: Peter Smith, 1978.

Maze, Rick. "Panama Harassment Down, U.S. Officials Say, despite Reports." *Army Times*, October 24, 1988, p. 8.

Meehan, John F., III. "The Operational Trilogy." *Parameters* 16, no. 3 (Autumn 1986): 9–18.

Meigs, Montgomery. "Unorthodox Thoughts about Asymmetric Warfare." *Parameters* 33, no. 2 (2003): 4–18.

Mendel, William W. and Floyd T. Banks, "Campaign Planning: Getting It Straight." *Parameters* 18, no. 3 (September 1988): 43–53.

Metz, Steven. "The Ideology of Terrorist Foreign Policies in Libya and South Africa." *Conflict* 7, no. 4 (1987): 379–402.

Metz, Steven and Raymond A. Millen. *Future War/Future Battlespace: The Strategic Role of American Landpower*. Carlisle Barracks, PA: U.S. Army War College, Strategic Studies Institute, March 2003. http://www.carlisle.army.mil/ssi/ (accessed August 24, 2003).

Miksche, Ferdinand O. *Attack: A Study of Blitzkrieg Tactics*. Reprint edition. Art of War Colloquium publication. Carlisle, PA: U.S. Army War College, 1 December 1983.

Mish, Frederick (editor in chief). *Webster's Ninth New Collegiate Dictionary*. Springfield: Merriam-Webster, Inc., 1987.

Moran, Lord. *The Anatomy of Courage*. Garden City Park, NY: Avery, 1987.

Murray, Williamson and Thomas O'Leary. "Military Transformation and Legacy Forces." *Joint Force Quarterly*, no. 30, Spring 2002, 20–27.

Nadler, David A. and Michael L. Tushman. "Beyond the Magic Leader: Leadership and Organizational Change." In *The Management of Organizations: Strategies, Tactics, Analyses*, edited by Michael L. Tushman, C. O'Reilly, and David A. Nadler, 505–519. New York: Harper & Row, 1989.

———. *Competing by Design: The Power of Organizational Architecture*. New York: Oxford University Press, 1997.

———. "A Diagnostic Model for Organizational Behavior." Research paper no. 4, Columbia University Graduate School of Business, New York, November 1975.

———. *Strategic Organization Design: Concepts, Tools, & Processes*. New York: HarperCollins, 1988.

Naveh, Shimon. *In Pursuit of Military Excellence: The Evolution of Operational Theory*. London: Frank Cass, 1997.

Naylor, William K. *The Principles of Strategy*. Fort Leavenworth, KS: General Services Schools Press, 1920.

Newell, Clayton R. "Exploring the Operational Perspective." *Parameters* 16, no. 3 (Autumn 1986): 19–25.

Nolan, James E. "The Concept of Cooperative Security." In *Global Engagement and Security in the 21st Century*, edited by Janne E. Nolan. Washington, DC: The Brookings Institution Press, 1994.

Northrop Grumman. "Northrop Grumman Chosen to Proceed with Developing Solid-State Laser Technology for Military Applications." News Release. January 5, 2006, http://biz.yahoo.com/pz/060105/91947.html (accessed April 14, 2006).

O'Ballance, Edgar. *Terror in Ireland: The Heritage of Hate*. Novato, CA: Presidio Press, 1981.

O'Brien, William V. *The Conduct of Just and Limited War*. New York: Praeger, 1981.

"Operations to 30 June 1919." National Archives, M917, Reel 10, Graves, 13–14.

Owens, William A. "The Once and Future Revolution in Military Affairs." *Joint Force Quarterly*, no. 31 Summer 2002, 55–61.

Pockrass, Robert M. "The Police Response to Terrorism: The Royal Ulster Constabulary." *Conflict* 6, no. 4 (1986): 287–305.

Posen, Barry R. and Andrew L. Ross. "Competing U.S. Grand Strategies." In *Strategy and Force Planning*. Newport, RI: U.S. Naval War College, 1995.

Quirk, Robert E. *An Affair of Honor: Woodrow Wilson and the Occupation of Veracruz*, edited by Richmond M. Lloyd. New York: W.W. Norton & Company, 1967.

"Report Exonerates Crew of Vincennes." *Kansas City Times*, August 20, 1988, A–1 and A–14.

Romjue, John L. "AirLand Battle: The Historical Perspective." *Military Review*, 66, no. 3 (March 1986): 52–55.

———. *American Army Doctrine for the Post–Cold War*. Fort Monroe, VA: U.S. Army Training and Doctrine Command, Military History Office, 1996.

———. *The Army of Excellence: The Development of the 1980s Army*. Fort Monroe, VA: U.S. Army Training and Doctrine Command, Office of the Command Historian, 1993.

———. *From Active Defense to AirLand Battle: The Development of Army Doctrine, 1973–1982*. Fort Monroe, VA: U.S. Army Training and Doctrine Command, Historical Office, June 1984.

Rosen, Stephen. *Winning the Next War: Innovation and the Modern Military*. Ithaca, NY: Cornell University Press, 1991.

Runals, Stephen E. "A Different Approach." *Military Review* 67, no. 10 (October 1987): 44–49.

Sarkesian, Sam C. (ed.). *Combat Effectiveness: Cohesion, Stress, and the Volunteer Military*. Beverly Hills, CA: Sage, 1980.

Scales, Robert H. *AAN Roundtable: Summary of Comments*. Fort Monroe, VA: U.S. Army Training and Doctrine Command, Office of the Deputy Chief of Staff for Doctrine, July 7, 1997.

———. "Cycles of War: Speed of Maneuver Will Be the Essential Ingredient of an Information Age Army." *Armed Forces Journal International* 134, no. 12 (July 1997): 38–42.

Schelling, Thomas C. *The Strategy of Conflict*. Cambridge, MA: Harvard University, 1976.

Schill, Charlie. "Treating Delayed Trauma." *Army Times*, October 24, 1988, 22.

Schneider, James J. "Foundations of Military Theory." Advanced Military Studies Program Course 1: Syllabus AY 88/89, SAMS, Fort Leavenworth, KS, June 28, 1988.

———. "Foundations of Military Theory." Advanced Military Studies Program, Course 1 Syllabus, SAMS, Fort Leavenworth, KS, U.S. Army Command and General Staff College, 1988.

———. "The Theory of the Empty Battlefield." *Journal of the Royal United Services Institute for Defense Studies* 132, no. 3 (September 1987): 37–44.

———. "The Theory of Operational Art." Draft, Theoretical Paper No. 3, SAMS, Fort Leavenworth, KS, March 1, 1988).

———. "Vulcan's Anvil: The American Civil War and the Emergence of Operational Art." Theoretical Paper No. 4, SAMS, Fort Leavenworth, KS, June 16, 1991).

Senge, Peter, Art Kleiner, Charlotte Roberts, Richard Ross, George Roth, and Bryan Smith. *The Dance of Change: The Challenges to Sustaining Momentum in Learning Organizations*. New York: Currency/Doubleday, 1999.

Shalit, Ben. *The Psychology of Conflict and Combat*. New York: Praeger, 1988.

Sheftick, Gary. "Army to Reset into Modular Brigade–Centric Force." Army News Service, n.d., http://www4.army.mil/ocpa/read.php?story_id_key=5703 (accessed March 13, 2004).

Siemieniec, Jack. "Chief of Staff Expands on Army Vision." Army News Service, January 31, 2000, http://www4.army.mil/ocpa/print.php?story_id_key=4162 (accessed July 6, 2005).

Simpkin, Richard E. *Race to the Swift*. New York: Brassey's Defense, 1985.

Smith, Bryan and Richard Ross. "From to Golf to Polo." In *The Dance of Change: The Challenges to Sustaining Momentum in Learning Organizations*, by Peter Senge, Art Kleiner, Charlotte Roberts, Richard Ross, George Roth, and Bryan Smith, 108–111. New York: Currency/Doubleday, 1999.

Sokolovskiy, V.D. *Soviet Military Strategy*. Edited and translated by Harriett Fast Scott. New York: Crane, Russak, and Company, Inc., 1985.

Spanier, John. *Games Nations Play*. 5th edition. New York: CBS College, 1984.

Spector, Ronald H. *Eagle against the Sun: The American War with Japan*. New York: Vintage Books, 1985.

Stillman, Richard J. *Public Administration: Concepts and Cases*. 6th edition. Boston: Houghton Mifflin Company, 1996.

Stouffer, Samuel A., Arthur A. Lumsdaine, Marion H. Lumsdaine, Robin M. Williams, Jr., M. Brewster Smith, Irving L. Janis, Shirley A. Star, and Leonard

S. Cottrell, Jr. *Studies in Social Psychology in World War II. Volume II; The American Soldier: Combat and Its Aftermath*. Princeton: Princeton University Press, 1949.

Svechin, Aleksandr A. *Strategy*. Minneapolis: East View, 1992.

Thakur, Ramesh. *Peacekeeping in Vietnam: Canada, India, Poland and the International Commission*. Edmonton, AB, Canada: The University of Alberta Press, 1984.

Toffler, Alvin and Heidi Toffler. *War and Anti-War*. New York: Warner Books, 1993.

Townsell, Tonya K. "Enhancements in Store for Future Stryker Brigades." Army News Service, December 23, 2003, http://www4.army.mil/ocpa/read.php?story_id_key=5536 (accessed March 16, 2004).

Trainor, Bernard E. "U.S. Sides with Captain of Vincennes." *Kansas City Times*, August 20, 1988, A-15.

Trebilock, Craig T. "The Myth of Posse Comitatus." *Journal of Homeland Security* (October 2000). http://www.homelandsecurity.org/journal/articles/Trebilcock.htm (accessed December 8, 2005).

Triggs, Marcia. "New Vision: More Brigades—Smaller but Lethal." Army News Service, October 8, 2003, http://ww4.army.mil/ocpa/read.php?story_id_key=5300 (accessed March 16, 2004).

U.S. Air Force. *The U.S. Air Force Transformation Flight Plan*. Washington, DC: U.S. Air Force, November 2003. http://www.af.mil/library/posture/AF_TRANS_FLIGHT_PLAN–2003.pdf (accessed May 11, 2004).

U.S. Air Force Research Laboratory (AFRL). "Active Denial System." Fact sheet, AFRL, Kirtland Air Force Base, NM, September 2005, http://www.de.afrl.af.mil/ (accessed April 14, 2006).

———. "Air Force Builds Portable Laser Weapon." Fact sheet, AFRL, Wright Patterson Air Force Base, n.d. http://www.afrl.af.mil/successstories/2005/emerging_tech/DE-S-06-01_Final.pdf (accessed April 14, 2006).

———. "High Powered Microwaves." Fact sheet, AFRL, Kirtland Air Force Base, NM, September 2002, http://www.de.afrl.af.mil/pa/factsheets/ (accessed April 14, 2006).

U.S. Army. *The Annual Report on the Army After Next Project to the Chief of Staff of the Army*. Fort Monroe, VA: Deputy Chief of Staff for Doctrine, U.S. Army Training and Doctrine Command, July 1997.

———. *Army Values*. http://www.army.mil/ArmyBTKC/gov/values.htm (accessed July 23, 2006).

———. *FM 1: The Army*. Washington, DC: U.S. Government Printing Office, June 2005.

———. *FM 3-0: Operations*. Washington, DC: U.S. Government Printing Office, June 2001.

———. *FM 3-0: Operations*. Washington, DC: U.S. Government Printing Office, February 2008.

———. *FM 26-2: Management of Stress in Army Operations*. Washington, DC: U.S. Government Printing Office, 1986.

———. *FM 100-1: The Army*. Washington, DC: U.S. Government Printing Office, 1986.

———. *FM 100-2-1: The Soviet Army: Operations and Tactics*. Washington, DC: U.S. Government Printing Office, 16 July 1984.

———. *FM 100-5: Field Service Regulations—Operations*. Washington, DC: U.S. Government Printing Office, 1962.

———. *FM 100-5: Operations*. Washington, DC: U.S. Government Printing Office, 1982.

———. *FM 100-5: Operations*. Washington, DC: U.S. Government Printing Office, 1986.

———. *FM 100-5: Operations*. Preliminary Draft. Washington, DC: Department of the Army, 21 August 1992.

———. *FM 100-6: Large Unit Operations. Coordinating Draft*. Fort Leavenworth, KS: U.S. Army Command and General Staff College, September 30, 1987.

———. *FM 100-20: Low-Intensity Conflict*. Washington, DC: U.S. Government Printing Office, 1981.

———. *Oaths of Enlistment and Oaths of Office*. http://www.army.mil/cmh–pg/faq/oaths.htm (accessed July 31, 2006).

———. *The Principles of Strategy for an Independent Corps or Army in a Theater of Operations*. Fort Leavenworth, KS: The Command and General Staff School Press, 1936.

———. *Providing the Best Quality Force to Our Nation: A Commitment to Excellence*. Washington, DC: U.S. Army, March 31, 2004. http://call.army.mil/products/ACP/acprefs.html (accessed January 9, 2005).

———. *The United States Army Posture Statement, Fiscal Year 2001*. Washington, DC: U.S. Army, 2001. http://www.army.mil/aps/aps_pdf.htm (accessed June 17, 2005).

———. *Unit of Employment (UE) Operations. White Paper Version 3.1*. Fort Leavenworth, KS: Combined Arms Doctrine Directorate, Combined Arms Center, April 20, 2004.

———. *The United States Army 2004 Army Transformation Roadmap*. Washington, DC: U.S. Army, July 2004, viii–xi. http://call.army.mil/products/ACP/acprefs.html (accessed January 9, 2005).

———. *The United States Army 2005 Posture Statement*. Washington, DC: U.S. Army, February 6, 2005. http://www.army.mil/aps/aps_pdf.htm (accessed June 17, 2005).

———. *United States Army Transformation Roadmap 2003*. Washington, DC: U.S. Army, November 1, 2003. http://www.army.mil/2003Transformation Roadmap/RoadmapFull.pdf (accessed April, 14, 2004).

———. *The United States Army White Paper: Concepts for the Objective Force*. Washington, DC: U.S. Army, n.d. http://www.monroe.army.mil/futurescenter/oftf/Key%20Docs/white_paper.htm (accessed March 13, 2004).

U.S. Army and U.S. Air Force. *FM 100-20/AFP 3-20: Military Operations in Low Intensity Conflict*. Washington, DC: U.S. Government Printing Office, 1990.

U.S. Army Training and Doctrine Command (TRADOC). *TRADOC Pamphlet 525-3-0: The Army in Joint Operations: The Army's Future Force Capstone Concept 2015-2024, Version 2.0*. Fort Monroe, VA: TRADOC, April 7, 2005.

———. *TRADOC Pamphlet 525-3-2: The United States Army Concept for Tactical Maneuver, 2015-2024, Version 1.0*. Fort Monroe, VA: TRADOC, October, 2, 2006.

U.S. Congress, Senate. "Loans to Foreign Governments." S. Doc. 86, 67th Cong., 2nd sess., 1921.

U.S. Department of Defense. *Joint Publication 3-0: Doctrine for Joint Operations.* Washington, DC: Government Printing Office, September 10, 2001.

———. *Joint Vision 2010.* Washington, DC: Joint Chiefs of Staff, Pentagon, 1996.

———. *The National Defense Strategy of the United States of America.* Washington, DC: U.S. Government Printing Office, March 2005.

———. *Quadrennial Defense Review Report.* Washington, DC: U.S. Department of Defense, September 30, 2001. http://call.army.mil/products/ACP/acprefs.html (accessed January 9, 2005).

———. *Transformation Planning Guidance.* Washington, DC: U.S. Department of Defense, April 2003. http://www.oft.osd.mil/library/library_files/document_129_Transformation_Planning_Guidance_April_2003_1.pdf (accessed January 9, 2005).

U.S. Department of State. *Papers Relating to the Foreign Relations of the United States, 1917, Supplement 2, The World War, Volume 1, Message acting secretary of the treasury to the secretary of state,* July 6, 1917. Washington, DC: U.S. Government Printing Office, 1932.

U.S. Joint Forces Command. *Major Combat Operations Joint Operating Concept. Version 1.1.* Draft Working Paper, U.S. Joint Forces Command, Suffolk, VA, J-9, June 8, 2004.

U.S. Marine Corps. *Concepts and Programs 2004.* Washington, DC: U.S. Marine Corps, 2004. http://hqinet001.hqmc.usmc.mil/p&r/concepts/2004/toc1.htm (accessed May 11, 2004).

U.S. Navy. *Naval Transformation Roadmap: Power and Access...from the Sea.* Washington, DC: U.S. Navy, n.d. http://www.onr.navy.mil/ctto/docs/naval_transform_roadmap.pdf (accessed May 23, 2004).

Walker, David M. "9/11: The Implications for Public-Sector Management." *Public Administration Review,* 62 (Special issue) (September 2002): 94–97.

Wass de Czege, Huba. *Task Force Modularity White Paper Part III: Brigade Units of Action.* Unpublished manuscript prepared for the chief of staff of the Army, May 24, 2004.

Williamson, William A. "Campaign Planning." *Parameters* 14, no. 4 (Winter 1984): 20–25.

Wilson, Woodrow. "The Study of Administration." In *Public Administration: Concepts and Cases,* by Richard J. Stillman, 6–16. 6th edition. Boston: Houghton Mifflin Company, 1996.

Winton, Harold R. *To Change an Army: General Sir John Burnett-Stuart and British Armored Doctrine, 1927–1938.* Lawrence, KS: University Press of Kansas, 1988.

Wright, Quincy. *A Study of War.* Chicago: The University of Chicago Press, 1971.

Zimet, Elihu. "High Energy Lasers: Technical, Operational, and Policy Issues." *Defense Horizons* (October 2002): 1–9. http://www.ndu.edu/inss/press/nduphp.html (accessed April 14, 2006).

Index

About the Author

John M. House is the executive director for Army Wargaming and Operations Analysis for AgileCast, Inc. He is a retired Army colonel with over 32 years of active duty and civilian experience in military operations and has written approximately eighty periodical articles and newspaper columns on a variety of military subjects. Since retiring from the Army in 2001, he has worked as a consultant and government employee in several positions. Dr. House has been a part-time university professor since 2006, teaching in Columbus State University, Northcentral University, American Public University, and TUI University.